Praise for *Aging with Agency*

"*Aging with Agency* is the definitive book on aging, why it matters, how to reperceive it, how to experience it positively, and how to support aging friends and family. Beginning with a history of attitudes on aging, Peters provides thorough reviews of the ideas of the major proponents of positive aging—Jung, Maslow, Erikson—as well as lesser-known figures like Naomi Feil, Bill Thomas, Viktor Frankl, Allan Chinen, Lars Tornstam, Al Power, and Thomas Kitwood. Drawing on her thirty-plus years of experience with the elderly, Peters offers primers and perspectives on memory loss, and she adds invaluable chapters on activities and practices that can help both the aging and their caregivers to thrive in the 'afternoon of life.' In the final section, she assesses the various options for living environments and identifies the red flags that the elderly and their families must watch for in making arrangements for end-of-life care. This book is a must-read for everyone who anticipates growing older."

—SUSAN MEHRTENS, PhD, president,
Jungian Center for the Spiritual Sciences

"Sandi Peters has written a practical book on the soulful aging process. She combines many years of service to the aged with integrated wisdom to create a real primer of understanding of critical spiritual passages in the aging process. Grounding her work in Jungian analytical psychology, she challenges the reader to maturation, searching for meaning in diminishment, finding hope in loss and grief, and living our personal myths in depth through the dying process. Her research is available to us in a very readable way. As a formator of spiritual directors, I will advise anyone journeying with an elderly person to read this book for guidance and insight."

—DONALD BISSON, FMS, D.Min.,
founder of the Center for Jungian
Christian Dialogue

"An enthusiastic endorsement for *Aging with Agency!* This truly transformational work can benefit a wide variety of readers: elders themselves, educators, mental health therapists, pastoral counselors, spiritual directors, retreat leaders, and professional and personal care providers. Even younger people—including millennials—who fear their own aging and are seeking something realistically positive about the later stages of adulting can find hope in these pages.

Sandi Peters has taken a wide-ranging, friendly approach to the process of maturing, with emphasis on the development of the inner life of the person as the ultimate challenge and raison d'être for optimal living in the last decades of human life. Her focus on the potential for growth in the works of Jung, Maslow, Erikson, and Tornstam creates a quality of anticipation that growing old could actually be exciting—a process to look forward to.

Peters does more than present theoretical ideas, however. She is very practical and realistic in her presentation and discussion of memory loss and the specifics of living environments. The chapters on meditation and inner-life practices are particularly helpful. The text is rich with references to other works, and the resource guide is an added bonus.

As a gerontologist, I recommend this book—especially to those burdened by a negative view of societal and personal aging. They are in for a wonderful (and useful) surprise!"

—JANE THIBAULT, PhD, professor emeritus in the Department of Family and Geriatric Medicine at the University of Louisville School of Medicine; author of numerous works on the intersection of aging and spirituality

"We live in a society with elderly people, but very few elders. There just have not been enough guides from the first half of life to the second half. Great elders reveal both a brightness and a sadness. They mirror you rather than asking you to mirror them. *Aging with Agency* is a guide to developing the kind of awareness that moves us from being old to being wise. Through story and example it counsels the reader to ripen rather than decline as the years unfold. It encourages movement toward gratitude and authenticity as the inner work of the second half of life is graciously embraced."

—FATHER RICHARD ROHR, OFM,
founder of the Center for Action and
Contemplation; author of *Falling Upward:
A Spirituality for the Second Half of Life*

"Sandi Peters's book *Aging with Agency* offers a wise and pragmatic framework for understanding the universal trajectory of aging, illness, and death. In charting how best to navigate the many changes of these life transitions, she highlights the seminal work of Jung, Maslow, and the Eriksons, and she draws on her own years of experience in working with aging populations. Particularly helpful is her understanding of the challenges, difficulties, and options available at the end of life. This wonderful book is an inspiring wake-up call to explore our own relationship to growing old and to be strong in advocating for truly compassionate care."

—JOSEPH GOLDSTEIN, teacher; founder
of Insight Meditation Society in Barre, Massachusetts; author of *Mindfulness: A Practical
Guide to Awakening*

"This remarkable book presents a profound—and profoundly challenging—new paradigm of aging. Drawing on her extensive clinical experience, Peters extends the Jungian view that aging is a time for individuation and spiritual development. She argues that such inner growth continues even with cognitive impairment and dementia, but only if caretakers recognize and foster the process. In losing memory, the elder is not simply disintegrating but is transitioning from ego to Self, as Jungians put it, or more generally, from this world to all worlds."

—ALLAN B. CHINEN, MD, psychiatrist
in private practice in San Francisco; clinical
professor of psychiatry at the University of
California, San Francisco; author of *In the
Ever After: Fairy Tales and the Second Half
of Life*

"What a refreshing landscape Sandi Peters, thought leader for our particular era of aging, invites us to explore in *Aging with Agency*. It reminds me of the beauty and comfort of my garden, without which it would be difficult to live in these critical, changing times. This garden also affords me the seasons of pruning and attending to my nonbearing magnolia tree, which are concrete challenges of growth. So it is with this book, as it opens us to the fruits of being present to our inner world. Peters draws upon her decades of study and clinical care to lead us down secure paths of presence, inquiry, and practice to come upon our own particular inner garden—one that needs our attention and can sustain us through life's most difficult experiences. *Aging with Agency* explores how to access this stream of life's flowing water in challenging living environments and even when undergoing memory loss, where she shows us that our deepest self is not abandoned in memory loss."

—MARITA GRUDZEN, MHS, associate
director emerita, Stanford Geriatric Education
Center, Stanford School of Medicine

Aging WITH Agency

Aging WITH Agency

Building Resilience, Confronting Challenges, and Navigating Eldercare

SANDI PETERS

Foreword by Drew Leder, MD, PhD

North Atlantic Books
Berkeley, California

Published by
North Atlantic Books
Berkeley, California

Cover art and design by Jess Morphew
Book design by Happenstance Type-O-Rama

Printed in the United States of America

Aging with Agency: Building Resilience, Confronting Challenges, and Navigating Eldercare is sponsored and published by the Society for the Study of Native Arts and Sciences (dba North Atlantic Books), an educational nonprofit based in Berkeley, California, that collaborates with partners to develop cross-cultural perspectives, nurture holistic views of art, science, the humanities, and healing, and seed personal and global transformation by publishing work on the relationship of body, spirit, and nature.

North Atlantic Books' publications are available through most bookstores. For further information, visit our website at www.northatlanticbooks.com or call 800-733-3000.

Library of Congress Cataloguing-in-Publication data is available from the publisher upon request.

1 2 3 4 5 6 7 8 9 KPC 25 24 23 22 21 20

This book includes recycled material and material from well-managed forests. North Atlantic Books is committed to the protection of our environment. We print on recycled paper whenever possible and partner with printers who strive to use environmentally responsible practices.

*To the many elders who trusted me with
their inner life, and my many teachers
who showed me the possible.*

CONTENTS

FOREWORD

Imagine you're walking on the beach. You're an elder, or a friend or family member of an elder, or a professional in the field of eldercare. What does it mean to grow old well? you wonder. How to meet all the many challenges one must face? How also to embrace the rich opportunities of later life?

A woman wanders up to you (this is a bit of a fairy tale) and says, "Come with me, learn from me. I offer *knowledge*. I will teach many things that will help you deal gracefully with growing old, including those elements of aging people most fear: needing assistance with daily living, experiencing the loss of loved ones, perhaps suffering cognitive decline and memory loss. Being knowledgeable, being prepared, is always to the good."

But then a man wanders up from the other direction on the beach. "You should come with me," he says. "I offer you more than just knowledge; I offer *wisdom*. I will teach you how later life is a special time and how you can use it to go deeper into oneself and grow closer with others—and even with the Divine."

Hmm; both sound important. You stand there by the sea, wondering which person to follow. Knowledge is as innumerable as the grains of sand on this beach, so in your mind you call the first messenger "Sandi." But as your gaze falls on the large rocks that form a natural pier, you reflect that wisdom is like a rock that withstands shifts of wave and tide; you think of Jesus saying to Peter (from the Greek *petrus*, meaning "rock") that he will be the rock on whom the church is built. So in your mind you call that second guide "Peter."

You still waver—knowledge or wisdom? Sandi or Peter?—and this book magically appears in your hand, and it's written by none other than *Sandi Peters!* (I said this was a fairy tale, but I never promised it would be a good one.) You laugh. You leaf through the book and find that it includes both knowledge and wisdom—practical need-to-know information alongside deep spiritual teachings—all designed to help us grow old well.

But what does that mean? Let's continue to play with words, such as the phrase "grow old." To "grow," according to the dictionary, is to "increase; develop into maturity." But do we experience our aging process as a time of increase and development? Not usually; not for most, and not in our culture. Instead of "growing old," perhaps in twenty-first century America we should call it "*shrinking* old." Our society and its institutions and media, right down to insulting birthday cards, often portray later life as a time of shrinkage—physical, cognitive, social, financial. Don't we fear our physical mobility shrinking, along with our cognitive skills, creativity, independence, and time left on earth? It's no surprise that many of us oscillate between dread and denial of the aging process.

So much for "growing." What of the word "old"? Etymologically it derives from the ancient Indo-European root *al*, meaning to "grow, nourish." There's that word "growth" again, and the rich resonance of "nourishment," which can take inward and outward forms. But we don't tend to have nourishing associations with the word "old." The word connotes something out of date, slow, over the hill; the very opposite of sexy, vital youth, or the shiny excitement of the new. Who gets excited about an old idea, an old sofa—or, for that matter, an old person?

This book helps us to shift into a whole new paradigm of growing old. In many ways, this is also the recovery of an old paradigm of growing old, one associated with many ancient and traditional cultures that revered the figure of the elder. The elder was associated with wisdom, spirituality, compassion for other people, and care of the earth "unto the seventh generation." But we have to do our inner work to become an elder; it's not just a matter of chronological longevity.

From this perspective, the process of aging, when embraced, can be fulfilling and transformative. We're eldering ourselves. Often when we're young we're simply too busy, too preoccupied with ego formation and with building a family and career, to have much focus on soul development. Aging brings losses but also opportunities for exploration and deepening. In later life we can feel nourished by the long life journey we have taken, the other lives we have created or touched, the unlived life we can still experience as we explore new activities and unexpressed sides of the self, and even the eternal life that shines bright within and without. This book is a guide filled with knowledge and wisdom to help us wander into the wilds of later life with greater assurance.

To use a more technological metaphor, perhaps this book is like a Swiss Army knife, a kind of "tool of tools." Such a knife might include a corkscrew, tweezers, scissors, a screwdriver, or a number of other tools so its owner can use the appropriate implement to address a variety of challenges. Analogously, different chapters in this book are designed to help us meet different later-life challenges. How do you access resources on aging within your community? How can you accept and work with memory decline—your own or a loved one's? How and when do you locate optimal arrangements when living independently is no longer an option? *Aging with Agency* offers pragmatic help for these and many other questions.

It is not just outward challenges that this book is designed to help with, but also those inward challenges of becoming an elder. Peters teaches that we can continue the process of soul growth even though the body's powers are diminishing. In fact, she shows us that diminishment, when worked with skillfully, often provokes soul growth. When power, status, wealth, and health are diminishing, that situation provides the needed time, and the severe challenges, that accelerate the search for God and true Self. She quotes gerontologist Jane Thibault's notion that aging creates a kind of "natural monastery." Just as a monk chooses to stay immobile in order to go on a spiritual journey—to simplify life in order to free up time and energy for soul work—so the austerities of aging may gift us with a monastic experience whether we choose it or not.

But whether we choose it or not can make all the difference. As Peters writes, "We all most likely know old people who refuse to be elders. Unwilling to face the challenges of working with their shadows and re-visioning their values, they attempt to return to a time when life was easier or more satisfying. They may be old, but they refuse to move into the aging process and instead cling to former, outworn modes of thinking, behaving, and feeling."

The result can be the stereotypically sad, bitter, self-righteous, or self-pitying curmudgeon. Perhaps we've known such old people or at times been one ourselves. This book is designed to help us, and our loved ones or clients, avoid such a fate. How so? Again, there is no single answer—we need knowledge and wisdom of many sorts—so here too the book, like a Swiss Army knife, offers many tools for soul work. It teaches us about the Eriksons' stages of development, Maslow's hierarchy of needs, and Jung's notion of the Self and its individuation as we incorporate our repressed shadow side. Peters offers many different techniques of meditation, whether on the cushion or while striding through the world. She supplies questions and exercises to help with inner exploration. She draws on examples from many secular and religious sources. She herself is deeply steeped in different spiritual traditions, both Western and Eastern. This book will unfold the psychospiritual tools appropriate for you, or perhaps for the aging family member or client you are assisting.

So I hope you enjoy this book and find it of great use. May you discover knowledge and wisdom that inspire you. A famous chapter in the ancient Chinese text Tao Te Ching reads, "The journey of a thousand miles begins with a single step." Right here, right now, ever begins the journey again, no matter how long stretches the path behind.

Drew Leder, MD, PhD
Professor of Western and Eastern philosophy
Loyola University Maryland, Baltimore

INTRODUCTION

This is the key sign that you are aging and not merely spending time—gradually you discover your original self, your own pristine way of being.

—THOMAS MOORE, *Ageless Soul: The Lifelong Journey toward Meaning and Joy* (New York: St. Martin's Press, 2017)

I once had a professor who assigned us ten books to read for one class. As we all groaned, he responded by saying that if we got only one thing out of a book, that was enough. What I want the reader to get from this book is the following:

- There is meaning to be found in older age. It is possible to find meaning even if we suffer physical or memory impairment.

- The way to fulfillment in old age is through exploring and developing our inner world.

For many, aging brings crisis, whether because of a deteriorating body or mind, choices that must be made, or changes in our interior or exterior landscape. The word *crisis* has its roots in the Greek language, meaning "to separate, decide, judge." Unanticipated and unwanted events give us pause. They separate us from our business-as-usual modes. We all get kicked out of our gardens of Eden sooner or later. For some, it happens in infancy; for others in childhood, adolescence, or midlife. No matter how long we've managed to escape the ravages of uninvited change, they inevitably arrive in old age with infirmity and loss, including memory loss.

In a famous Buddhist scripture, a woman named Kisa Gotami comes to the Buddha utterly distraught because her son has died. She begs the Buddha to restore him to life. He agrees to do so if she can bring him a mustard seed from a house untouched by death. Of course, she cannot, and her failure becomes her blessing: the realization that there is crisis in everyone's life. Loss, grief, disappointment, uncertainty, illness—these are what connect us to others and to the deepest part of our being. Like it or not, aging includes loss because it includes change. Whether your outlook is secular or religious, shifting gears internally to fully embrace aging in all its aspects is the central task of later life.

For many years, I facilitated a discussion group called Aging Matters. The group's name had a double meaning that conveyed the gravity of the topic. The questions (matters) we encounter as we age do matter, because our response to them can make the difference between aging as an experience of discovery or aging as a battleground. Every spiritual tradition offers a set of propositions that posit some answers to the fundamental questions of life, or at least some guidelines for how to approach them. Aging demands that we examine multiple propositions, no matter their origin, from the perspective of present experience.

If we do not have a context for understanding our experience in old age, we can end up depressed or despairing. If we do not have an affirmative vision of aging and cannot find meaning in our many experiences of loss and change, we easily get overwhelmed and are hard-pressed to stay positive. This book grows out of three concerns I have about aging in this society:

- our culture's tendency to assume and encourage a continuation of midlife goals and values into old age

- the medicalized environment of care so often provided to elders

- the prevailing attitude of fear toward aging, especially toward those living with memory loss, which results in a disregard of the elderly and treating both aging and memory loss as tragedies.

I have written this book to address these concerns. It is the book I have searched for and wanted to read. It is written for all those who take aging seriously and want to reimagine this time of life.

The word "agency" in the title comes from the root *ag-* in medieval Latin, meaning "to drive, draw out or forth, move." It is an apt analogy for the intention of this book. Older adults reading this book will be guided in how to deepen through the changes of aging while building the resilience to live fully. By "resilience" I mean not only the ability to bounce back from adverse circumstances, but also the underlying psychic strata that facilitate this response. Family members caring for elders will gain valuable insight into what might be going on below the surface for their loved ones, thus improving their capacity to assist. They will also receive tools to make their caregiving journey feel less burdensome. Professionals in the field, currently influenced by cognitive behavioral therapy, will be able to add a depth perspective to their approaches to care. Readers who are biased, as many are, by cultural models that deny or circumvent the aging process will realize that aging is much more than what current thinking allows. My hope is that this book will inspire facility administrators to develop and implement programs that address psychological and end-of-life issues for all the elders in their care, and that it will alert families and elders to the terrain of aging.

Our present cohort of older adults is immensely diverse. An individual's or group's cultural, health-related, and socioeconomic characteristics will alter the way they perceive and assimilate this book's content. It is my hope that discipline-specific gerontologists who read this work will translate its theories and practices for the population of older adults they serve.

The first part of the book focuses on the tasks of aging as understood through the lens of developmental psychology. The middle section explores the experience of memory loss and offers time-tested contemplative practices that enhance our ability to remain present during challenging times. The final chapters offer practical information to help us make more informed choices and navigate care options more effectively.

We live on at least two different levels of reality: that of ego, the many voices in our head that we are most familiar with; and that of soul. When

I use the word *soul*, I am not referring to some fixed essence, but rather to a force or energy that is in all life and wants life to be fully expressed. One of my most significant teachers has been the Swiss psychiatrist C. G. Jung (1875–1961). He calls this energy or force *Self*, and he holds that its purpose is wholeness. To ego, the thrust of Self can sometimes feel as if we are being directed, or even propelled, where we would rather not go. This is reminiscent of the saying attributed to Jesus in the Bible (John 21:18) that when we get older, someone else will lead us where we don't want to go. In our day, this someone is usually an adult child or a social worker. However, we can also be led by our fate. We do the best we can to avoid *X*, *Y*, or *Z*, and it happens anyway. When Self manifests in life, it almost always throws a wrench into projects and plans. It can feel very personal; in reality, it is, and it isn't. It is personal in the sense that our life is being acted upon. It isn't personal in the sense that we are not special (exalted or condemned) because of the action of Self.

We are each part of a larger whole. Our experiences, past and present, are part of that larger whole—one of the ways in which the whole manifests. A perspective that sees all that happens to us as part of this larger vision would never make it through a logic course. Nonetheless, this is what I have come to understand through my life experience, years of study in the disciplines of philosophy, theology, and psychology, and my work with oldsters. ("Oldsters" is a term coined by Ashton Applewhite in her book *This Chair Rocks: A Manifesto against Ageism*.)

My understanding of soul overlaps with religion but is not constrained by it. A Buddhist monk once said, "The personality [i.e., ego] never gets enlightened." At the time, I found this statement to be very disappointing. It took me quite a few years to comprehend the truth of what he was saying. The ego part of us just wants things to be easy. It almost always resists change. The deeper part of us, however, wants to grow—to be enlightened. This book is addressed to that part of all of us.

This book ranges over history, philosophical inquiry, psychology, gerontology, life-span development, and spirituality in an attempt to ground the aging experience in a meaningful context. Great thinkers create theories. These are the Einsteins, Freuds, and Jungs of the world.

Others' creativity lies in synthesis. I am one of these. I have tried to integrate the thoughts of others from various disciplines and perspectives, along with my own experiences, into what I hope is a rich, deep, compelling picture of the aging process. I want my arguments to move you to consider possibilities beyond the physical body and current medically based prejudices, especially for those with cognitive challenges. If I succeed in helping you refrain from foreclosing on other possibilities, I have fulfilled my goal.

In 1985, I left theology school and shortly thereafter embarked on a path that would change my life forever. I became deeply involved in the lives of two older women, both of whom were part of a faith community in which I participated. Through my association with these two women, I received an education in the needs of elders, the services available to them, and eventually the care settings that many elders reluctantly call "home" in the final years of life.

The early part of my work was mostly helping frail but cognitively intact elders "age in place," meaning to remain in their homes and communities. As I was privileged to enter the homes and inner sanctums of these elders' lives, I became aware of issues of loneliness, loss of purpose, helplessness, anxiety, and depression. Working in a large urban area, I often discovered that financial resources had little to do with quality of life in old age. Too often I would go into the homes of financially secure older adults who could and did purchase services they required, but they still struggled with feelings of unhappiness, worthlessness, and abandonment. On the other hand, many elders living in the poorer section of town in dire material circumstances were often cheerful, optimistic, and seemingly well adjusted.

The difference between these two groups was stark and troubling. What I noticed was that the economically poorer elders had learned the arts of connection and resiliency. Because their lives had not been easy, they took less for granted. They had been forced to develop internal resources, often resulting in humility and faith in God or the universe. They also had strong community ties that were not broken by their infirmity. Indeed, my visits would frequently be punctuated by neighbors popping in to say hi or checking to see if they needed anything. Contrast this with one elder I knew who was isolated in her home in the affluent area, where family and friends—if they were around at all—were inaccessible for various reasons. This elder spent her days with paid caregivers who often didn't speak English clearly. Having perhaps been sheltered from some of the vicissitudes of life, older adults like these had not been required to develop what I think of as "spiritual muscle." Now, at a time of vulnerability, they had few internal resources to sustain them.

I observed this difference at a time in my life when I started practicing Buddhist meditation and was developing a keen interest in the contemplative life. These influences gradually led me to see the aging experience as a potential crucible for awakening. This in turn led me back to an early interest in Jung and an exploration of life-span development. Although Jung's theories are mostly discredited by the contemporary emphasis on scientific, evidence-based approaches to the body/mind question, they offer an unequaled scope and vision to the aging.

This book couples Jungian thought with the work of life-span theorists and contemplative spiritual practices from around the world. In these pages, there are the beginnings of a road map that can not only turn the tide of ageism in our culture but also potentially move that culture toward a more humane and meaningful future for all ages.

Any book on aging cannot leave out the reality of cognitive decline. It is my belief that memory loss is not necessarily exempt from Self's/soul's thrust toward wholeness. How this looks will necessarily differ depending on whether an elder is compromised in this way. There is a tremendous amount of fear starting in midlife and escalating with age about losing one's faculties. These concerns are merited; however, our attitudes toward cognitive decline—and those living with it—need a significant face-lift. Having walked alongside many older adults who struggled with memory loss, including my beloved aunt, I can attest to the ongoing presence of Self/soul, despite appearances to the contrary. It is my hope that this book will soften readers' attitudes towards memory loss and bring some needed rebalancing to the subject.

Choosing a good environment in which to spend our later years goes a long way toward supporting us in the tasks of elderhood. The many facilities older people call home in our society are woefully inadequate to helping elders age with dignity and meaning. Most people pointedly avoid looking at these facilities, hoping they will never have to end up in one. Unfortunately, an ostrich approach exacerbates the situation for us all. What is needed is an informed, educated public willing to raise its voice for change so the specter of fear can be changed to a spirit of confidence.

It is my sincere hope that this book will be of benefit to the many elders who are now facing—and who one day will face—challenges of isolation, stigmatization, and loss for which there is currently little provision other than medication. For family members concerned for their own well-being as well as that of the elders they love, I hope this book leads them to consider elders' psychological and spiritual well-being alongside physical and safety needs. Finally, I hope professionals of various persuasions will find inspiration to broaden their outlook regarding what is possible and will actively encourage elders in their care to seek life and not just safety.

May this book contribute to greater ease with aging.

May it offer insight into the potential of old age and cognitive loss for the elder and for those caring for them.

May it, in some small way, affect our societal attitudes toward the last stage of life so the full journey of our lives can be supported, nourished, understood, and allowed to deepen within us.

1

Why Am I Still Here?

At one time or another, each of us is brought to the cliff's edge. At such moments we can either back away in bitterness or confusion, or leap forward into mystery.

—PHILLIP SIMMONS, *Learning to Fall: The Blessings of an Imperfect Life* (New York: Bantam, 2000)

What is the purpose of life in old age? Where do we find meaning and hopefulness when our usual supports are taken away? This is a challenge throughout life. It is even more challenging as we grow older. Aging is a stressful time. It calls for a radical change in and reorientation toward how we live our lives. Many of us arrive on the doorstep of aging woefully unprepared. We assume this stage of life will be like the ones that went before; therefore, we haven't developed the particular skills we need to meet this time of life.

When persistent calls from the body demand attention; when we start losing friends and abilities; when we make changes in our lives, even the welcome ones, we are subject to the perils of stress. For the most part, work—in whatever capacity we knew it, whether as executive director, trash collector, homemaker, or teacher—no longer distracts us from facing ourselves. Children are grown and often not living nearby. Our bodies, and sometimes our minds, decide to go on vacation or take a leave of absence. Our energy flags in the middle of a project. Society, if it sees us at all, dismisses us as irrelevant. These are changes we don't like.

On my seventieth birthday, an eighty-year-old friend with white hair took me out to dinner to celebrate. Each time the server came to our table, she looked at and spoke to me, not my dining companion. I became increasingly uncomfortable about this; thinking that perhaps I was overreacting, I asked my friend if she noticed it too.

"Oh, yes," she replied. "It happens all the time." Since my hair has not yet turned white, I was immune. It's not only vanity that encourages women to get rid of the gray or white in their hair; not being seen is the greatest motivator. I didn't speak up at the time. I felt awkward, and I didn't have confidence in voicing my observation without criticism creeping in. The incident plagued me for weeks afterward until I wrote a letter to the restaurant describing what I saw and asking management to talk with the servers.

What happened in this situation was completely unconscious on the server's part. This is the insidiousness of ageism. It is so much a part of our culture that we don't even notice it. It seems a formidable task to find meaning amid so much that pulls in the opposite direction. Yet this is the task we are called upon to undertake in old age. In the above example, the first step was to notice what was happening. Instead of internalizing and passively accepting the situation or making light of it, the next step is mustering the courage to name it for what it is; next would be to look internally for the patterns that keep it in place. Teasing these out and working with them develops spiritual muscle. Another name for this quality is resilience. Resilience allows us to reframe a situation so that instead of seeing it as an easily dismissed annoyance, we can view it as an opportunity to be a change agent, both within ourselves and—if we're courageous enough—in society.

In small settings and in large ones, our approach to the question "Why am I still here?" has an enormous impact on how we experience old age. The question is not limited to the person experiencing aging, however. It also encompasses the elder's family members and friends who are called upon to make decisions they are often ill equipped to make. When it comes to aging, we live in a society of denial. No one really wants to face this severe time of life. We think "sufficient unto the day is the trouble thereof," as the Bible says, and we imagine that when the time comes to "do something" about an aging parent or friend, a solution will automatically appear.

Solutions do appear, and they are often not what's best for the old person. It is true that situations like these contain many unknowns that make it impractical to formulate definite or precise plans. However, we can educate ourselves about the types of services that are available and especially about the needs of people at this time of life. Too often I have seen families move a parent out of the home with the best of intentions only for the parent to then languish, become ill, or adopt uncharacteristic traits. This is particularly true for people with memory loss. If the parent has been moved to a care facility, staffers tell the relative that the memory loss is an "expected decline." In some cases, it is; but in too many cases it is the result of thoughtless decision-making and bad social policy.

Family members caring for an aging relative often act out of uninformed but good intentions. One such incident that stands out for me is that of a ninety-four-year-old woman I'll call Mary, who had early-stage memory loss. (Throughout this book, elders cited as examples are composites of older adults I have worked with through the years. If they resemble someone the reader knows, it is because these situations and stories are ubiquitous.)

Mary and her husband, who was watching out for her, moved into a high-end care facility. When he unexpectedly died of a stroke, the facility moved her into their locked memory unit, even though she was less advanced in her cognitive loss than the other residents. Mary could easily have maintained her life in the section of the facility where she and her husband had developed relationships; she was very social and found these relationships sustaining. But the couple's three children, who lived out of state, and their fiduciary (the person who managed their finances) were not concerned about Mary's move. The facility told them it was for Mary's safety, and they went along without question. The fiduciary did not want to get involved and did not see this as her role. The children wanted Mary to be safe and were told by the facility this was what was needed. Other options were not made available. Mary had a longtime friend who tried to intervene by explaining to one of the daughters that the placement was inappropriate, but the daughter was not interested in discussing the matter. It was much easier to go along with the professionals than to question what was happening.

The facility benefited in two ways from this arrangement: they decreased their liability, and they could charge more money for Mary's care. Mary, on the other hand, did not benefit at all. She now found herself "incarcerated," as she put it, and she took to sleeping most of the time to escape her situation. Actually, her response proved fortuitous. Others in such a situation might have gotten depressed or started expressing anger; if Mary had done that, the next step would have been for the facility to medicate her. That too would have been normalized and rationalized so that someone unfamiliar with memory loss and facility management would accept this course of events as necessary.

There was no good outcome for Mary and no good reason this had to happen. Several factors allowed this situation to prevail: ignorance on the children's part, indifference on the fiduciary's, and liability concerns coupled with economic incentives for the facility. This is what can pass for eldercare in the United States today.

When an elder is limited in her ability to meet her own needs, it is incumbent upon family members and professionals to provide for her. In too many instances, the only need deemed necessary to meet is safety. When we discuss the theories of Abraham Maslow in chapter 5, we will see that safety is one of the lowest needs humans have. Eldercare too often gets reduced to this level, and we are complicit with this state of affairs when we fail to educate ourselves. We are so much more than our bodies. As we age, bodies slowly decline, but under the right circumstances, spirits can still flourish. When we are involved in eldercare, either for ourselves or for a loved one, it is critical to take the inner world into account along with bodily needs. As in the other stages of life, old people have good days and less-than-good days. Unfortunately, having a preponderance of not-good days is too often the result of circumstances that can be ameliorated. Life can be meaningfully lived and enjoyed to the end.

Tribal society valued the old ones because of their usefulness. The elders carried the traditions and knowledge that helped the tribe thrive. Today, technology has made the wisdom of the elders obsolete. Instead of young people going to old ones for advice, the reverse happens. Older adults, immigrants to high-tech culture, consult with the young natives on how to work smartphones and computers. Since the United States has a very youth-oriented, extroverted society, the experience that comes from living a long life no longer holds value. On top of that, many older adults, influenced by the culture's predominant values, do not see their own experience as valuable. Hence we have a void in meaning for late life.

In the past, religions were able to successfully fill that gap through moral injunctions. In Judaism and Christianity, the directive to "honor thy father and mother" is the fourth of the Ten Commandments. The Koran exhorts followers to honor, respect, obey, and be kind to their parents. Filial piety is a hallmark of teachings in Confucian philosophy and Asian cultures. Today's Western society does not seem to have internalized these instructions. Even when adult children do want to care for their parents, too much gets in the way: distance, work responsibilities, child rearing, lack of awareness of what's needed and available, and for the vast majority, lack of adequate financial resources.

Likewise, for the oldster, past societal models of aging are not helpful because they are outdated or negative. Prior models frequently confined the older adult to a small range of identities, e.g., images of kindly Grandma in the rocking chair or baking cookies for a church event, or Grandpa showing a young man how to plow a field. Most of these roles are obsolete. Pejorative images of befuddled but amusing older people have taken their place. Care facilities that house older adults reflect this ambivalence. Lip service is paid to respecting elders, but in actuality, older people are often infantilized. Attention is paid to safety and medical issues, but little regard is given to what might be needed for an old person to truly flourish rather than simply existing.

In short, elders face social and cultural displacement. Many older adults find themselves living out various versions of outdated options while trying to fashion a life that feels significant. Most people are caught off guard by aging. In addition to coping with the very real physical, social, and economic changes that attend aging, present-day elders often do not have a good psychological understanding of what aging entails, and they lack the tools they need to address the new challenges facing them. Uncertainty is evident in both the outer-directed question "What to do?" and the inner-directed question "How to be?" We can't go back to tribal or religious values. We are living in a liminal time—betwixt and between, as cultural anthropologist Victor Turner put it. Prior values and outmoded ways of doing and being have fallen away, but nothing has yet taken their place. Something new must emerge. We have to do our best to forge our own understanding and purpose for the last stage of life.

One of the many tasks of growing old is to ask questions and explore possible answers. To do that, let's consider the story of Linda, a married woman who has several children who have families of their own and now live in other parts of the country. She worked as an accountant and retired at age sixty-seven; her husband, Bill, five years her senior, had already retired. Their plan had always been to travel the country in their RV once they were both retired.

It too often happens at this stage of life that one or the other partner falls ill. In this case, Bill fell off a ladder while fixing their roof and shattered his hip. While in rehabilitation, he contracted septicemia, a blood infection. The infection was treated successfully, but the stress of surgery and illness left Bill unmotivated and depressed. He was never able to mount the effort to do his physical therapy exercises, so when he was discharged home, he was in a wheelchair. This situation changed their plans and hopes for the future. Linda became a caregiver, and Bill, unused to being an invalid, continued to slip deeper into depression.

This is a good example of some of the surprises that happen as we age and of our different approaches to dealing with those surprises. It took Linda a certain amount of self-searching, lots of questioning, and some letting go to arrive at a life worth living for her. Initially she just reacted and threw herself into caring for Bill. Her goal was to get him back to his old self so their life could continue as it had been. She went out of her way to be cheerful and attentive; she fixed Bill special dishes and generally tried to make him happy. Bill, however, did not respond as she hoped he would.

When Bill was a child, his father deserted the family, leaving his mother—who had never worked outside the home before—to raise three children on her own. Getting even the basic necessities of life was problematic for Bill's family. He was a pudgy, silent child who was often the butt of jokes at school. When he reached his teens, he vowed to himself that he would never give people the chance to ridicule or feel sorry for him again. He lost weight, took up weightlifting, joined the football team, and learned to be macho.

Over the years of being married to Linda, Bill's need to always appear strong and in charge mellowed. His relationship with Linda and their children allowed his original nature to return. After his injury, however, he once again felt like that helpless, tormented child. In the face of loss, he reverted to the one coping style of his teen years that had been successful, and his need to feel strong reasserted itself. Bill was stuck. He was unwilling to face the fear of his present situation, which would have led him to question his coping strategies from his earlier years, when being macho had masked his vulnerability.

Once Linda realized she would not be able to bribe, love, or cajole Bill out of his present adaptation, she took stock of her own situation. How was she to lead her life, now that she had a dependent husband and that they could no longer live out their dreams as they had planned to do? It was not easy for Linda to recognize and separate her need to take care of Bill from her need to take care of herself. She had always relied on Bill to take the lead in planning and decision-making. Now that he refused to perform these tasks, they were left to her.

Linda did not have a good sense of herself. She had been so busy working and taking care of the house that she had not developed many of her own interests. She did have some good friends, however, and it was to them that she turned now. These women encouraged Linda to try new things. She began taking classes in t'ai chi, ceramics, and Spanish at the local senior center. She found she had a facility for language; since she lived in a town that was close to the border with Mexico and many Mexican migrants in her area needed help, Linda started volunteering, doing paperwork and child care for migrants. In the past she had been somewhat apolitical, but now that she was so close to the issue of immigration, she found herself speaking out on behalf of the rights of those she was helping. When a mother and her two children needed an immigration sponsor, Linda offered her home to them.

Linda found her life enlarging instead of contracting. She discovered that she had skills and talents that had gone unused. She found a purpose that was deeper, richer, and more valuable than the original plan of traveling the states in an RV, despite how pleasurable that might have been. The presence of the migrant family in their home also helped to lift Bill's mood, because the children reminded him of his own children when they were young. This brought him out of his enclosed shell. While he never made an attempt to get out of his wheelchair, his isolation and depression were mitigated.

What can we learn about the question "Why am I still here?" from this story? Linda and Bill were plunged into an existential crisis, like many who live into their later years. We cannot control the circumstances that befall us as we age. We are all vulnerable all the time. The only control we're guaranteed to have is over our response. If we approach our aging with an expectation of loss, when the losses occur—and they will—we will contract. We will withdraw into a shell, as Bill did. While there is always hope, it is much more difficult to remain open once we have allowed the crust of old protective habits to take over.

All of us arrive in old age, as Bill did, with coping styles that are less than optimal. Sometimes we need protective armor just to get through the life that has been given us. The presence of such armor is not the problem. The difference between the past and the present is that we do not need to hold onto those old habits. Age offers us the opportunity to look at the many pushes and pulls that formed us and that continue to play out in our lives. We can stop, look, evaluate, and make new choices.

Bill did not stop to ask himself what he was feeling, where it came from, or what images and memories accompanied his impulse to shut down. He went on autopilot. Sometimes in the moment that's all we can do. Later, however, we have the ability to come back and reassess. We can bring psychological awareness and attentiveness to our inner world. Who is talking inside our heads, and what stories are they telling? These stories are not innocuous. They are often the drivers behind our action or inaction. Bringing them into the open—where there is light, and where we can engage with them—is the way to freedom. Had Bill engaged his inner world in this way, he might have seen how his early child-hood experiences were influencing his present condition. He could have sought help from a social worker or a psychologist. Even talking with his wife would have been salutary. He might have been able to break out of the prison that was locking him into, and replicating, his childhood feelings of insecurity and depression. Such a development could have then given him the incentive to push through his resistance, work hard on his rehabilitation, and leave the hospital walking on his own. Of course, if he had done that, he and Linda might have been able to realize their dream of traveling, and Linda's newfound sense of purpose in working with immigrants might never have come to pass.

Linda went in the opposite direction from Bill. She discovered new aspects of herself, forged new identities, and found strengths she didn't know she had. Instead of contracting in the face of disappointment, fear, and the unknown, she expanded. From the perspective of this book, this is the essence of what it means to grow old. When we encounter the inevitable changes of aging, we need to find ways to enlarge our vision and perspective to embrace them. This is not easy, but failure to do so often results in leading a truncated life.

The difference between an elder and an old person is that an elder has chosen to open to change rather than shut it out. That doesn't mean the person is able to do this all the time, but the intention and desire to remain open are primary. We are all fallible and make mistakes. We often take two steps forward and one step back. We don't need to evaluate ourselves on how successful we are in being open; the point is how often we make the effort. We can't always succeed in being who we would like to be, but each day is offered to us anew. Linda's response to her new situation gave her life renewed purpose. She found a way to fashion a new life for herself, one that allowed her to continue experiencing her vitality.

It is possible to do what Linda did at any age. For those who live into their eighties and nineties and who also have some level of infirmity, a bit of ingenuity and deep self-knowledge are required to figure out what is needed to maintain a vital connection to life. Often the answer has more to do with being than with doing. When we finally have the time to really listen to those in our lives and reflect back to them what we are hearing, this is a tremendous gift we can give. Watching the sun fully set, taking a meandering walk in our neighborhood, joining a group of people who share our interests, and becoming involved politically (even from the comfort of one's home) are all ways of connecting inside and outside. One elder friend of mine who is almost blind belongs to a poetry writing group, another spends much of her day knitting caps for low-income families, another cooks soup for the homeless at a nearby church each week, another is writing her memoir, and still another participates in senior center programs via her landline phone. There are countless ways to stay connected to others and to oneself.

When we approach life with an attitude of exploration and curiosity, we are assured of finding what we need to turn old age from contraction to expansion. When a family member or friend applies the same attitude to their care of an older adult, what often is experienced as a burden can turn into a mutually life-enhancing adventure. Victor Frankl, the

Viennese psychiatrist who survived a concentration camp, said we can endure any *what,* as long as we have a *why.* This book is intended to guide the reader through the territory of aging by offering a psychological road map of our internal landscape. The thinkers and theorists I discuss in the following chapters all illustrate various dynamics inherent in moving from the consciousness characteristic of the first half of life to that characteristic of the second half of life. Each approaches the territory from a different perspective, yet like different instruments in an orchestra, they all harmonize to give us a view of the kinds of psychological and philosophical terrain we are likely to encounter. Much of the book focuses on what each of us can do to maximize awareness of internal dynamics and thus enrich our understanding of ourselves and others.

If our care needs require us to rely on others to provide for us, whether in our homes or in a care facility, then it becomes indispensable to appreciate the value of interdependence. It is not solely up to the older person to struggle with the growth of consciousness. The work of consciousness-raising also falls to family members, professional caregivers, facility administrators, and institutions. When we can no longer create meaning for ourselves, we need to be able to rely on others to help us with that task. Of utmost importance in all cases are education and attitude. These are the two pillars that make the difference between seeing aging primarily through a pessimistic lens or a balanced one. Being informed is the first step on a long road of adventure, one I hope readers will take up with some measure of confidence and hopefulness as a result of this book.

2

Growing Old:
Past and Present

It remains to be seen whether we can build postmodern courses
of life that are both socially just and fulfill our needs for love and
meaning.

—THOMAS COLE, *The Journey of Life:*
A Cultural History of Aging in America
(Cambridge, UK: Cambridge University
Press, 1991)

A desire I have always had and that has grown stronger with age is to know the history of things. I frequently pursue this question personally. What are the forces acting on me from childhood that led me to make the choices I make and to see things the way I do today? How do these factors influence my present attitudes, biases, strengths, and weaknesses? As we saw in chapter 1, assessing the impact of personal history on our lives gives us greater freedom of choice in the present.

As my years in the aging field turned into decades, that same spirit of inquiry caused me to wonder what it was like for old people before our modern era. Of course, I knew that many elders in bygone days continued to live at home or with family and that they had a role within that family. As society became more urbanized, however, elders were left behind. How did we get to the place we're in now, where so many old people live outside their original communities, and care facilities are increasingly the norm? Is this simply progress? Is it a positive development? This chapter is an attempt to give the reader a sense of how questions of aging were addressed in the past, particularly with regard to housing and medical care. If you're interested in doing additional research in this area, know that much of the information in this chapter came from these sources:

- www.seniorliving.org/history/1776-1799
- https://medicine.jrank.org/pages/1243/Nursing-Homes -History.html
- https://rincondelrio.com/the-history-of-nursing-homes-from -almshouses-to-skilled-nursing

The personal problems that individual elders, family members, and professionals faced in the past are important clues in determining best options for today. The societal problems older adults grapple with today are mirrored in the problems of yesteryear. Although each older adult faces a different set of circumstances and responds uniquely, the factors that enable or thwart forward movement are societal. We are embedded in a larger political and social context that has a very real impact on the choices that are available. As we explore challenges of the past, my hope is that readers will become more attentive to issues of aging in their own lives and communities.

One of the best examples of larger political forces influencing individual choice in aging has been, and continues to be, the area of housing. In recent years, federal monies from the U.S. Department of Housing and Urban Development and state monies that fund construction of low-income housing or offer subsidies to landlords for low-income tenants have all but dried up. Affordable housing options for those aged sixty or older who do not own their own homes are scarce. In the San

Francisco Bay area, all federally and state-funded senior housing buildings hold a lottery to fill openings when they occur. If a senior is lucky enough to get into the lottery, she can then look forward to being on a wait list for at least five years. This means that just when social ties are most important, many seniors must leave their long-term community because, once they retire, they may not have the income to sustain the high cost of rents in urban areas. The demand for affordable living options when care is required is even more dire. Financing housing is one of the greatest hurdles to most of the issues discussed in this chapter. If we wish to take advantage of, promote, or negotiate policies, programs, and services to make life satisfying in older age, what we learn from history can provide a corrective so we do not have to repeat the mistakes of the past.

Aging Comes of Age

Aging became an area of study in its own right in the early twentieth century. What prompted its emergence was the recognition that longevity was increasing and that, as a result, older people were experiencing more chronic diseases than infectious ones. In his 1903 book *Etudes on the Nature of Man,* Eli Metchnikoff (1845–1916), a Nobel laureate and professor at the Pasteur Institute of Paris, introduced the terms "gerontology" (the study of aging) and "thanatology" (the study of death) into the modern lexicon. *Geron-* comes from the Greek *geras,* meaning "old man; to become ripe." When combined with *-ology,* meaning "a branch of knowledge," gerontology is the study of older people. Interestingly, according to one of my textbooks on aging, the word *geron* also refers to the process by which an animal sheds its skin. Becoming ripe and shedding one's skin are the views of aging advocated in this book. This will become evident as we explore life span in later chapters. The capacity for ripening is an apt metaphor for many in the field of gerontology today, including many baby boomers.

Around 1909, Ignatz Leo Nascher (1863–1944), an Austrian-born physician, coined the term *geriatrics* to designate care of the aged as a medical specialty. He saw the causes of aging as having to do with senescence, a natural decline, as opposed to the thinking of his time that attributed aging to pathology. As in so many instances, it turns out to be both/and rather than either/or. For instance, Alzheimer's disease is clearly a brain pathology and not a natural part of aging. At the same time, we now know that there are changes in the brain as we age and that some loss of mental agility is due to a natural decline. The same can be said for many other diseases affecting older adults. Arthritis is seen as normal wear and tear of the joints; however, there are some forms, such as rheumatoid arthritis, that involve a dysfunction of the autoimmune system, which makes them pathological. The point is that when it comes to the diseases of old age, there are generally multiple factors at work. Informing ourselves about a diagnosis is important because it helps us make more informed choices about our lifestyle and about how we psychologically approach the condition.

After World War II, geriatrics emerged as a distinct discipline in medicine, and gerontology emerged in social science. The American Geriatrics Society was founded in 1942 to promote health, independence, and quality of life for older adults. The Gerontological Society of America was founded in 1945 with the goals of educating scientists, decision makers, and the public about issues in health, behavioral and social policy, and higher education. There is now a plethora of organizations committed to better understanding the aging process and improving quality of life for older adults.

Over the course of the twentieth century, life expectancy in the United States rose dramatically. In 1909, people usually died at between fifty and fifty-three years of age. By 1945, that figure rose to between sixty-three and sixty-seven years of age, and by 1998, life expectancy reached seventy-three to seventy-nine years of age. The upward trend in longevity holds true worldwide. It is expected that by 2030, older persons will outnumber children aged nine years and younger, and that by 2050 more than 20 percent of the US population will be aged sixty-five or older, compared to 13.7 percent today. This compelling knowledge challenges us to continue developing resources to meet the varied needs of old people. It is a sobering and galvanizing task. The potential for innovation at many levels is the gift and power of these statistics.

To understand the impact of societal aging is to get a glimmer of our own attitudes toward growing old. Just as our childhood experiences influence our adult choices and attitudes, societal pressures and expectations are also consequential. They have an enormous, though often hidden, significance for how and what we notice. How do you approach your aging? Do you run for Botox, color your hair, and send ageist birthday cards, or do you unabashedly acknowledge your years? What about allocation of resources? Do you subscribe to the "greedy geezer" myth? Do you believe that old people are "over the hill" and should make way for the young? What do you see as the goal of late life? What might be the optimal living situation for yourself, or for other older adults, in old age? Are there models of independent or community living in late life that you find appealing? If so, what and where are they?

Our answers to these and many more questions are often directly related to the influence of the society within which we live. Unless we make a conscious choice to consider possibilities outside the norm, we inadvertently go along unthinkingly with what our culture values and defines as appropriate.

Looking Back: A Brief History of US Eldercare

The history of care provision for older adults both with and without memory loss is long and complex. As will become evident, society has certainly moved forward in terms of providing care; however, the underlying issues that proved troublesome in the past—especially the economic issues—continue to bedevil the present.

Before the Industrial Revolution (1820–1870) and its attendant mass migration to urban areas, families and the community took care of old people. Until the Great Depression (1929–1939), most states still had laws requiring children to care for parents. While this is no longer the case, most children today still feel some level of moral obligation to at least oversee their parents' care, if not to directly care for them.

Depending on the personalities involved and the type of relationship between adult child and parent, this arrangement can be a godsend or a nightmare. Usually, parental need for help falls at the exact time in life when an adult child is most stressed with their own children's needs, career demands, and economic pressures. In the best circumstances, the adult child is sensitive to the parent's history, preferences, and desires and seeks to help the parent maximize their autonomy and choice. Unfortunately, many children are unable or unwilling to put in the time and effort necessary to ensure a good outcome for the parent. In these circumstances, the older person is left to struggle on their own or to turn to professionals who, hopefully, will have their best interests at heart.

Historically, elders without families went to tax-supported poorhouses or almshouses. The poorhouse supported anyone who was indigent, including children, the mentally ill, alcoholics, disabled individuals, and old people. It does not take much ingenuity to imagine what it was like to have such diverse groups living together, nor the kinds of challenges likely to emerge. To make matters worse, poorhouses were fraught with corruption and expensive to operate, and they had a bad reputation. Eventually, the poorhouse was split into the "deserving poor" (e.g., children, mentally ill people, and elders) and the "undeserving poor" (e.g., alcoholics and vagrants). At the end of the nineteenth century, boards of charity were set up in several states as regulatory bodies to oversee the institutions.

In light of the difficulty of housing older adults with other dependent populations, some philanthropic organizations established "homes for the aged." While these homes did fill a need and were helpful to single and widowed older adults, they had significant drawbacks. Homes for the aged often afforded old people little control over their lives. In addition, the old people who lived there were expected to help with the daily maintenance of the home, which effectively disenfranchised frail or sickly older adults. Additionally, many only admitted certain old people, such as those with good character, those who could pay a fee, or those affiliated with the sponsoring religious or ethnic group. Because homes for the aged had such stringent requirements, they often excluded those most in need. On the positive side, some of them were designed to include children as well as elders. The world of eldercare in our day has circled back to recognizing the value of having children and elders intermingle. Innovative programs of eldercare include intergenerational activities, and some even have a child day care attached to an eldercare facility.

Today, in place of homes for the aged, we have facilities for those who can afford to pay—often substantial sums—for their care. For those who are economically disadvantaged, less optimal choices are available. As long as an older person is cognitively intact and able to exercise control, they can have a fairly good life in a facility. Once a degree of memory loss or physical dependence sets in, however, autonomy is severely curtailed. In the last resort, what is most frightening about aging is loss of control. While control is often an illusion even in the best of times, that fact does not become apparent until we are faced with frailty or find ourselves dependent in some way. This is one of the reasons why it is so important to acquire some introspective tools and adopt an attitude of curiosity earlier in life. It is also one of the reasons why it is important for us to pay attention to what is going on in the world of eldercare. We may one day find ourselves or a parent in need of services. What do we want for our care in our later years? We need to become informed advocates now so we can have an impact on our futures and mitigate some of the social and psychological effects of dependence.

As an example, let's consider the case of Joyce, who moved into an assisted living community with an attached care center when she was eighty-five. At the time, she was independent. She made friends in her new environment, participated in several program offerings, and volunteered at a nearby elementary school.

Joyce had had a hard life. She grew up in a small, rural community as an only child. Her mother had mental health issues and was in and out of institutions. During these times she stayed with an aunt and uncle. Her uncle sexually abused her. She never told anyone about this abuse because he told her no one would believe her, and she believed him. In high school, she engaged in promiscuous behavior and drinking. When an itinerant musical group came to town one weekend, she ran away with the drummer to California. They broke up shortly after arrival, and she was faced with the choice of either living on the streets or working to pay her way. She had always had an affinity for animals, and she found a low-paying job in an animal shelter. It took many years, many jobs, and several near-death experiences before she took control of her life. In her midthirties she discovered Alcoholics Anonymous. Through the relationships she formed at AA, the philosophy of life she embraced during that time, and the psychological understanding she developed while seeing a good psychotherapist, Joyce eventually worked her way out of her childhood trauma. In her early forties she went to school to study social work, graduated with an MSW, and started a career working with abused children.

When Joyce had a stroke at the assisted living facility, she was moved to the attached care center. Even though she now required care to meet her basic needs, she was able to maintain her equilibrium and identity. What Joyce brought with her to this new living situation was an attitude that looked at life's glass as being half full rather than half empty. She had learned this skill as a result of her years of hardship and suffering. In the care center, she often expressed gratitude to the staff who assisted her, used humor on difficult days, and soon became a staff favorite. Friends from the assisted living section visited her, and the teacher and children from the school where she volunteered came weekly to do a program with her and the other residents. Joyce was exceptional in her ability to draw deeply on inner resources and create meaning in each situation.

Most of the housing restrictions in the early homes for the aged were aimed at excluding immigrants from taking advantage of resources. The current divide in both American and European society over the presence of immigrants and the resources they consume is just the latest instance of a long-standing issue that seems to come to the fore whenever problems of access arise in times of economic challenge. Of course, the contributions of those immigrants are rarely taken into consideration. In our own day, immigrants and minorities provide the majority of care for elders in urban areas. In California, they labor in vineyards and the Central Valley to harvest the fruits and vegetables that feed people all over the country.

Few Americans are willing to do these kinds of jobs. What does justice mean in this situation? Americans are polarized on the issue. In our personal lives, when we come to a juncture that seems to require an either/ or response, such as deciding whether to move from our home or remain in place, the best resolution comes from taking time, factoring in personal preferences, exploring options, and talking things through with knowledgeable others as well as friends. This is a pattern legislatures could also choose. The resulting outcomes would most likely be more creative, more reflective of multiple values, and less polarizing.

In the nineteenth century, to address ongoing problems in finding housing for burgeoning populations in the United States, federal, state, and local governments began to build institutions to house people. In 1845, Congress made land grants to states so they could build asylums. Many mentally ill poorhouse and almshouse inmates were transferred to these institutions; among them were elders with memory loss. As resources were freed up following the Civil War (1861–1865), laws were passed that moved children and others with special needs from poorhouses to specific facilities for them. By the early twentieth century, there were asylums for the mentally ill, specialized housing for the disabled, and orphanages for children. Old people were left behind, so that by the 1920s nearly 70 percent of all residents in almshouses were old people. Contributing to this situation was a growth in longevity. Between 1900 and 1930, average life expectancy increased by ten years. By the time the Great Depression hit in 1929, the number of elders living in poorhouses, coupled with the public fear of these places, forced the federal government to act.

In 1935 President Franklin Delano Roosevelt signed the Social Security Act into law. The act created a precursor to Medicare, the Old Age Assistance program, which, together with matching grants from states, provides monies for medical care for older people. The program was intended to abolish the dreaded almshouses by ensuring that old people had sufficient resources to be independent. The catch, however, was that only those old people who lived independently or in privately owned residences were eligible for the program. This meant elders living in almshouses had to move to private situations or be excluded. What happened next is a good example of how shortsightedness, hasty decision-making, and lack of comprehensive planning result in unfavorable outcomes.

The states, which funded county almshouses, transferred these institutions to private control so residents would be eligible to receive Social Security assistance. In their haste, however, they failed to establish regulations for the homes. Regulations didn't come about until 1967, when the first standards for nursing homes were implemented. Most readers are familiar with the periodic horror stories about abuse in some nursing homes in our day, despite the myriad regulations in place. It is not hard to imagine what the circumstances were like when there was minimal accountability and lucrative funds. Even though institutionalized elders now received Social Security checks, the money went to the cost of their care. The elders who benefited the most were those who were able to continue living in their own home or community. This is also true in our day. Social Security funding is a safety net for many low-income Americans.

As I write this book, for the last several years some members of Congress have put forward proposals to privatize the Social Security program. Often such legislation is proposed without a comprehensive sense of its ramifications or a knowledge of the relevant history. If history has anything to tell us, it is that privatization inevitably leads to various forms of abuse. In our day, many of the problems with care facilities stem from a profit-driven motive. This is so because we have not yet been able or willing to recognize and deal with human greed. Perhaps one day we will value generosity more than self-interest. Until that time comes, we need checks and balances on the darker impulses of human nature. The notion that privatizing the Social Security program will help people is a dangerous fiction.

Enter the Medical Model of Care

In 1954, Congress passed the Hill-Burton Act, which provided funds to hospitals and health-related facilities so they could modernize and expand. The nursing home industry as we know it today originated from this stimulus. Old people who were too sick to live in an almshouse had nowhere to go, so they would often spend prolonged periods in hospitals or sanitariums. To deal with this situation, funds from Hill-Burton were used to convert old hospitals to nursing homes or to build nursing homes attached to hospitals. At the time, policy makers saw this as a reasonable solution for housing sick old people. These nursing homes thus became the primary option for older adults with limited financial resources or who needed assistance. The debate over national health care currently raging in the United States has its antecedents in this time. What is the government's obligation to care for the sick, old, infirm, or poor? Over the years, various initiatives to provide care for infirm populations have been proposed, and numerous interest groups have opposed them. In the late 1950s, nursing home costs associated with old people brought the debate front and center.

Old people were now living in nursing homes, but the cost of care kept rising. In response, in 1965, the federal government created Medicare and Medicaid. These programs were a boon to elders living on Social Security benefits, whether in their own homes or in small congregate living sites. They now had more discretionary money because they did not have to use their Social Security checks to cover health care costs. While Medicare did also help elders living in facilities, it did so indirectly because the money went to pay for their care. The funds, however, were insufficient to cover costs, and quality of care was sacrificed. Most facilities had to look elsewhere for financial stability, and that came then, as it does now, in the form of Medicare reimbursement for rehabilitation services.

Although Medicare and Medicaid do not provide care to all Americans, and the amount they pay for care is often below what private insurance pays, they offer a model that has worked successfully (albeit with some hiccups) for older adults and the poor for more than fifty years. Yet, as with so many other well-intended efforts, several unanticipated and unfortunate consequences resulted. Primary among these was that nursing homes proliferated, and the medical model of care for old people was born.

The number of nursing homes in the US grew by 140 percent between 1960 and 1976. Between Hill-Burton funds for construction and Medicare reimbursement for services, private industry had discovered a golden goose. Just as no one wanted to go to an almshouse, now no one wanted to go to a nursing home. Yet for those without familial or economic resources, the nursing home was the only option. Older readers may remember visiting these places. They housed many old people with no reason to be there other than their age. Some nursing homes were habitable, usually those in more rural communities or small towns where workers and residents had a history. Other nursing homes were abysmal. Profit went into the pockets of unscrupulous owners and administrators, while quality of care was poor and quality of life was virtually nonexistent. Inadequate, unpalatable food, absence of consistent medical care, and lack of screened and trained staff were too often the case. In essence, the nursing home replicated the earlier almshouse or poorhouse.

Lawmakers started enacting some standards in the early 1970s, but their focus was on the unsustainable cost of these homes. This led to a shift away from caring for old people in institutions and toward providing care in community settings, a shift that continues to this day. In 1965, the Older Americans Act established the Administration on Aging to encourage community-based services. As part of that effort, federal regulations require Area Agencies on Aging (AAAs) to operate in almost every county in the US and to provide vital information and services to older adults and family members. Each AAA has its finger on the pulse of the community and can refer callers to appropriate resources. Everyone reading this book should familiarize themselves with their local AAA so that when the time comes you will know where to turn. (Find your local AAA at https://eldercare.acl.gov.)

The medical model of care became prevalent in eldercare because Medicare tied a facility's financial reimbursement to the patient's specific medical conditions. This fee-for-service model is still in use today. When an older adult goes into a facility following surgery or the onset of another medical condition, they are there for rehabilitation. As long as they continue to make progress, Medicare pays for the service for up to one hundred days (as of this writing). Once the patient is determined to have reached their best level of functioning—which may be well below what they are actually capable of—funding is discontinued, and the patient is discharged. On the face of it, this model makes sense; however, according to Beth Baker, author of *Old Age in a New Age* (see entry in appendix B), coupling rehabilitation with Medicare payments further pushed nursing homes toward a medical model of care.

The medical model, which continues to dominate health care in the US, is based on an illness approach to care. When we visit our doctor, it is usually because we are having a problem we want fixed. For the most part, we don't expect our doctor to ask about our lifestyle or diet. We want our specific problem addressed and a pill to make it go away, if possible. The doctor is trained to treat problems and not to stray too far beyond the presented symptoms. This approach is problematic because it does not take into account all the other factors that can affect a symptom, such as grief, anxiety, depression, or financial hardship. In all these situations, it is likely that the person's physical symptoms mask or indicate psychological concerns. Treating the body without addressing these other important areas amounts to neglecting the whole person. This is exactly the problem of situating long-term care within a medical model. The medical model privileges concern for the body over concern for the person's psychological, social, and spiritual needs.

A hospital is a place where we go temporarily to heal. Submitting to the impersonality of a sterile environment, an institutional schedule, mass-produced food, and detached care is almost bearable because it is temporary. Such a setting is not conducive to a well-rounded life. We are also finding that it is not particularly conducive to healing, either. Nevertheless, the hardship is manageable because we know it will not last over the long term. A hospital is not a home. However, for older adults who have no other choice but to live in the hospital-like setting of a nursing home, life is grim. Not only is the environment barren, but residents are seen as their disease rather than as individuals. There is an emphasis on efficiency and completion of tasks associated with bodily care rather than on recognizing the old person's social and emotional needs. Within a medical model, elders become stroke victims, "feeders" (those requiring assistance with eating), or—when confined to bed and lacking the ability to interact—"vegetables." Few people would choose such circumstances as a way to end their days.

Throughout the 1950s and 1960s, widespread concern about the perceived lack of care in nursing homes grew until it reached a crescendo. In 1970, Maggie Kuhn (1905–1995), a retired social worker, founded the Gray Panthers, a grassroots organization dedicated to social change. The Gray Panthers advocated for higher standards in nursing homes, and in 1987, their efforts helped secure the passage of the Nursing Home Reform Act, which was part of a larger budget bill called the Omnibus Budget Reconciliation Act (OBRA). The nursing home provisions of OBRA were intended to ensure that residents living in nursing homes receive high-quality care by revising care standards. This was a significant step toward improving conditions, and like so much else, it had another side: it created a plethora of regulations, paperwork, and bureaucracy. Among those working in the field it is now jokingly remarked that nursing homes are second only to the nuclear industry in terms of government regulation. Regardless, OBRA has improved conditions in these environments. Although many nursing homes are still a long way from being life-giving places, egregious wrongdoing has been mitigated.

At the height of their expansion, nursing homes housed old people without regard to diagnosis. Today nursing homes are distinguished from other care environments—such as board and care, dementia or memory care, and assisted living—by housing mainly elders who require round-the-clock nursing care. The chapters on facilities at the end of this book discuss the advantages and disadvantages of these environments as well as what to look for when choosing one.

Aging in Place

Even with the changes brought about by OBRA, many older adults wanted—and continue to want—to remain in their homes and communities. Because of this, federal and state governments increased funding for community-based programs. When I started working in aging services in the mid-1980s, the term "aging in place" was just coming into vogue.

It refers to alternatives to facility living and services that help elders remain in the community. This idea opened a lucrative marketplace for new services, such as concierges, home-delivered gourmet meals, care in the home, and transportation.

The future of eldercare is likely to look very different from what is presently offered. While large-scale corporate-run housing for economically advantaged, independent seniors and assisted living facilities continue to proliferate, there is a great need for below-market-rate housing for independent middle- and low-income seniors, as well as affordable options for those who need daily assistance. As mentioned earlier in this chapter, funding for these kinds of housing options has been severely curtailed. Clearly, the issues of the past are alive and well in the present. As Congress continues to seek ways to rein in the costs of health care and eldercare, the need for advocacy in this regard is imperative. Without the supports that make life safe and stable, older adults' ability to find purpose and meaning in later years is severely curtailed. Creating conditions for a robust elderhood for everyone requires elders, family members, caregivers, and politicians to champion laws and programs that improve access to services. In researching the history of aging in the US, the one fact that stands out for me is that it has always been the demands of the average citizen that have pushed lawmakers to find ways to improve the aging experience.

Many creative people are seeking new ways to address some of the challenges facing older adults. The saying "necessity is the mother of invention" helps explain the current trend toward smaller-scale and mixed communities. Multigenerational households, cooperative housing, cohousing, "Golden Girls" arrangements (several older adults living together), and the village movement (fee-based local organizations that offer social and educational programs and trained volunteers to elders living at home) are just some of the options gaining momentum. For example, geriatrician Bill Thomas, who played a significant role in revolutionizing care in nursing homes, is now working on a project called Minka that is developing small prefabricated houses that can be used to create community housing.

Technology is likely to play a significant role in providing solutions to some older living challenges. Ride-sharing companies such as Uber and Lyft now offer taxi services for older adults who don't have a smartphone. There are also apps that can be installed in the home to remind seniors to take medication, and apps for family members to monitor the movements of their loved one in the home. Aging 2.0 is a loosely knit group of tech entrepreneurs who bill themselves as "a global network of innovators" dedicated to the design of user-friendly, practical tools for the aging market. We are just beginning to discover what may be possible as tech puts its resources into product design.

We started this chapter by asking how we arrived where we are now with eldercare—and whether the current state of eldercare is a positive development. I leave it to readers to make their own determinations. As we followed the labyrinthine path of the past, we witnessed the ongoing struggle to address unanticipated emerging problems, mostly in the arena of health care and housing. We also saw how formulating quick solutions without taking into account multiple facets of a problem often creates more problems.

As individuals and as a society, we cannot simply react to changing circumstances. If we want stability, good fiscal accountability, and well-being, we must be proactive. What we have seen on the macro level often repeats itself on the micro level. What society struggles with on a grand scale, individuals struggle with in their own lives. In both instances our tendency is to throw whatever resources we can muster at a problem and hope it goes away so we can move on to the next order of business. This is not an effective strategy for meaningful or viable change.

All of us, if we live long enough, will be consumers of services for older adults. If we are willing to look aging in the face without turning away, we are assuming responsibility for our future selves. We can use what we learn about our particular circumstances and needs, and what we learn about wider community efforts, to improve the experience of late life. Armed with knowledge, we can make informed choices for housing, medical care, relationships, and end-of-life care for ourselves, our loved ones, and our neighbors. If we do not take the time to educate ourselves, we will find ourselves reacting, and in a time of crisis we will be like the leaders of the past, who made hasty, poor decisions. We cannot afford to stand by and let others decide how we will live in old age. It is up to us to become advocates.

The most enduring change that seems to have emerged in the last hundred years is the increasing recognition of the distinct needs of older adults. This recognition must embrace care of the inner world as well as the body. If we look at the models and options for aging currently available and do not like what we see, it is up to us to be creative and make our voices heard. I can think of no more positive way of bringing meaning to the experience of aging than to initiate new ideas, designs, and services for the benefit of all. Efforts to create innovative options to meet current and future needs are in their infancy. We all need to turn our attention to the task of ensuring that old age is something we can look forward to rather than avoid.

3

An Introduction
to C. G. Jung

Every problem, therefore, brings the possibility of a widening of consciousness, but also the necessity of saying goodbye to childlike unconsciousness and trust in nature.

> —C. G. JUNG, "The Stages of Life," in *Structure & Dynamics of the Psyche,* translated by R. F. C. Hull, 2nd ed.; vol. 8 of *The Collected Works of C. G. Jung,* edited by Herbert Read, Michael Fordham, Gerhard Adler, and William McGuire (Princeton, NJ: Princeton University Press, 1969)

This chapter offers a perspective on how to approach aging by considering the psychological theories of Swiss psychiatrist C. G. Jung. Jung was both a scientist and a mystic, although for much of his life he took great pains to eschew the term *mystic* because of its pejorative connotations in scientific circles. With the rise of behaviorism—and the subsequent dominance of its progeny, cognitive behavioral therapy—in the US,

Jung's thought has been all but brushed aside in mainstream circles. Few academic psychology programs teach his work, and his writings remain obscure and unknown among the general populace. My hope is that this book will help to bring Jung's psychology out of the closet.

Jung's body of work is a direct outgrowth of his personal experiences of grappling with his interior world and that of his patients, and then conceptualizing what he discovered. His psychology is so vital for older age because he insisted that the second half of life has a depth and breadth unique to itself. One of his most frequently quoted remarks, from his essay "The Stages of Life," states the following: "A human being would certainly not grow to be seventy or eighty years old if this longevity had no meaning for the species." For Jung and his followers, late life is about becoming an explorer of the inner landscape, and Jung gave us a set of concepts to guide this exploration.

When a person's children leave home and their career no longer occupies center stage, they are faced with the question of what their anchor is at this time of life. This was the compelling question facing Frank, a retiree who went into the navy as a young man. He met his sweetheart in a small Texas town while on leave, and together they and their children lived in various locations in the US and overseas. When he retired from the service, he secured a government job that kept him happily productive until his health failed. A heart attack followed by knee surgery that didn't heal properly turned Frank from an active to a passive older person.

Frank had never been drawn to introspection, and he thought all psychology was hogwash. He and his wife had taken care of his parents in their later years, and neither parent had provided him with good role models for aging. He enjoyed socializing, but like many men, he depended on his wife to keep the social connections going. His only real pastimes were reading novels and watching TV. Although encouraged by his wife and children to try new things and explore hobbies, he staunchly refused. When his wife died, he moved into an assisted living facility, but because he had few social skills, he spent the majority of his time in his room. Whenever family members or friends suggested he try some of the programs at the care facility, he always came up with some excuse for why he didn't want to go.

Frank is an excellent example of someone who was unable and unwilling to explore the possibilities aging offered him. Unfortunately, his experience is all too common. In order to be able to take advantage of our elder years, we must be willing to open the door to our inner world and be curious about what is taking place inside. By the time the effects of aging hit Frank, he had adopted an inflexible stance toward life. Obstinacy has its place, but not when it comes to negotiating the twists and turns life throws at us. Frank never let me delve deeply enough into his background to determine what caused his rigidity, but I suspect it was a protective mechanism. Something or someone had wounded him when he was young, and unlike Joyce in chapter 2, who eventually sought help for the effects of her childhood abuse, Frank kept his tough shell to the end. Had he been willing to explore his inner world, as Jung recommended, his life might have been filled with richness, depth, and meaning.

I was first exposed to Jung in my late twenties in an undergraduate class on psychology as literature. I distinctly remember the stories resonating inside me as nothing before had ever done. I started reading Jung's writings and attending lectures on his ideas sponsored by the Jung Society in Washington, DC. This enthusiasm lasted until I moved to California for graduate school and could not find comparable study opportunities. My interest in Jung slid into the background until it was rekindled twenty years later when I entered spiritual direction training. By that time, I had been working in the field of aging for ten years. As I once again delved into Jungian thought, the correspondence between his psychology and what I was seeing in my work with elders was stunning. Over the years, Jung's thought has helped me contextualize the challenges and potential of my own journey as well as the journeys of the elders with whom I work. Jung's work conveys a level of meaning that melds the psychological and the spiritual into life-giving wholeness.

In the field of consciousness studies, there is currently a lively debate on the question of where consciousness resides. Is it in the brain or in the mind? As with most controversies, there are cogent arguments on both sides of the question. This debate is not new. It goes all the way back to Plato's Forms, which he conceptualized as residing predominantly outside the psyche as opposed to within it. In today's scientific climate, many researchers would like to reduce mind to brain. These scientists believe mind is nothing but brain, and when we understand the intricacies of brain, we will understand mind.

The distinction between brain and mind may sound academic, but it has bearing on how we think about aging. If we think we are our brain—the physiological set of neural components that allow the body to function—and the brain malfunctions as it does in memory loss, then we are left with a very mechanistic idea of personhood. This mechanistic notion plays out in the attitude we take toward those with memory loss and exacerbates our fear when we consider our possible future. It also limits our vision of what is possible when undergoing memory loss because such a view cannot account for experiences such as inspiration, spirit, and insight that can come to the fore in old age. The brain/mind controversy is also reflected in the medical model of aging discussed in chapter 2. There, the focus is on bodily deficits, which of course includes the brain. This leads to a lopsided approach to care in which bodily needs are emphasized and other types of needs neglected.

Jung's ideas, on the other hand, explore the intangible interior domain of mind or consciousness, a potentially endless region for exploration.

Reflections on the Road of Life

Jung's life is an excellent illustration of his psychology. He dedicated his life to making the unconscious conscious, and as a result he left posterity a phenomenology of the interior world. This body of concepts offers the reader a lens through which to explore their experiences. Each person's life reflects their psychology, although we are often not conscious of this correspondence. I have chosen to use Jung's life as a jumping-off point for reflection on the forces that act upon us throughout life and that cry out for recognition in our elder years because his amazing life is public knowledge, and it displays both typical and atypical events.

One of the gateways into the unconscious and unknown within involves exploring our memories. Thus, as this book explores the stages of Jung's life, each section of our journey will present personal-reflection questions to help the reader metabolize the material by exploring their memories about the corresponding stage of their own lives. By reflecting on these questions, we begin to notice patterns and conditions that pushed us one way instead of another. As we move through the major influences in Jung's life that allowed him to discover his "myth," as he called it, follow along in your own life with the various characters and choices at each stage.

Our first set of reflections will explore memories from across the first half of life.

REFLECTION   *What experiences from your younger years are distinctive? What about your teen years? When you moved out of the house? When you started a career? When you got married? Looking back from this vantage point, what is missing in these periods? What strengths and weaknesses did you bring? What and who influenced you? How?*

In his memoir, *Memories, Dreams, Reflections* (New York: Vintage Books, 1961), Jung says his mother was frequently hospitalized and therefore absent. This made her emotionally unavailable, and he describes her as depressed. Jung also recounts having otherworldly, uncanny experiences around her that frightened him. Jung took after his mother temperamentally, and he too seemed prone to unusual experiences early in life. His autobiography is replete with childhood tales about frightening dreams, daydreams, images, and thoughts that went well beyond usual childhood fantasy. Today he would be considered a precocious child whose imaginative powers were particularly acute. Speaking of his response to his experiences with his mother, Jung says: "The feeling I associated with 'woman' for a long time was that of innate unreliability.... That is the handicap I started out with" (*MDR*, 8). Here he is engaging in just the kind of reflection that readers of this book are encouraged to undertake.

REFLECTION   *What were your experiences with your mother? What legacy do you carry from her? How does it benefit you? How does it get in your way? Do you follow in her footsteps, or has your path significantly diverged? What early childhood experiences stand out for you? Who and what most influenced you for better and for worse?*

From his father, Jung received a legacy of doubt. His father was a parson, and the family was rather poor, but what was most disturbing to Jung was his father's relation to his faith. He says, "My poor father did not dare to think, because he was consumed by inward doubts. He was taking refuge from himself and therefore insisted on blind faith" (*MDR, 73*). This was particularly painful to Jung because he had a religious sensibility but was unable to turn to his father for answers. The quest for the meaning of God became a hallmark of his life and his psychology. In his middle years, he carved the Latin inscription *Vocatus atqua non vocatus deus aderit* (Called or not called, God is present) over the lintel of his Lake Zurich house.

REFLECTION   *Were you raised in any religious tradition? Do you still follow it? How has it shaped you? If you no longer adhere to your faith of origin, have you substituted anything? At what point in your life did you begin to doubt? Who and what, if anything, helped you with that exploration? What about finances? Did you always have enough food? Did you have to wear secondhand clothes? If so, did that bother you? Were you aware of economic differences with your friends? How did you feel about that?*

Jung was an only child until he was nine years old, and he characterized his early years as lonely. When he started school, it was with mixed results. On the one hand, he had others to play with; on the other hand, he discovered that he was a different self in the presence of others. This discovery later grew into what he called his "No. 1" and "No. 2" personalities.

Personality No. 1 is the core ego: the one who lives in the here and now, makes plans, admonishes us, and wants to be successful. Personality No. 2 observes No. 1 but is interested in things beyond the daily round. This part philosophizes, lives in the past, seeks a broader vision, is impractical, sees images, and is often misunderstood by the world. No. 2 is the inner person, and although Jung never equated it with Self, it shares more characteristics with that aspect of our interior world than with the ego. Jung says, "In my life, No. 2 has been of prime importance, and I have always tried to make room for anything that wanted to come to me from within" (*MDR*, 45).

> REFLECTION   *Does this talk of two different personalities within have resonance with you? We all have multiple figures within; however, they can often be distilled down to two major characters, as when we find ourselves pulled in seemingly contrary directions. One side wants to buy a house, and the other side wants to travel. One side wants to get involved in some neighborhood group or service community, while the other doesn't. One voice says you are useless, and another says you can be capable. These are examples of the polarities of life that will be discussed in the next chapter. Can you make a list of the polarities that have engaged you most deeply in your life in the past and in the present?*

Jung went off to university to study medicine. As he neared the end of his studies, he grappled with deciding what his specialty would be. He knew he would need to start earning money immediately upon graduating. While he was studying at home during this period, a series of inexplicable phenomena occurred. A solid walnut table top spontaneously split down the middle where there was no seam; a few days later, a solid steel bread knife broke in two. No one seemed to be able to explain these events. Shortly thereafter, Jung heard of some relatives who were consulting a medium, and he joined their group. He documented all these events, and they formed the basis of his doctoral thesis, titled "On the Psychology and Pathology of So-Called Occult Phenomena." Still, he was undecided about his profession until he picked up a textbook on psychiatry for his exams. He discovered, to his shock, that this subject matter dovetailed with his lifelong interest in the interior world. In later life, Jung would call these kinds of meaningful, acausally connected coincidences "synchronicities." With that experience, he finally found his niche.

REFLECTION   *Events are called synchronicities when they involve a meaningful coincidence. Often, synchronicities occur through dreams, reveries, intuitions, or when ruminating about something. When have such experiences come together in a way that seemed unlikely or surprised you? Perhaps you had a dream about someone you hadn't talked with in many years, and soon thereafter you received a letter or a phone call from that person. Or perhaps you got lost on a trip and ended up in a small town you had wanted to visit but didn't think was on your route. Maybe you heard a song or a discussion on the radio that directly addressed your concern of the moment. Everyone has these experiences, often more frequently than we realize. However, we need to be open in order to notice them. As we age, we have more time for this kind of awareness.*

In the winter of 1900, Jung completed his studies and became an assistant to Eugene Bleuler (1857–1939), a noted psychiatrist at Burgholzli Psychiatric Hospital in Zurich. Bleuler was interested in hypnotism and was a follower of Sigmund Freud (1856–1939). He assigned Jung the task of administering a word-association test to patients. During this test, Jung would say a word, and the patient would respond by saying the first word that came to mind. Jung conjectured that a delayed response indicated a possible gap in the patient's ability to perceive things within themselves. This gap is an example of a *complex* (discussed in chapter 4). These experiments made Jung famous in the world of psychiatry. Bleuler suggested Jung send his results and conclusions to Freud, and this initiated a correspondence between the two that changed the direction of Jung's life.

REFLECTION   *At what point in your life did you experience success, however you define it? What factors and people contributed to it? Did success come easily, or was it a struggle? What stood in your way? Were you able to work through it, or did it stymie you? Was your career marked by one direction, or did it switch? If it changed, what prompted the move? What do you struggle with today? What is your direction? What are your successes?*

During the years 1907–1913, Freud and Jung enjoyed a deep and mutually beneficial friendship. At their first meeting, it is said that they talked thirteen hours straight without a break. Freud, the older of the two, saw Jung as his heir apparent, and at first so did Jung. As his thinking developed, however, Jung found himself at odds with some of Freud's theory. Jung's early history of psychic experiences with his mother, occurrences in his own life, and research in the paranormal, coupled with his extensive reading in philosophy, myth, and religion, gave him a broad base for theorizing about the psyche. Although Jung did not want to break with Freud, who had become a father figure for him, it was inevitable. Knowing it would create an irreparable rift in his relationship with Freud, in 1912 Jung published *Symbols of the Unconscious*. To distinguish his work from Freud's psychoanalysis, Jung called his method analytic psychology.

REFLECTION   *Often, we have to break with the very people who helped us get where we are. Children have to leave home and make their own way. Employees sometimes have to leave a company or a mentor to establish themselves or further their career. Did you ever have a mentor in your work? Were you ever a mentor? What was that relationship like? What happened to it? How did you feel at the time? Did you allow yourself to feel, or did you push things to the side because it was too painful to deal with or you didn't have the time? If you have children, how did you feel when they started separating from you and your values? What about old friends whom you outgrew, or who outgrew you? How did you handle the loss?*

Prior to his split with Freud, Jung found himself at the beginning of what today we would call a midlife crisis. Their rupture exacerbated the situation. Jung says, "A period of inner uncertainty began for me. It would be no exaggeration to call it a state of disorientation. I felt totally suspended in midair, for I had not yet found my own footing" (*MDR*, 170). Thus began what Jung called his "confrontation with the unconscious." While the height of his distress only lasted four or five months, the aftermath continued for the next eighteen years. During this time, Jung focused most of his energy on his internal world and what he was discovering there. While he continued to see patients and publish, he also recorded his experiences and painted his visions in notebooks that he later transferred to the *Red Book,* which was published in 2009, forty-eight years after his death.

> REFLECTION   *How old were you when your carefully constructed world first started disintegrating? What were the precipitating factors? How long did it take for you to put yourself back together again? What did you learn about yourself during this time? How did the experience change you? Do you think it made you a stronger person or not? How do you see this time now from the vantage point of years?*

At the age of sixty-eight, Jung broke his foot and then had a heart attack. In talking about this experience, he describes a vision of being high above the earth, looking down on it in every direction, and then approaching a temple made of a dark block of stone. Just as he was to enter the temple, the form of his doctor appeared, and he knew he was being summoned back to earth. He did not want to return to what he called "the box system" and the "drab world" again. It took him three weeks to make up his mind to live. During the day he'd feel depressed, but at night he'd enter a transformed state. Afterward, his nurse told him "it was as if you were surrounded by a bright glow" (*MDR,* 289), something she had observed in people who were dying. Jung died seventeen years later in 1961, at the age of eighty-five.

> REFLECTION   *It is not uncommon for people to experience a health crisis early in their retirement and then go on to live many more years. Have you ever had a health crisis or been close to death? What about a loved one? What stands out for you about this time in your life? Did it change you? If so, how? If you were able to resume your life as it had been, did you have to modify your behavior in some way? Was that distasteful for you or not?*

The Two Halves of Life

One of the basic ideas Jung articulates is that our early years are most often spent exploring the world and building our reputations, careers, and families. For the most part, our focus is on an outer-driven existence, as it should be. Our energies in the first half of life are what the mythologist Joseph Campbell (1904–1987) called "heroic." In the heroic journey, success and achievement are the highest goals. Psychic energy is devoted to conquering. What we conquer is not as important as the fact of conquering it. Goals can range from having one's own business to creating a family to becoming enlightened; no matter what the goal is, the goal is all. We see this in Jung's life through his persistent quest for a specialty in school, bolstered by his urgent need to earn money, and finally his achievement of notoriety in the world of psychiatry. Ideally, the reflections following each stage of Jung's storyline prompted your recognition of your own heroic quest and the sacrifices, difficulties, and successes you experienced along the way.

In his wonderfully accessible book *Falling Upward*, Franciscan priest Richard Rohr describes the first half of life as *building*. On the external level we climb the ladder of success, however we define that. On the internal level we construct an identity, set boundaries, establish ourselves, and forge a self. This holds true for the majority of us, unless we've had a particularly traumatic childhood or have experienced grave illness or loss. In such cases, a person's trajectory will often be different because upheaval can force us to go inside and discover deeper resources. Rohr describes the first half of life as the "loyal soldier" who must be discharged before we can embark upon the second half. He says, "To let go of the loyal soldier will be a severe death, and an exile from your first base.... Discharging your loyal soldier will be necessary to finding authentic inner authority" (49).

Crises in life, whether large or small, are the places where we are challenged to let go of the old and open to the new. It seems Jung's midlife crisis was precipitated by internal forces rather than external circumstances. He was very ambitious and highly intuitive, and he was living in an exciting social climate. Jung was an integral part of a nascent group, headed by Freud, that was exploring the deeper reaches of the human mind. It was uncharted territory, and Jung was eager for the challenge. For most of us, neither the social climate nor our particular situations are so emotionally charged. Unless we are precipitated into crisis by an external event such as divorce, illness, layoff, or death of a spouse or child, the shift occurs incrementally. If we have achieved our goals, we may wonder, "Is this all there is?" If we believe we have not been successful, we can become depressed. In either instance, we begin to question some of the most fundamental tenets that have held our lives together. This time of life is often referred to as second adolescence because once again we ask questions such as: Who am I? Where am I going? Who am I going with? What's the point and meaning of life? Old answers no longer serve. Just as the world opened before us years ago and demanded an explanation for its being, it now reopens.

In the book *Jung and Aging,* Jungian analyst James Hollis describes late-life development this way: "The second half of life is a persistently compelling subpoena to sort through that immense internal traffic we all carry and to discern what is true for us" (205). Those who try to cling to outworn ideals, values, and suppositions because the thought of questioning them is too fearsome will fail to mature. By refusing to examine the ideas that have brought us to an impasse, we cannot discover what is true for us. Without the ability to embrace the ambiguity and mystery of life, we miss the potential of late life.

The second half of life is about dismantling the edifices we've created in the first half. Finally freed of family, work, and (hopefully) economic impediments, we now have the time to go back, pick up the pieces, and see how they fit into the mosaic of our life. Society's current proclivity for viewing old age as an extension of midlife contradicts this trajectory and is detrimental to our psychological and spiritual well-being. When old people tell stories, they are naturally engaging in this kind of life review. In many ways, Jung undertook this task during his years of writing in his notebooks that became the *Red Book.* Still, once he reached his early eighties, he felt the need to go back and review his story.

Busyness and activity are tendencies that are likely to remain highly valued throughout life and that need opportunities for expression.

However, too often in our culture we use them to avoid painful places. This is another danger of extending midlife into the elder years. It is only by turning toward the changes and challenges of older age that we develop the wisdom and resiliency to live fully until we die.

It is a paradoxical axiom that the only way to actually move through a painful state is to engage with it. For this we need time to be, time to contemplate, time to revisit old hurts and make peace with them, with others, and with ourselves. This is an essentially introverted endeavor. It takes tremendous courage to confront our past, particularly when we have been exposed to trauma, as most of us have to varying degrees. It is so much easier to allow the culture's emphasis on acquisition, entertainment, youth, and productivity to distract us from the task of introspection. Unfortunately, when we do not process and integrate emotionally charged past experiences, they go underground, into the unconscious. There they remain until a stimulus provokes them. Then, like a sleeping dragon, they awaken.

When we do engage the multiple facets of our inner life, we become like the California buckeye. An old buckeye often has several large trunks extending horizontally rather than vertically from the main trunk. Miraculously they manage to hold themselves partially upright. From them grow smaller trunks, and from these, endless branches. A mature tree can be eight or more feet in diameter. Buckeyes are stunning. In the spring, they produce long brackets of flowers that perfume the area. In the same way, an old person who engages the aging process becomes a person of compelling beauty.

This chapter has taken us on a journey through our own lives by following the life of Jung. Parental figures, our early childhood environment, school days, choice of career, and eventual crises and loss of health are like colors in the palette of life. It is helpful to imagine one's life in this way. What colors would you give to these various phases of your life? Can you begin to see the outlines of something greater than the individual episodes? As we move into the next chapter, we will encounter a map that may bring more clarity and perspective to the whole.

4

Mapping the Terrain

The bothers, impediments, and dreaded symptoms of later years change in significance as we find their purpose.

—JAMES HILLMAN, *The Force of Character and the Lasting Life* (New York: Random House, 1999)

Jungian psychology concentrates on potential development in later life by offering a unique map of consciousness. Just as a map of the world makes it easier to grasp the bigger picture, a map of Jung's theories can give a coherent framework for reflecting on our experience and making it relevant.

One of the best ways to understand something is to see a visual depiction of it. On the next page is an image of the concepts discussed in this chapter. Before we begin, it is important to remember that concepts are ways of understanding and mapping what otherwise can be a confusing and seemingly impassable terrain. Concepts can be likened to territorial maps. Just as in reality there are no dividing lines between the states in the US, concepts are not concrete. In the course of time, the map of psyche may be redrawn. Until then, we use imagination, cognition, and language to help us communicate with each other and navigate the world. In so doing, we expand our knowledge and control over both ourselves and our world.

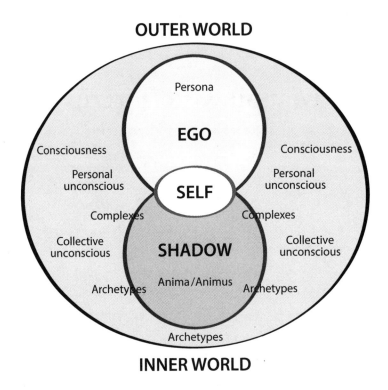

In Jungian psychology, the gestalt of figure 1 is called psyche. It is the whole picture of the inner world in which various entities have their role. The first thing to notice is the distinction between consciousness and the unconscious. Put simplistically, these could also be called "what we are aware of" and "what is hidden from our awareness." However, a caution is necessary at this point. Defining consciousness is a difficult task that involves the brain/mind controversy discussed in chapter 3. Is consciousness caused by brain firings and misfirings, or is it something more? What does it mean to be conscious? Do animals have consciousness?

Is the stream of consciousness that we all experience actually conscious when we experience it, or only upon reflection? These questions are my attempt to introduce complicated topics in a way that makes them accessible and hopefully incites an interest in further investigation.

In addition to Jung's concepts, two seminal ideas from archetypal psychologist James Hillman (1926–2011) are helpful to understanding late-life development. Hillman was an early student of Jung, and in 1959, he became the first director of studies at the Jung Institute in Zurich. As his opening remark at the beginning of this chapter suggests, once we find a meaning for our discontentments, they become bearable.

By familiarizing ourselves with the various components of our internal world, we bring them into the light of day or consciousness. This is the meaning and purpose of the second half of life for Jung. He called this personal struggle for consciousness "individuation." By this he meant that as we investigate and develop knowledge of and tolerance for the various aspects of our personality and history, the fragments become integrated into a whole. To be individuated is to be the individual you were meant to be.

Hillman introduced the word *daimon* into the lexicon of psychological thought. The word comes from the Greek and means "lesser god, guiding spirit." In *The Soul's Code*, Hillman states, "The soul of each of us is given a unique *daimon* before we are born, and it has selected an image or pattern that we live on earth" (8). The *daimon* is that unique energy within each person that seeks individuation, meaning that each of us seeks to be whoever or whatever we are called to manifest in the world. We don't often think of each of us as having a calling. What if we did? Would that change how you see your life and the way circumstances shaped you? Seeing life in this way makes each life matter. We are not mere cogs in some capitalist machine. Each of us is called to contribute something to the world, and old age is the time to see the overall pattern. We don't need to subscribe to the notion of reincarnation or God's plan to grasp what Hillman is talking about. He often used what he called the "acorn theory" to explain his theory of the *daimon*. An acorn, given the proper conditions, grows up to be a tree; it never grows into a flower or a bush. It follows its *daimon* to become what it is called to be. Similarly, humans also have a calling embedded within them.

Hillman saw the *daimon* as not being interested in experiences that make the ego feel good, but rather in ensuring that the "soul's code" is known and acted upon. In his view, the missed opportunities, imbalances, and psychic debris that inevitably clutter any life can be understood and embraced when looked upon from the perspective of the *daimon*. In *The Soul's Code* Hillman offers numerous examples of how the *daimon* is visible in the lives of well-known personalities. One story that has always stood out in my memory concerns the well-known Spanish bullfighter, Manolete. Apparently, when he was young, Manolete was an exceedingly delicate, bashful child who always hid behind his mother's skirts. Hillman asks, "Were her 'apron strings' a metaphor, or was he already using her apron, her skirt, as a cape?" (16). In Hillman's thinking, Manolete already had a premonition of his *daimon* as a child. It so frightened him that he shied away from an active life.

The point is that our darkest, most judged and rejected qualities have some positive element. Not feeling adequate, worthy, or good enough contains the seed of humility and a sense of equality with others—the opposite of hubris. Looking at our emotions in this way is like finding a treasure stored in what we've long considered the toxic dump of our internal neighborhood. Instead of ridiculing ourselves for what we lack or hanging onto the hurtful events we've been subjected to in life, Hillman's perspective encourages us to re-vision other possible meanings to explain what happened. In essence, he challenges us to rewrite our stories.

We don't need fame to feel the call of the *daimon*. When we experience an energy, urge, intention, or voice that is persistent in calling us to a task, an act, or an accomplishment, we are experiencing our *daimon*. A friend of mine in her early sixties who wanted something meaningful and financially viable to do after retirement enrolled in a spiritual direction training program. To her surprise, she found herself living in an altered state of consciousness for about six months. She began having synchronous experiences and felt like she was living in a magical realm. She was. Two things were happening. One was that her *daimon* came through (she is an incredibly insightful, empathic social worker); the other is that she activated the energy of an archetype, the universal instinct for healing. Eventually the constellated energy returned to the unconscious, but it left her with a fresh understanding of and approach to her interior.

My writing this book is another example. I felt compelled to voice what I've learned in my years of eldercare experience in a form I hope will be helpful for others. The effort oscillated between being a joy and a burden. To heed the call meant exercising discipline and having much less time to be with friends or do things I really enjoy. It meant sacrifice. Whether this book is "successful" in terms of the outer world is secondary to the *daimon*'s insistence that I write it. What calls have you not been able to heed in your life? Do you still hear them? Can you consider that these calls are not simply random firings but meaningful summonses to live out your *daimon* before leaving this earth? We tend to think in large terms, but one's *daimon* can be as simple as being kind. The Dalai Lama says, "My religion is kindness." That is no small thing. Bringing kindness to your part of the world can uplift the people around you. Like teachers who never really know the impact of their teaching, you may never know the ripples that your kindness creates.

Hillman's book *Force of Character* presents another useful concept, "infolding," for understanding aging. This term refers to a turning inward that happens with age. Older adults are no longer on an expansive upward trajectory. Instead, they are moving inward toward the unknown, toward being rather than becoming. Hillman trusts that the symptoms of later years help with this inwardness. When the purpose of these symptoms is understood, attitudes toward them change significantly. This is not unlike the attitude shift mentioned in reference to the *daimon,* where we are called to reconsider the parts of life that did not go as intended. For Hillman, it is in the fragmentation and disempowerment of old age that character is revealed.

The meaning of a symptom is as varied as the people who have the symptom. For the sake of simplicity, let's take the example of arthritis. How does that symptom relate to an elder's life? What message might soul be trying to communicate? Perhaps the elder was always fiercely independent, and arthritis is now forcing the person toward interdependence. Or perhaps looking good was a high priority, and now the elder is being challenged to let go of their external image. Or perhaps the elder was a type A personality, and arthritis demands a reduction of multitasking in favor of an increased awareness of the moment. One symptom can have multiple meanings. When a symptom is fought, denied, or otherwise neglected, the possibility of seeing it within a larger perspective is lost, along with the possibility of benefiting from it in some way.

Hillman sees old-age symptoms as an initiation into another way of life. They are purposeful from the perspective of the soul's thrust toward individuation. In Hillman's view, whatever goes on in life is intelligible and as such gives light. To embrace the task of elderhood is to welcome all that comes, thereby widening one's perspectives. What if the symptom is the very precondition for movement toward wholeness?

To continue on our journey through the psyche, we're going to follow the story of Sarah, an elder I once knew. As we go along, see if you can relate these concepts to your personal experience.

REFLECTION   *Identify some aspect of your life that is currently problematic. Perhaps you are grappling with changes in lifestyle that are unwelcome; perhaps you are providing care to a loved one and feeling the strain of too much responsibility; perhaps you are questioning yourself in some way. Life presents us with endless events, large and small, inner and outer, that elicit uncomfortable or unwanted thoughts and feelings. As you read about a concept, try to apply it to your present situation. In this way, you will make the material your own, and you will develop a useful way of reflecting on the experiences in your life. This is one of the primary ways to find meaning in life.*

Sarah was a fairly healthy woman in her late seventies who moved to an upscale senior community to be close to one of her children. Her son called me in to work with her because she was not adjusting well to the move, and her small apartment was a mess. The son thought she needed a housekeeper. Sarah was in need, but of much more than a housekeeper. She was not participating in any of the community offerings, nor was she eating communally. Instead she would go to the dining room, request a to-go meal, and return to her unit. She was also drinking more than was healthy for her.

Shortly after her husband's death, Sarah had sold her home of thirty-plus years and moved from a small midwestern town to an area of the country where she told me she did not fit in. She said she didn't have an interest in the activities offered by the community, and she had enough engagement with her children. The reality was that the children were too busy to be able to provide her the kind of support she needed, despite wanting to do so.

Sarah's situation is not that rare. Whenever we undergo major life changes, such as the death of a spouse or moving from one part of the country to another, we enter a liminal space. We are no longer functioning in ordinary time but are somewhere in between. This situation activates whatever was not fully metabolized in our earlier years.

Projection

To understand what Sarah was going through, we need to explore the concept of *projection*. Since projection is such a common occurrence, it bears mention in any discussion that has the intention of opening awareness to the inner world. Projection is a defense we unknowingly use to cope with difficult experiences or emotions. It was originally identified by Freud as the way we assign our unacceptable thoughts and beliefs to others. A classic example of projection in a marriage is when a spouse who is having an affair accuses the other spouse of infidelity. Older people who have a paranoid component of their personality will often accuse their care partners or children of stealing from them. The older person feels powerless because they need help from the caregiver. Possessions represent power. The accusation is an attempt to restore a sense of control.

It is impossible not to engage in projection. Whenever we make assumptions, we are projecting. When we assume others feel the way we do about things, we are projecting. When we expect others to be able to do something we can do without much effort, we are projecting. Thankfully, it is possible to become aware of our projections. Indeed, this is one of the most revealing methods of self-inquiry. Have you ever noticed how you spontaneously make up stories about people you pass on the street or meet at a gathering—or even about those closest to you, whom you have known for a long time?

Many years ago I used to do long silent retreats. There would be a hundred other people on retreat, and invariably I would pick out two or three who either rubbed me the wrong way or to whom I felt positively drawn. Whenever I would pass by them or see them in the food line, I would find myself fantasizing about who they were. Before long I would have created a story about each of them that I was sure had at least some accuracy. At the end of the retreat I made it a point to have a conversation with the person if for no other reason than to validate my suppositions. Fully 90 percent of the time, my ideas about the person had no correspondence with reality. This was very humbling and informative. While this experience wasn't part of the intended result of a silent retreat, it stayed with me long afterward. Now I find it amusing to watch myself concoct stories about others. It is a wonderful way to flesh out my projections and prejudices.

Projection is closely tied to the shadow (which we'll discuss later in this chapter). Like the shadow, we project our good qualities as well as those we scorn. When we idolize another and think we can never be like them, we have denied our own qualities that draw us to them. While it is true that we cannot be "like them," what they are showing us is our own potential. Paying attention to what draws us is just as informative as noting what repels us. If we refuse to own our darkness and our light—if we don't pay attention to our story-making tendency—we'll likely be misled into assuming that what we think is so is actually so. This leads to many problems that create unnecessary suffering. If we develop a sense of humor about our minds, our projections won't be so terrifying, unreachable, or distasteful. Instead they can become excellent opportunities to learn about ourselves, cultivate detachment, and grow in wisdom. Take one day and try to notice your projections, both the attractive ones and the repulsive ones. At the end of the day, make a list of your projections, and see if you can trace their origins and foundational desires.

Ego

Although Jung did not come up with the concept of ego (the word comes from Latin, meaning "I" or "self"), he did make use of it. Ego is the center of the conscious personality. It is the command center for the various voices in our head that keep a running commentary on all our experiences: what we had for breakfast, something our friend said last night, the pregnant woman we see on the street, our plans for a holiday, our fear about an upcoming doctor's appointment, and on and on. The Pixar film *Inside Out* is a hilarious, poignant, and fairly accurate depiction of this part of our inner world. Ego evolves out of Self, just as consciousness grows out of the unconscious. It is all those aspects of our self that lie on the surface, such as personality, identity, cognition, and continuity. Ego manages memory, executive functions, feelings, imperatives, and sensory data—in short, all that we experience on a daily basis. Yet these experiences are only a small part of the entire psyche. Ego is like the manager, whereas Self is the CEO.

We need ego. If you were involved in the spiritual movements of the 1960s, you might remember the misguided effort to get rid of ego. Growth is not about getting rid of or transcending ego, but about learning to harness and direct it from a deeper place within. Problems with the ego arise in later life because ego has been in charge for a long time and is now fully under the illusion that it runs the show. (This is not true for those who have been exposed to mental or physical suffering earlier in life.) The saying "life is what happens while you're busy making other plans," often attributed to musician John Lennon, is a good example of ego making plans and Self putting forth a different agenda.

Sarah's ego kept trying to assert control and to deny that she needed help. It was overwhelmed. Too many losses in too short a time had overpowered her coping ability. Whatever skills she may have developed to meet life's challenges were unavailable. The death of someone we love brings back memories of prior deaths, losses, and the big questions of life. In her conversations with me, it became apparent that Sarah had not been able to process these experiences. She arrived in her new home with much psychological baggage but no way to unpack it. She was also no longer a prominent member of a small community; now she was just another senior in a large group of seniors. She had lost status, which implied losing the kinds of social opportunities that go along with it.

On top of grief and loss, Sarah was also facing issues of lost identity and role transitions. She responded by shying away from making new friends or engaging in a new life. She did not have—nor was she willing to create—the supports needed to successfully negotiate the recent changes in her life. Alcohol became a way of easing the tension.

Jungians believe ego begins in very early childhood as a nucleus within Self. Ego and Self are connected throughout development by what is referred to as the ego-Self axis. In healthy development, the ego maintains a connection with Self. This maximizes our chances for resiliency later in life. The first half of life is about ego development; the second half is about ego yielding to Self. When the early environment does not adequately meet the child's needs, or when there is early trauma, the axis does not develop or is weak. In adulthood, a weak axis might manifest as narcissism, lifelong feelings of inadequacy and insecurity, or even a tendency to eschew limits, as in the myth of Icarus, who flew too close to the sun. The older person with a weak axis refuses to make a will, plan for death, or remove rugs that might cause her to fall; she insists she can do what she clearly cannot do; she acts as if she thinks the world revolves around her moods and wishes; or she always asks, "Why me?" These are all examples of recoiling from reality. Of course, we all do this to some extent. Getting stuck in these patterns is what creates blocks and suffering.

When we feel adrift or out of sorts and have difficulty making decisions, it is often due to a disconnection within. These feelings can serve as a warning light indicating that it is time to turn inward. Ego has been severed from its power base, Self. Interestingly, in times of vulnerability such as grief, depression, or anxiety, it is easier to connect with the deeper current within because ego is temporarily off-line. Loss of control makes us humble, and humility is one of the doorways to greater awareness. This is why so much spiritual and psychological literature talks about the redemptive aspect of suffering. In a May 2019 episode of NPR's *Forum*, *New York Times* columnist David Brooks spoke about his newest book, *The Second Mountain*, and how it relates to suffering. He said (and I paraphrase) that suffering either breaks you or it breaks you open. Those who endure crush the ego and come into themselves. He could well be describing the journey of old age, where the many assaults to pride, body, mind, and identity seem designed to break open the old so something new can be born. This is what Hillman describes as the process of infolding.

In his latest book, *How to Change Your Mind*, author Michael Pollan has a fascinating section on what current neuroscience is calling the default mode network (DMN) and its relation to ego. The DMN is a network within the brain that seems to act as a gatekeeper (just as ego does) for what comes into conscious awareness, either from outside ourselves or from within (i.e., the unconscious). When the DMN is suppressed, as happens under the influence of psychedelic drugs, we are much more susceptible to both outer and inner forces rising into consciousness. Pollan's discussion of the DMN seems to corroborate my observations of elders with memory loss whose egos no longer act as custodians. The DMN is located in the frontal region of the brain, where functioning is impaired in cases of memory loss. This helps explain why older people with memory loss often experience repressed emotions coming to the surface, and why they disregard social cues—an area also regulated by ego. This may also explain why, as we age and have more leisure time, long-forgotten memories return in moments of reverie, when the threshold of consciousness is lowered. The material Jung processed during his crisis, which eventually became the basis of his psychological theories, might also be related to the DMN temporarily being suppressed. It is exciting to contemplate the possibility that in the future, science and psychology might have a meeting of the ways, as Jung so fervently advocated.

REFLECTION   *As you read through this description of ego, how has it resonated for you? Where are the places you find yourself holding on, and where are the places you find it easy to let go? What is the difference? If you are caring for an older person who is stuck, how might you use what you learned in this chapter to facilitate how you approach the person? How might you use the material to bring more awareness and fullness into your life?*

Persona

The persona is the face we show the world. It is part of our ego structure and is conscious. I think of the persona as a hat on a rack. Before going out the door, we don a face mask to meet the day. We have multiple masks, and we choose which one to put on based on the circumstances we expect to encounter. We use a persona when we want to make a good impression or conform to inner or outer expectations. We all carry within us a plethora of exhortations that we internalized from family, peers, culture, and idealized notions of how things should be. If we allow it to, age gives us the freedom to evaluate these expectations, keep what enhances life, and discard what doesn't.

Sarah was unwilling to put aside her persona of being okay and in charge. She felt she had to put up a good front. Older adults often feel this way. They want to hide infirmity or difficulties. One of the biggest impediments to older people using a cane or walker is their persona. When it comes to their children, oldsters are particularly reluctant to expose any potentially damning weakness. They are afraid their vulnerability might result in unwanted change. It is indeed unfortunate that many children, in their zeal to protect the parent, often overcompensate and pressure a parent into actions the parent is not yet ready to take. I don't know how willingly Sarah agreed to the move her children asked of her. Nor do I know if their request stemmed from Sarah genuinely sharing what she was feeling, thus frightening her children, or if it was more of a move of convenience. I do know that her persona of competence was her defense against bewilderment and further encroachment on her fragile stability. However, Sarah's persona was harmful to her. In her desire to protect herself, she actually increased her risk.

Others become so identified with a role or aspect of self that they think this is who they are. If a person has identified with their job or beauty or physical prowess and then they lose it, they are in a doubly vulnerable situation. There is the loss itself, and then there is the loss of the face they used in their world. One persona that older women have a hard time relinquishing is "looking good." Much of this has to do with a cultural emphasis on youth. Feminists have made some inroads here, but it's up to older people themselves to help change the culture by refusing to be compliant with the demands of an outmoded persona.

Many years ago, a friend of mine who vacationed in Bali brought back the welcome magazine from her hotel room. On the front cover was a toothless older woman with a wide grin, holding a basket of fresh vegetables. This image was what Bali chose to represent their culture. What a far cry that is from what we find in the United States. As a swimmer, I am saddened that so many older women who used to enjoy being in the water now won't go because wearing a bathing suit exposes varicose veins and bulges. Because their skin is no longer taut and their body no longer svelte, they give up an activity that improves both mental and physical health and vitality. I certainly understand how hard it is to go against the grain; however, if we don't swallow our pride and jettison these cultural notions of beauty, we will all remain captive to them, at the expense of lessening our potential joy. In the May 2011 issue of *The Sun,* James Hillman offers a reframe applicable to all of us: "To show one's face is part of having the courage to show who one is. And coming to terms with your own face takes a lifetime.... As you get older the relationship between your face and who you are matures. They blend together. Your true self shows more."

REFLECTION   *How comfortable are you with your face? Your body?*
What are some of the masks you wear? When do you wear them, and with
whom? Have you willingly let go of some of your masks? Have some been
abruptly torn away? If so, have you made peace with that? How? When
we consciously use a mask, it can be helpful. When we forget we are using
a mask or we put one on to please the external or internal "fashion police,"
we are doing ourselves and our peers a great disservice.

The Personal Unconscious

Jung believed the personal unconscious comes into prominence during
the second half of life because we cannot pay sufficient attention to it
in the busyness of our early years. The personal unconscious is all those
thoughts, experiences, and memories that are unique to each of us but
have been repressed, rejected, or forgotten. As we age, these parts seek a
voice. It is not uncommon to experience memories of people and events
from the past suddenly present in the current moment. Sometimes these
occurrences have emotions attached that beg to be recognized. For older
adults, as for most people, content from the personal unconscious tends
to be related to unresolved grief, loss, disappointment, hurt, betrayal,
divorce, death, addiction, or suicide of a child, spouse, or parent. Relationships with a family member or friend that were broken off in the
past can cause unconscious material to arise in the present. Incidents
of unfairness or betrayal that we either experienced or perpetrated can
return in the form of an upwelling of the personal unconscious.

Something like this happened to Gail, a woman in her late seventies.
She had had a remarkably healthy life, but now her body was beginning
to break down. She needed to have a hip replacement, yet she continually put it off. When I met her, she was using a walker and was in great
pain whenever she moved. She was terrified of surgery. Over time her
story came out: when Gail was three or four years old, her older brother
went into the hospital for surgery and never came home again. Her religious family told her Jimmy went to be with God, but she noticed that
this explanation did not make her parents happy. In fact, Jimmy's death

cast a pall over the family, and three years later, Gail's parents divorced. Over the years Gail did not think much about this time in her life. She repressed the emotional trauma from it. Now, in addition to her hip pain, she was experiencing disturbing dreams at night and memories of Jimmy in the day.

She began working with a therapist and discovered there was a connection among all these experiences. Her refusal to have a hip replacement was linked with her childhood fear that if you go to a hospital for surgery, you never come out again. Of course, over her long life, she had visited friends in hospitals and had seen them recover; however, when it came to herself, her experience with her brother and its aftermath still unconsciously dominated her thinking. Gail's memories of her brother and her distressing dreams began arising in response to her present situation. Psyche was giving her an invitation to revisit that time in her life, sort through the emotions, and come to a more encompassing understanding. Had she avoided this call, it is likely Gail would have ended up in a wheelchair and died before her time. As it was, she did have the surgery, which turned out successfully, and as of this writing (eight years later) she's still alive.

Sometimes memories arise for no apparent reason. This is what Gail initially thought. However, if we give ourselves space to ruminate over them, they can surprise us with content we had totally overlooked or forgotten. Often there is a situation in the present that is stimulating the memory, and we now have the chance to repair something or re-experience it from the perspective of our later years. Whatever was neglected or avoided earlier in life tends to come into the foreground in late life. Paying attention brings meaning to seemingly pointless emotions, memories, and thoughts. Too often we avoid these confrontations with the unconscious by involving ourselves in various projects. Despite a given project's worthiness, we need to recognize this impulse as a strategy used by the ego to deflect attention from difficult but life-giving introspection.

The personal unconscious is not just personal; it is also social. A good example of the personal unconscious in US culture has to do with relations between white people and people of color. Many white people are not aware that they have a built-in bias against people of color. When asked if they are prejudiced against blacks, for instance, many whites will sincerely say they are not. To prove this, they will say they have black friends, or they too experience racism, or they also grew up in poor neighborhoods (notice that this statement equates black with poor). At the same time, they will often act in ways that show prejudice, such as feeling bodily tension when they walk by a black person (especially a young man) on the street, or voting in ways that disenfranchise black people.

I once got into a heated discussion with a friend who insisted she was not biased but who ranted about "welfare moms" in her neighborhood who were black. When I attempted to point out the advantages she'd had growing up, she insisted she grew up poor. This was true, but she still could not see that she had grown up in an intact family and community in the countryside. These beginnings gave her the inner means to climb social and financial ladders to success. Growing up in a ghetto, where violence is just outside (and sometimes inside) the door of your home, with minimal access to good public education, is not conducive to equality. My friend's bias and anger blinded her to this reality. Many other societies do not share in this US bias, perhaps because those societies do not share the same history. A good book that discusses this cultural lacuna is *White Fragility: Why It's So Hard for White People to Talk about Racism*.

Another social example from the personal unconscious is ageism. Being overly solicitous or talking loudly to an older person, telling someone they don't look their age, trying to hide one's own age, and sending birthday greetings that poke fun at growing old are all examples of a societal age bias that we unconsciously live out. At its base are the rejection and fear of aging that live within us. This bias is not universal, because other societies value old age and elders. As we develop skill at introspection, it is very gratifying to identify the origins of personal as well as cultural biases, preferences, and ideas. Make a list of beliefs you have about the way things are or should be, and then try linking that list with your cultural, ethnic, and socioeconomic identity. The next time you find yourself remembering an event from the past, pull it out of the depths and explore it from these various angles. You can also do this with physical symptoms.

Complexes

Complexes are related ideas and emotions, primarily based on childhood experiences, that have been repressed into the personal unconscious. Jungian analyst Murray Stein uses the image of electrons circling a nucleus within an atom to describe a complex. The originating experience (memory) is the nucleus, and our response (emotions) is the electrons. Together they make up the complex. In *Jung's Map of the Soul,* Stein explains complexes this way: "Complexes are what remain in the psyche after it has digested experience and reconstructed it into inner objects" (49). Jung likened complexes to "a shadow government of the ego" because they are split off from the conscious mind (ego) and act autonomously, like subpersonalities.

Complexes happen as a normal part of development. Some common behaviors that indicate the presence of a complex include slips of the tongue, lapses of memory (especially for things we do not want to remember or do), misunderstandings in communications, writing something we didn't intend, and disliking someone as soon as we meet them for no good reason. Particularly strong complexes for some women are Earth Mother, Sex Goddess, and Martyr. Men can be subject to Don Juan and Hero complexes.

Complexes become problematic when they are denied. We notice denied complexes because they are highly charged with emotional energy. Someone has "pushed our buttons." Such complexes are often rooted in childhood experiences of trauma. This does not mean the precipitating event itself had to be traumatic, but our response to it was. Experiences of fear, shame, worthlessness, defensiveness, being out of control, disappointment, self-destructive behaviors, frequent accidents, whininess, continually choosing people who can't meet our needs, resistance, and particularly strong emotions are often rooted in complexes.

Sarah was in the grip of a complex that told her she had to keep it together no matter what. This is common, especially for those who grew up in toxic or unstable environments. If we felt we always needed to be good or not be seen to avoid negative attention, or if we internalized any number of other injunctions children absorb without the need for explicit words, we can develop a complex. When we are in the grip of a highly emotionally charged complex, we are no longer in control. (That is, our ego is not in control.) In such circumstances, we often feel compelled to act on our ideas and are unable to let them go. Based on my years of work with cognitively impaired elders who have problematic behaviors (e.g., acting out angrily, being paranoid, or crying episodes), I believe these people are trying to discharge and resolve early complexes that have arisen now that the ego, the gatekeeper, is dissolved.

A common way in which complexes are revealed is when someone crosses a personal line for us. If the issue is very important, we tend to perseverate, replaying the situation or conversation over and over and over again in our minds. When we notice we are doing this, it is a signal that we are caught. We need to step back, take a breath, and see how much consciousness we are able to actually bring to the subject. This is very difficult because we are blinded by our emotion in these situations. Depending on the strength of the complex, it could take multiple periods of reflection to gain even a bit of clarity. Most likely the complex has its origin in a particularly painful event. Shame is often one of the hidden ingredients. This can make us hesitant to expose our feelings to another, yet it is unlikely we will get at the source on our own. It is important that the person we choose to help us is trustworthy, empathetic, and capable of unbiased listening; otherwise we risk reinforcing the complex. Getting an outside perspective and having someone listen to us, especially a trained professional, will greatly increase our chances of successfully identifying the root cause of the complex. Dreams—especially the ones that disturb our equilibrium—often offer us an avenue to material lost in a complex. Chapter 11 suggests several methods of exploring dreams that can be helpful.

Examples of complexes pertinent to older age include repeating the same story over and over. This is often an attempt to integrate an experience into life. Repetition is the way Self tries to let ego know that something needs healing. Forgetting to take medication or refusing to use ambulatory devices can point to an unacknowledged heroic complex. Running into similar problems repeatedly—for instance, we can't find the right doctor, no medication helps, our friends disappoint us, or repair people don't do a good job—is often a sign that a complex is at work. Other complexes associated with older adults include hoarding or not wanting to spend money on their care. This is true for many who scraped by during the Great Depression or grew up in poverty in any era. Complexes can be carried on generationally as well. There is now a field of study called epigenetics that posits a genetic link between the experiences of prior generations and the responses of present generations. For instance, research is now showing that descendants of Holocaust survivors have altered stress-related hormones.

Although complexes are challenging to unpack, the reward for doing so is worth it. They actually are gateways into deeper levels of our interior world and to opportunities to discover the forces working within us. Despite the discomfort they cause, they are psyche's way of getting us to wake up. Jung often said the purpose of life is to reclaim more and more from the unconscious. That's exactly what we do when we bring a complex out of the dark. It's not the presence of a complex that is problematic but our lack of awareness of it. Some complexes lead us to become champions of social causes. For instance, a childhood experience of injustice can provide the passion for activism. When present in positive ways, complexes lend us energy to realize our goals. The first step in working with complexes is to pay attention to what provokes strong reactions. The second is reflection and discussion. Complexes activate archetypes that reside in the collective unconscious.

The Archetype of Self

Self is the quintessential archetype around which the whole psyche revolves. Jung conceived Self as the ordering principle that unifies the unconscious with consciousness and partakes of both. Self is also the ground within the psyche that seeks wholeness for each person. Although Jung himself did not capitalize Self when he talked about it, his followers have done so to distinguish it from other interpretations of self or ego. In keeping with this usage, when I use the term Self as Jung did, it is capitalized.

In his book *The Mana Personality*, Jung describes Self as "an unknowable essence which we cannot grasp ... since by definition it transcends our powers of comprehension. It might equally well be called the God within us" (Vol. 7, 238). For those who believe in a traditional God, Self can easily be understood as God's will. Zen Buddhists call it the face you had before you were born. While Self lends itself easily to religious concepts, it is not bound by them. Suffice it to say that Jung's concept of Self has as much relevance to nontheists as to theists. It provides a way of understanding where inspiration, awe, and insight have their source. When Hillman describes the *daimon*, he is referring to the Self archetype that has an agenda for our life. Throughout this book Self has a prominent place because it provides a framework and incentive for the work of old age.

Erich Neumann (1882–1948), a writer, student of Jung, and psychologist, believed that Self exists before ego and consciousness take form. As noted earlier, ego grows out of Self, and in healthy development there is a strong relationship between the two. Acceptance comes from the Self through this axis. When the axis between the two is weak, good therapy can help restore or strengthen the connection. When we are feeling at odds with ourselves, it's often because we have lost touch with this ground within.

Experiences of grief, alienation, longing, loss of trust, dread, despair, and other difficult situations can bring awareness of Self to the foreground. This is the gift of such experiences. French existentialist Albert Camus (1913–1960) is credited with saying, "In the midst of winter, I found an invincible summer." American poet Theodore Roethke (1908–1963) put it another way: "In a dark time the eye begins to see." Both examples point to something ineffable we can experience when we explore unhappy states and trust that there is a gift waiting. In the example of Sarah, instead of turning toward the source of her suffering, she turned away from it. Her ego misguided her by trying to protect her and keep her safe. Unfortunately, ego's definition of safety is to maintain the status quo at all costs. Self is not concerned with this. Self pushes us where we would rather not go in the interests of individuation.

Jung said, "To this day God is the name by which I designate all things which cross my willful path violently and recklessly, all things which upset my subjective views, plans, and intentions and change the course of my life for better or worse." When I first encountered this quote many years ago in *Ego and Archetype* (Baltimore: Penguin, 1974 [101]), by psychiatrist and Jungian analyst Edward Edinger (1922–1998), I was shocked. The sentiment expressed is so discontinuous with what most of us imagine when we think of God. As Jung's psychology and much inner work transformed me, I have come to appreciate this statement, and I encourage the reader to grapple with it.

A healthy connection with Self is what brings meaning to our lives. Writing in *Jung and Aging*, Jungian analyst Lionel Corbet says, "Meaning refers partly to the ability to discern a pattern, to make connections between otherwise disparate events in one's life, so that they can be seen as weaving into a coherent theme which has moved through the course of one's life" (227). This is what Jung called "finding your myth." It is also Hillman's *daimon* and what the Eriksons called integrity, as we will see in chapter 6. As an elder is able to appreciate, understand, and put the pieces of their life into a whole, they are fulfilling the destiny of their life and bringing meaning to it.

REFLECTION   *What is your philosophy or belief about God? Do you experience something beyond yourself? What gets you up in the morning? What do you think is the purpose of life? Have you felt guided in your life? If so, can you identify the points when you did? Does any part of us continue to exist after we die? If so, what?*

The Collective Unconscious and Archetypes

If you review the map of psyche, you will notice that the collective unconscious occupies half the territory of the psyche. This is the home of archetypes, that emotionally charged element of a complex noted earlier.

While I was writing this book, I became so gripped by the material that sometimes I became a road hazard to drivers when I got behind the wheel. As relevant thoughts and ideas for specific sections pushed their way into my consciousness, I felt compelled to write them down, regardless of whether I was driving at the time. Likewise, sleep was endlessly disturbed as psyche either kept me awake or woke me up with yet another idea or example that had to be recorded. These very sentences I'm typing came from the middle of the night. In short, a power or energy from a more mysterious part of myself took over. It was both exhilarating and exhausting. It was also unnerving to the ego, who was unseated from her throne of command and oversight. During this process, I was possessed by archetypal energy. This is not an infrequent occurrence when engaging the creative process. It takes hold of you; you don't take hold of it. Even with the lessened energy that comes in later life, we can be subjected to this upwelling when we engage in something that activates or releases our *daimon* or the archetype of creativity.

One way to think about the collective unconscious is to look at the difference between our older reptilian brain, which is the seat of our shared instincts, and our neocortex, which developed later and reflects more individualized experience. The collective unconscious is like instinct in that it is common to all human beings, whereas the ways in which a person is conditioned by family, society, ethnicity, and personality is more like the neocortex, in that these factors determine the unique way in which a person responds to life.

The collective unconscious is one of Jung's unique contributions to psychological thought. He considered it the deepest level of psyche, common to all humans, instinctual, and the opposite of individual. This is the place of myths, fables, parables, and fairy tales that give us a symbolic language for understanding our experience. The characters in these stories are archetypes, patterns, images, or energies linked to universal experiences. They are part of what it means to be human, regardless of where you are in the world or when in history you live.

Usually, although not always, archetypes have a personal "hook" or pull based on individual circumstances of birth, upbringing, experience, education, and the like. Suppose you and a friend are at a party and the host neglects to welcome the two of you personally. If you are particularly susceptible to feeling slighted—perhaps because, as the third child in your family, you were often overlooked—you may take offense. Your friend, on the other hand, who was an only child and received much parental attention, does not even notice. If the emotion of being discounted was sufficiently strong, you might find yourself ruminating on it for days while continuing to feel its effects. When you were a child, you did not have the tools to understand and integrate the feelings and thoughts you had about being ignored, so they lodged in your personal unconscious and formed a complex. Once there, a complex attracts a corresponding archetype like a magnet.

In our example, instead of dismissing the offended feeling as irrelevant, or privately lambasting the host for lack of etiquette, a wise response is to stop and explore any associations you can make with the feeling. This can lead to the root cause. Just as we pull a weed from the garden by its root, so too we can work with feelings at their roots. This doesn't mean they never surface again; however, the more we do this, the less reactive we will be to the next occurrence of the triggering behavior. In this way, we gather invaluable information about ourselves, which in turn helps us create a life in which we are freer to be who we are because we are less controlled by circumstances from the past.

Every culture has relatively similar mental images of such archetypes as mother, warrior, lover, and child. These can manifest in positive or negative ways. If we have a positive experience of mothering in childhood, the mother archetype manifests as nurturing. If our childhood experience of "mother" is negative, when the archetype arises in our awareness it may evoke feelings of personal inadequacy, neglect, abandonment, or despair. The Wizard of Oz prominently features both aspects of the mother archetype: the good witch, Glinda, and the Wicked Witch of the West. Because change is often fraught with anxiety and is such a constant in aging, the mother archetype arises often. It can be seen in the feelings we have toward ourselves and others as we negotiate our lives and adapt. Are we gentle or critical? Do we feel a basic sense of trust and support, or do we feel fearful and pessimistic? Whatever response we have, it is likely rooted in our experience with our mothers as a child and our response to that experience.

The father archetype elicits different responses. A stern, emotionally detached father can lead offspring to be rigid, overly intellectual, or too prone to idealizing others. An engaged, compassionate father, on the other hand, can cause his children to feel more able to take risks and be more emotionally secure. If we take the time to link current emotional responses with influential conditions from the past, we can get a perspective that helps free us of habitual responses.

Another archetype present in old age is death. There's the final death at the end of life, and there's the series of small deaths that can feel relentless as we age. There's also a limit on the horizon that we now find ourselves taking into account. Lurking in the background of consciousness, and more prominently in the unconscious, is the awareness that each experience could be the last of its kind. This is especially true when the experience is special, such as a trip to another country. The way we approach death or loss is influenced by personality, experience, and attitudes absorbed from our families, cultures, and peer groups. Some elders are quite comfortable making plans for their death and talking openly about it with their loved ones, while others avoid the subject.

Usually those willing to discuss death are also those willing to tackle the practical decisions about where and how to live in old age. Those who are uncomfortable with dying are often those who end up refusing to address the circumstances of their life until a decline in mental or physical health precipitates a change.

Sarah was caught in the grip of powerful archetypal forces, primarily the archetypes of grief and loss. Suffering and grief are the price we pay for being human. Sarah did not understand that her feelings of grief, and its cousins—disconnection, abandonment, disorientation, anxiety—are part of a larger journey; nor did she have a map for the wilderness. Bowing to the forces of grief is hard and scary work, yet it is the coin we pay for admittance to new life.

REFLECTION   *Consider your relationship to loss and grief. Have you brought back treasures from your journey? If so, what are they? If you have managed to divert your grief, consider spending some time remembering your losses. See if you have any residue that has not yet been refined by tenderness. Set an intention to allow those unwanted, fearful feelings to surface, and when they do, hold them as you would hold a small child. Welcome them into your world and allow them to transform you.*

Archetypal Energy

The term "archetypal energy" is often used to describe situations when a person experiences an excessive constellation (i.e., gathering) or charge of energy. A good example is herculean energies coming to the fore in times of danger, especially when a loved one's life or well-being is threatened. Another example is encountering a very powerful dream figure, such as a family member, spouse, or friend who has died. When we wake up, we can't shake the memory, and we feel as if the dream was real. The emotion elicited by the dream is indeed real and has a life of its own at the psychic level. There is often a message for us that we must then decipher.

Another instance of archetypal energy is when there is deep anger or sorrow over a situation that does not warrant such depth of response. When we overreact, we say we feel out of control or are beside ourselves, and that is not inaccurate. An archetype from the collective unconscious has become activated, and we are flooded with its energy. This is where Sarah was caught. Because she had not faced her losses by bringing the feelings and thoughts evoked by the death of her spouse, her move, and her loss of status into consciousness, she was vulnerable to the archetypal reservoir of grief we all carry within.

When archetypal energy is constellated, we are dealing with both our personal emotion and with the emotion of the ancestors living in that particular archetype. All strong emotion gets some of its charge from the archetypal experience of being human. The rage periodically being released in the US today in the form of mass shootings and other acts of violence has archetypal energy at its base. The American Psychiatric Association has even developed a diagnosis explaining this behavior—intermittent explosive disorder—and has classified it as a lack of impulse control. Traditionally, society has had structures in place to contain this fury. There is an expectation of civility in discourse and a moral imperative to treat others with respect. As tradition breaks down, however, so too do the pillars that uphold it. These energies can be very destructive. They can also generate new solutions. Whether personally or socially, the outcome depends on bringing conscious awareness to the energy itself.

The gift of time in old age allows us to stop and examine these upwellings, whether in our personal lives or in the collective. A helpful question to ask is: what are the thoughts, feelings, and associations that accompany such outbursts? By identifying these we become familiar with the forces within us and in society. Once we're acquainted with these forces, we can better direct the powerful energies they unleash and perhaps make significant changes as a result.

REFLECTION   *What has been your experience with archetypal energy? Were you able to use it positively, or did it take you over? If it did gain the upper hand, how did you manage that? What have you learned from experiences in your life that have been overwhelming? Can you apply that teaching now to times when circumstances seem out of control or when you feel out of your depth?*

The Shadow Archetype

The shadow archetype has particular relevance for old age. The shadow consists of all those disowned qualities, both positive and negative, that have been locked outside of awareness. It shows itself in unconscious slips of the tongue, actions of ours that bewilder us, and dreams.

For some, the shadow we meet in old age is positive. We are all familiar with stories of older people who bloom in old age: those who discover a new skill, take up a long-deferred talent, finally feel strong enough to be assertive, or make decisions based on their own needs rather than the expectations or demands of others. In each instance, some part of the person was previously ignored, denied, or repressed. Painter, sculptor, and author Frederick Franck (1909–2006) shares some of his experiences along these lines in *Fingers Pointing toward the Sacred:* "I did not choose to paint, draw, carve or write; I just had to. My parents decided I would be a great doctor. Yet, instead of even a run-of-the-mill doctor, I end up as an old fellow who still fights his battle with life on pieces of paper" (247). Another example is someone who was denigrated in her family or early environment and thus grew up with a lack of self-worth. In her later years, with time to reflect on that early assessment, she begins to rearrange the puzzle pieces of her life, and a more confident, gutsy person emerges.

For many of us, the shadow reveals itself in old vulnerabilities of long standing that come to the fore in an immediate way. Like the Hydra, a many-headed serpent in Greek mythology, our historic weaknesses can return as age brings vulnerability. Deciding whether to stay at home or move can activate an unaddressed lifelong feeling of inferiority. The thought of moving to a new environment with strangers and being forced to socialize with them can raise the specter of unworthiness, insecurity, and perhaps even childhood shame. This may have been one of the elements in Sarah's story that impeded her willingness to make new friends. Awareness of inadequacy may never reach consciousness, and the decision to move is often left to fate. But these issues do not go away just because they are not confronted. Instead, they hide, biding their time until our ego control is weak, such as when we are physically or mentally compromised. In chapter 9 we will discuss how these issues often reemerge with memory loss and beg for healing. As we purge ourselves of material possessions in the last third of life, we are also called to unload internal belongings by resolving old issues and cleaning up our psychic debris.

For Jung, occasions that push the ego into places it would rather not go offer an opportunity to incorporate the shadow. When we find ourselves thinking, saying, or doing something uncharacteristic of us, our shadow is activated. Our shadow shows us the side of ourselves we don't want to see; it complements and balances our ego consciousness by showing us a positive or negative possibility of which we were not aware. When we pay attention to the shadow's appearances in our awareness, we have the chance to bring what otherwise lives in darkness into the light, thus becoming more balanced and whole. Coping with a failing body, making decisions about where to live, and questioning deeply held values and beliefs are disquieting events that are upsetting to the ego but are welcome to Self. We all know elders who are limited, not because of physical or cognitive ailments, but because they choose to perceive and interact with the world in outmoded ways. When we shirk the inner work required in late life, we tend to exist rather than live.

For the most part, strong emotion is less visible in the lives of older people. This is most likely because when we arrive at old age, many of us have developed skills to cope with emotion. Also we have less physical energy, so oldsters tend to husband what energy they do have more carefully. Our ability to change our lifestyles in accordance with what we really want to do and who we prefer to interact with may also contribute to lessening archetypal interference. Still, many old people hang onto unsettling emotional states, making it very hard for family members and caregivers to help them. Sometimes suspicion and paranoia are present; more often, these high-energy emotions are converted into less dynamic states such as selfishness, endless complaints, and fault finding.

Another aspect of shadow has to do with binary, black-and-white thinking. One of the natural developments in older age is a lessening of judgment because we can more easily see the bigger picture. However, we all have places where we're challenged. When we encounter these places inside ourselves or in others, it is a sure sign that something about ourselves has not been fully explored and embraced. As painful or counterproductive as it may seem, it is imperative that we move from either/or thinking and instead engage in both/and thinking. We do this by coming to know, learning to live with, and integrating the dark places within. No one is incapable of atrocities, despite our vehement protestations to the contrary. This is the meaning of archetypes. They are universal. That means each of us has the capacity for great evil and great good. I cannot stress this enough, because ego is amazingly resistant to any intimation that it might be culpable in some way. Those who mature in older age are able to recognize their capacity for hurting others and their impulses to do so. They can discipline themselves because they have faced their darkness.

REFLECTION *Where does the shadow manifest in your life? What pieces of your life do you shy away from? What emotions are you uncomfortable experiencing? Have you found yourself uncharacteristically drawn to interests that you previously eschewed? How judgmental are you at this time in your life? Do you hold tightly to things or people being right or wrong? What is your relationship to forgiveness? Are you holding onto events and people in the past who have hurt you because they were wrong? What about those whom you have hurt? Can you recognize the places of meanness, vindictiveness, and also deep caring inside of you?*

Opposites

In motivational theory, two psychological drives compete within us. The drive for homeostasis seeks to maintain equilibrium in a person's psychological economy; the drive to fulfill the appetites puts the individual at risk. A prosaic example from the world of elderhood is the desire to remain in one's own home, where one feels safe and secure (homeostasis), versus moving into communal living, where there are many unknowns.

Jung characterized these two drives as wishing to remain alive (the natural man/homeostasis) and wishing to grow (the spiritual principle). He noted that these drives often conflict. He saw the process of individuation as a struggle against nature, because nature tries to maintain the status quo, while Self pushes toward the unknown. The task of the second half of life is to release the known and embrace the unfamiliar.

Existential psychologist Rollo May (1909–1994) characterizes the struggle in *The Courage to Create:* "The unconscious seems to take delight in breaking through—and breaking up—exactly what we cling to most rigidly in our conscious thinking. A dynamic struggle goes on within a person between what he or she consciously thinks on the one hand and, on the other, some insight, some perspective that is struggling to be born. The insight is then born with anxiety, guilt, and the joy and gratification that is inseparable from the actualizing of a new idea or vision" (58).

Uncertainty seems to be the order of the day as we age, from the deeply philosophical/religious question "Is there a God?" to the mundane "Should I or shouldn't I?" Our natural tendency is to rush to choose one side or the other to avoid the discomfort of not knowing or doubting. Either choice can be debilitating or destabilizing. In keeping with his proclivity to face psychic turmoil head-on, Jung believed that holding the opposites in tension while each vies for power is one of the factors that allows individuation to proceed.

I don't know if Sarah was ever able to fully open to this time in her life. She was clearly being called to individuation, with loss and betrayal on one side of the scale and new life and opportunity on the other. To engage in this process requires allowing unknown, forgotten, or denied shadow elements to surface. It requires us to let them linger while we pay attention to the thoughts, images, dreams, and feelings they generate. The added time of older age is a bonus we can use to reflect and amplify whatever arises. The gift this gives us is the ability to thrive even in the midst of trying circumstances.

REFLECTION   *Managing conflicting emotions and making decisions without sufficient information is often the norm as we age. Are you aware of the push/pull of the opposites as they play out in your life? Where do they show up? What is your habitual response? When we're in the grip of indecision it can be agonizing to stay with the discomfort. Our tendency is to fly to one side of the dilemma or the other, but the benefit and eventual resolution can only be truly reached when we are willing to experience what's difficult.*

Anima/Animus

Jung believed that each of us has a contrasexual element within us. He called the feminine side of a man *anima,* and the masculine side of a woman *animus.* One of the most accessible ways of grasping this concept is suggested by Murray Stein in *Jung's Map of the Soul:* "The ways [people] actually feel about their own deeper inner selves characterize their anima or animus attitude" (130). What he means is that the attitude we have toward ourselves—critical and judgmental, or interested and attentive—tells us whether our anima/animus is developed or neurotic. An undeveloped anima in a man often manifests as moodiness, petulance, or vanity, while a developed anima allows for softness, relatedness, and access to feelings. An undeveloped animus in a woman typically shows itself in overly opinionated and controlling behavior, whereas when the animus is developed, a woman is strong and clear-headed.

The images of masculine and feminine we inherit from our parents have a substantial impact on our inner contrasexual figures. Many years ago I attended a consciousness-raising weekend where one of the exercises was to imagine our inner man and woman. My man turned out to be a cold, erect, impeccably dressed figure. He was my inner critic and judge. It has taken years and much inner work for that image to transform. Now, I often have dreams of kind, warmhearted men helping me in my life, which shows that transformation has taken place. Due to changing gender roles in present-day culture, the concepts of anima/animus have been criticized as being too culturally and historically bound. Be that as it may, for current oldsters and those entering the second half of life, we often see a lessening need for control in men and a greater independence in women.

REFLECTION   *Where do you stand in the present cultural debate in our society about gender roles? Do you dismiss or avoid the conversation? How strongly are you attached to gender roles? Have you found yourself engaging in activities or seeking friendships with those whom you at one time had no interest in cultivating? Are there certain talents you've discovered in yourself that you have historically thought of as either "unmanly" or "too masculine," "unfeminine" or "too feminine"? Have you surprised yourself by doing or thinking things that are new to you and that you have previously seen as gendered? Look for the interplay of these forces within yourself. Becoming aware of the ways we are conditioned to believe and behave can give us greater freedom in our lives.*

Individuation

Jung introduced the term *individuation* into the lexicon of psychological vocabulary, and it is pivotal to his psychology. It is intimately linked with Self, and it describes the process of becoming who one is meant to be. Jung says in *Individuation:* "The aim of individuation is nothing less than to divest the self [ego] of the false wrappings of the persona on the one hand, and the suggestive power of primordial images [archetypes] on the other" (Vol. 7, 174). In other words, individuation is the process whereby habitual, nonessential inclinations accumulated over a lifetime are relinquished to allow innate, core values, inclinations, and abilities to flourish. When this occurs, we are less vulnerable to being overwhelmed by archetypal energies because we have developed an interior sensitivity to them and the self-knowledge to recognize them.

Although individuation is not a theory of psychological development per se, it does suggest movement toward increasing maturity and differentiation. As noted by Jungian analyst Margaret Sullivan in *The Mystery of Analytic Work,* Jung was the first psychoanalyst to imagine an inborn human urge toward truth and wholeness. He proposed that the core human drive is to become the individual one innately is, and he specifically differentiated it from expectations stemming from the culture, one's family, or the personal ego. According to Sullivan, Self provides the ego with the impetus toward individuation. Instead of assuming that behaviors and moods that accompany aging or cognitive loss are simply due to lack of engagement, depression, or dysfunction in the brain, individuation suggests purposefulness.

I'm sure many of you have arrived at some point or other in life where you find yourself saying, "I'm done!" It usually has to do with some role or job that required you to adopt an attitude or behavior that allowed you to meet external and internal demands. It is now time to discard these mandates because the cost of keeping them is greater than their value. You have outgrown the need for them. Initially, there may be some guilt about releasing aspects of ego, and ego does not make the job easier. However, the energy that propels letting go at this time is the process of individuation. It can be likened to peeling an onion as we slowly, and painfully, remove the accumulated layers of a lifetime to discover our core.

Individuation calls for a shift in perspective at all levels. It is definitely not more of the same. In some ways, we're like teenagers, once again learning how to live in this world. Acquiring maps for this stage of life is crucial. Though individuation is not an easy task, it can be helpful to understand and remember that there is an inner guide—Self—that intends individuation for each of us. Adopting a sense of adventure, a willingness to entertain periods of discomfort, and an interest in the interior world makes for fullness of life.

As we turn to other guides for this journey in the following chapters, I leave you with Hillman's description of the path of growth from *The Soul's Code:* "The 'acorn theory' … holds that each person bears a uniqueness that asks to be lived and that is already present before it can be lived" (6).

5

Maslow's Hierarchy
of Needs and Aging

*[The] depths are not only the wellsprings of neuroses, but also of
health, joy, and creativeness.*

> —ABRAHAM MASLOW, *The Farther
> Reaches of Human Nature* (New York:
> Viking, 1971)

Now we'll explore the work of American psychologist Abraham Maslow
(1908–1970), most noted for his motivational theory of a hierarchy of
human needs that each individual seeks to fulfill. Maslow's hierarchy
of needs offers those interested in aging another lens through which
to examine the many experiences that unfold as we age. Various needs
in his hierarchy show up throughout our lives; however, as we live with
the changes brought about through aging, we can once again find ourselves grappling with needs both basic and transcendent. As we will
see in chapters 12 and 13, the first four levels of Maslow's hierarchy
have a special significance in old age because the losses, dependency, and

absence of meaning characteristic of this time of life bring them to the surface again.

Maslow is one of the few psychologists who studied *The Farther Reaches of Human Nature,* as one of his books is titled. He had an intense interest in the exception rather than the rule, and his later additions to his initial hierarchy reflect this interest. His hierarchy of needs begins with basic survival needs that allow life to flourish, and they increase in complexity until they reach what he called growth needs. Just as Jung's psychology grew out of his personal experience of grappling with psyche, so Maslow's hierarchy evolved over the years, as he evolved. It is unfortunate that the aspect of his work concerned with what he termed "metaneeds"—those impulses that go beyond survival to seek out altered states of consciousness and greater self-actualization—has been almost completely ignored. It is deeply relevant to the exploration of the interior world this book advocates.

Initially, Maslow described five basic levels of need that he considered to be biologically rooted and therefore hardwired in human beings. He believed these needs—which he called *D* needs, for *deficiency*—come first in order of importance because they are all dependent on things outside the self. They must be met minimally before a person can begin meeting higher-order needs. The basic needs are:

1. Physiological: food, clothing, shelter, warmth

2. Safety and security

3. To belong and feel loved

4. Self-esteem and recognition from the world and within one's self

5. Self-actualization or growth

Shortly before his death, Maslow added three needs that he called *metaneeds*—cognitive, aesthetics, and transcendence—bringing his hierarchy of needs to a total of eight. He distinguished the metaneeds from the first five needs by conceptualizing them as personal growth needs rather than satisfaction of deficiency needs. He also rearranged the order of the full list of needs by inserting the cognitive and aesthetic needs before self-actualization and adding transcendence at the end.

Between 1943 and 1954 Maslow continued to refine his thinking, culminating with the publication of his book *Motivation and Personality*. During these years, his theory became popular in business and management because it offered a way to understand the motivational needs of different workers and to use this understanding to incentivize a more productive workforce. As recently as 2014, the *Wall Street Journal* published an article titled "What Businesses Can Learn from Maslow's Hierarchy of Needs."

Eventually Maslow became interested in people he called self-actualizers—those who went beyond D needs to achieve their full potential. From Jung's perspective, these are the people who individuate: those who are able to integrate consciousness with the unconscious or ego with Self. In Maslow's interviews with self-actualizers, he noted that they had regular access to altered states. He coined the term "peak experiences" to describe these states. We all occasionally enjoy peak experiences when we are jolted out of our usual mode of being and find ourselves in a more expansive state. Self-actualizers experience this kind of state at a greater frequency that the majority of us.

Maslow came to believe that there are two basic ways of perceiving and thinking: D (deficiency) and B (being). D cognition is the way most of us see reality most of the time. B cognition is the way most spiritual traditions call us to see. From the perspective of this book, D cognition would be the way we ordinarily approach aging: with attitudes of bias, disdain, and fear. Jung called this the "natural man," the part of us based in instinct that seeks stasis. B cognition, on the other hand, is what this book advocates. It's a way of valuing, seeing, thinking about, and attending to the aging process that requires a broader, higher, or more depth-oriented mindset. Maslow reasoned that even though everyone does not actualize these values, there is a biological need for them, and a full definition of the complete human being must include them. His book *The Farther Reaches of Human Nature* details his thought on this topic.

As with so much else in life, it is possible to see Maslow's theories from multiple perspectives. At the risk of stretching his hierarchy beyond what he intended, below we'll review each of Maslow's needs, and we'll include a discussion of the interior or psychic level that corresponds to each need.

Level 1: Physiological

Physiological needs are driven by biological survival. Air, food, water, sleep, and a relatively constant body temperature are the most important of these, because without these things a person cannot survive. Housing is also included here because some sort of shelter is part of what allows us to meet these needs. Unless these requirements are met, we can't move on to the next level because our attention is occupied by the basics. The archetype associated with this level is the homeless man or the bag lady. Internally, we all carry the dread of this possibility. A hurricane, earthquake, mudslide, or other natural disaster can wipe out our home and can take this physiological foundation with it. There is also the symbolic dimension of psychic homelessness: being fragmented or alienated within so that it is impossible to find one's internal home.

It's easy to assume that most elders living in the developed world have these needs met. Unfortunately, there are many who have to make a choice between buying food, buying medicine, or paying the rent. When these elders live in cold or hot climates, they often cannot afford to operate the requisite heating or cooling systems. Because elder bodies are more susceptible to fluctuating temperatures, death is often the result.

When we are ill, our attention can be hijacked, and we can fall back to this level of fighting to simply meet our physiological needs. If we have trouble breathing, are in pain, or are chronically awake at night, our attention gets focused on these physical aspects. When we cannot count on a basic level of physical well-being and nurturance, the primitive brain can take over, leaving little room in consciousness for higher-level needs to emerge and be met. This is a good reason to cultivate a broader base of consciousness. While for the most part I am not a big fan of cognitive behavioral therapy because it tends to treat the symptom and not the cause of distress, it can be very effective when dealing with bodily issues. Chapters 10 and 11 explore ways of working with these kinds of discomforts so they do not take up all the real estate in our minds.

In Hinduism, the ancient Laws of Manu—one of the first written law codes in Asia—offer an interesting perspective by proposing a four-stage model of life: student, householder, forest dweller, and wandering ascetic. The final two stages imply living in a way that only minimally meets Maslow's first two levels of needs. Most people in the West who don't have those needs fairly well met are living in a state of anxiety. Maslow's rare individuals who live according to their metaneeds or *B* values find meaning in the deprivation. The caveat here, of course, is that this option is chosen and not forced on the person.

Level 2: Safety

Second-level needs relate to safety and have a high priority. For elders, these concerns range from living in unsafe neighborhoods or being a target for unscrupulous scammers to refusing to give up driving and living in facilities that limit an elder's freedom because of liability issues concerning potential falls. Whenever people are faced with a situation that feels overwhelming, instills fear, or evokes any strong emotion, the perceived need for safety arises. The person having this experience will choose one of three classic physiological responses—fight, flight, or freeze—according to their personality. These reactions are built into the amygdala, that part of the reptilian brain that has to do with survival. Even though many people in developed societies no longer regularly face life-and-death situations, the body does not differentiate between types of stress. Any stressful situation still elicits these primitive responses.

The fight response might come up for an elder who experiences anxiety in response to family pressure to move out of the home. The elder in this situation may lash out in defensive anger. Family members may become offended or wonder what is wrong with him or her, since this type of behavior was not demonstrated before. The situation can escalate and create negative feelings and misunderstandings on both sides. The culprit is this primitive need for safety and security that has not been recognized.

As noted earlier, archetypes emerge when people find themselves in heightened emotional states. In real time it can feel as if we are a victim of raw emotions, when in fact our reaction to something has ignited that energy. Elders living with memory loss in particular frequently respond to situations of coercion by reacting with fear or its protector, anger. The caregiver's task is to learn the signs of strong emotion. Attempts at denial, dismissal, judgment, rational explanation, or distraction are unhelpful. Recognizing and responding to the reality of the situation as perceived by the elder, and offering appropriate comfort, will defuse whatever has been activated.

The flight response is often used to avoid unpleasantness. We fly from discomfort in hopes that the threat will disappear. Unfortunately, as we learned in earlier chapters, what is ignored or actively repressed goes into the shadow and stays there until a moment of weakness or vulnerability. The elderly woman who is no longer able to safely maintain her home and who cannot or will not agree to move or get help in the home is pushing knowledge of her infirmity into the shadow. She refuses to acknowledge what is plain to others around her: that she is at risk and will most likely be forced to make a change by physical or cognitive circumstances. In his insightful and practical book *How to Say It to Seniors,* David Solie, CEO of a life insurance brokerage firm, attributes the unsettling behavior of older people to the fact that they're undertaking developmental tasks at odds with the world around them. During his career, Solie recognized the need to hear and address these concerns beyond surface dialogue.

When an elder is frail or has memory loss, security needs come more to the fore and are easily triggered. This is one of the reasons why the first commandment in forgetfulness care is not to argue with the person. Actually, this is a good strategy for all of us when dealing with others or even ourselves. Whenever emotions are heightened, arguing, rationalizing, and cajoling are fruitless endeavors that end up antagonizing other people, frustrating the caregiver, and creating unnecessary suffering. It is much better to recognize that there is an overwhelming emotion present that cannot be leaped over or ignored. Once the emotion is acknowledged and addressed through reflection and conversation, forward movement often becomes possible.

The freeze response can be seen when people feel pulled in contrary directions simultaneously. The resulting tension tends to paralyze the one who feels it. Exercising patience and compassion toward the unknown usually allows one option to emerge as the best choice. This can only happen, however, when one is willing to sit with the discomfort of indecision and not knowing, often for longer than desired. People often freeze when they receive a diagnosis that will require some kind of major life change, such as surgery or chemotherapy. At these times it is difficult to think clearly or make decisions. Psychiatrist Elisabeth Kübler-Ross (1926–2004) saw this as a grief response and called it shock. Once shock passes, it is possible to make decisions. Some elders, however, find themselves in an almost continual state of shock, and they respond by freezing and refusing to make decisions. They can take quite a while to work through this period. It can be difficult to recover from cumulative shocks and changes, making it all the more important to develop spiritual muscle ahead of time.

For an elder experiencing memory loss, the higher brain functions that regulate executive (decision-making) function are the first to be compromised, leaving the more primal areas that control emotion to gain and maintain ascendancy. In some ways, the elder's response to the environment is not unlike that of a child. Both react in ways that do not include cognitive processing. This means that occurrences such as loud noises, physical pain, flashing lights, rough handling, and inadequate support can be perceived as threatening.

The elder can use fighting, flight, or freezing to ward off or escape what is perceived as menacing. Both the child and the elder with memory loss require surroundings that have some kind of routine. In order to meet the safety needs of both, a predictable, orderly world is required. Similarly, elders who have a diagnosis of obsessive compulsive disorder and live with chronic heightened states of anxiety require the stability identified by level 2 needs for safety.

Elders without memory loss also want stability, of course. Here we are dealing with interior as opposed to exterior safety. By its nature, life is risky. The tendency to hunker down, be safe, not take risks, and avoid failure that some people display in later life is detrimental to their overall well-being. It can result in lessened social and psychological engagement, which puts the elder at risk for isolation. With a predictable environment and the ability to work with our internal mandate that wants to be safe, elders are able to turn their attention to other, less basic parts of their lives.

Level 3: Love and Belonging

Love, affection, and belonging are third-level needs in Maslow's hierarchy. He describes these needs as driven by the desire to overcome feelings of loneliness and alienation through giving and receiving love and affection. Most people get these needs met through family, friends, work, faith communities, and interest groups. When we are older, however, many factors conspire to limit our access to these usual sources of love and belonging.

Death is the largest contributor to isolation, particularly for those who live into their nineties. Frequently older people experience the death of a spouse or longtime partner. The surviving person must now take over all the tasks that were previously shared. This usually happens at a time when the survivor feels lessened energy and interest, but the demand is nonetheless urgent. Rather than spending time with others, the older person uses their energy on life maintenance. If a child dies, that is a blow that can affect people at such a deep level that it takes years to rebound, if ever. Once again, the elder's available energy goes into managing grief. Thankfully, more and more people are taking advantage of grief support groups. These not only provide a forum to discuss feelings but also play an important role in meeting the need to belong.

Another significant death-related loss that older people experience is that of the history shared with longtime friends. Death can be relentless in depriving us of familiar voices and anchors. When a longtime friend dies, a part of our history slides away. We lose an important "other" to reminisce and laugh or cry with about events in the past. The consequence can be a cumulative feeling of aloneness. To exacerbate matters, mobility challenges often keep elders close to home, and the loss of hearing or vision leads to reduced involvements in areas of interest that used to provide a sense of internal and external connection. Making new friends and developing new interests to replace those that are no longer available is an ongoing challenge, yet it is vital for psychological and ultimately physical health.

The aging-in-place movement, which aims to keep elders living at home for as long as possible, offers an array of services that are attractive to many older people who do not want to move out of their home. As long as an elder has some degree of mobility, remaining at home is a feasible option. When this is not the case, the consequent lack of stimulation and contact with others on a regular basis often results in a decline in mental and functional ability. With the baby boomer generation now reaching early old age, more people are emphasizing community living. Although boomers eschew institutions, there is great appeal in the idea of house sharing, co-ops, and cohousing. This model has much to offer as an alternative to the isolation that can come from living alone or moving to a facility. The village movement—which works to connect older neighbors with each other, provide volunteers, and offer interesting, relevant programs—also addresses this need.

In recognition of the potential pitfalls of isolation for elders, society provides organizations such as senior centers to help meet these needs. The problem with senior centers, however, is that too many older people refuse to take advantage of them. There is such a strong age bias in our culture that older people do not want to be seen in a senior-identified place. I have had many people aged eighty and older tell me they don't want to go to a senior center because it's full of old people! It's hard to make good choices when we are constrained by unacknowledged prejudices. It would be very life-enhancing for these older adults to review the basis of their thinking and free themselves of knee-jerk responses. For compromised elders, there is adult day care, although here too many refuse to go because change and the unknown are too scary. Others cannot afford the price of admission.

One innovative nonprofit program for homebound elders—named Well Connected, formerly called Senior Center Without Walls—offers free telephone-based or videoconferencing activity programs. It allows elders to engage in conversation and meaningful relationships without having to leave home. Many elders say this program has been lifesaving for them.

From the perspective of the interior life, one way to help meet the need for love and belonging is to find ways to give love first to oneself and then to others. If we live long enough, most people who walk the journey of life with us will die or move away. Cultivating younger friends, getting involved in groups, taking up hobbies that draw a wide variety of ages, and volunteering in places that support and nurture their volunteers are just a few ways to help ensure rich relationships in old age.

Level 4: Self-Esteem

The fourth level in Maslow's hierarchy, self-esteem, concerns both how we perceive ourselves and how others treat us. When we have self-esteem, we feel confidence and a sense of value. When this need is not met, we experience feelings of inferiority, weakness, helplessness, or worthlessness. While self-esteem needs can be challenging to meet for many across the life span, most people have areas in life where they feel useful and necessary. Consider how you meet your need for self-esteem. Is it through work, relationships, hobbies, political activism, athletics, volunteering, parenting, or a special ability? If you could no longer continue with whatever gratifies you, how would you respond?

Once frailty sets in—and sometimes even before that—one's usual sources of gratification need to be modified or abandoned. For those who are unprepared, the onset of frailty can erode their sense of purpose and usefulness. Without some kind of compensation for the loss of active engagement, elders too often end up clinically depressed. We can meet the need for self-esteem by ensuring that we have a wide range of interests and that we are prepared with alternate possibilities in case our life situation changes.

Years ago I came across a story written by a daughter about her father's progressive decline. She called it "My Father's Window Box." In the story, she describes how, after retirement, her father bought a several-hundred-acre farm. As his energy and health changed, he gradually modified what he took on. At the end of his life, in his nineties, he was satisfied taking care of the plants in a single small window box. This story is an excellent example of resilience. As her father progressively let go of project after project, he still found ways to keep alive some aspect of what brought meaning to his life. Sometimes we have to be a sleuth to find the right thing for us. It takes creativity and often the help of others to do so.

Amid the rapidly changing mores of society and the rise of technology, it is hard for some oldsters to feel that their presence is valued. Many speakers and writers have noted that the kind of knowledge elders offered in the past is no longer valued. When the focus is on technology, as it is in our society, the young are the carriers of know-how. Elders go to youngsters to ask for help with their various devices. While this can provide a good avenue for intergenerational connection, there is no guarantee that the relationship is one of reciprocity. Nor do all elders have access to young people.

An associated aspect of modern society that disenfranchises older adults is an emphasis on productivity. Elders do not produce. Elderhood is more about being than about doing. If society is to value elders again, and if elders are to value themselves, it will not be because of what elders know about the external world; rather, it will be because of what they know about the internal one. As faculties wane, interests and abilities change. As time becomes available for reminiscence and reflection, the possibility of mining the interior world grows. The theory of gerotranscendence, discussed in chapter 7, offers a positive vision of what happens naturally when elders embrace age. It will take time before such theories are integrated into the societal outlook at any meaningful level. A shift in perspective is required that places as much value on the internal landscape as on the external. Today's elders can be pioneers and leaders in this endeavor. What they discover and communicate can contribute to a shift in attitudes about aging. Recognizing this possibility and taking up the challenge can provide present-day elders with a sense of self-esteem and fulfillment.

Level 5: Cognitive

This is one of the metaneeds that Maslow added to his hierarchy toward the end of his life. By cognitive needs, he meant concern for meaning and knowledge: the desire to know and understand. This need pushes us as long as we are alive. It is analogous to the emphasis Jung placed on the meaning-making process of individuation. Loss of meaning is a common experience of old people. Having lived a long life and now being unable to do things that once brought them enjoyment, some old-sters are hard-pressed to find meaning in their existence. When I worked in a predominantly Catholic facility, the old people there brought meaning to their experience by saying they were in God's waiting room. This simple perspective belies a wise attitude. For them, there was meaning in being and waiting. That was enough.

When Jung said we cannot live the values of the second half of life according to the values of the first half, this is what he was referring to. Meaning in older adulthood needs to be discovered again as if for the first time. Unlike the first half of life, there are no rules or roles or givens. This can be a stumbling block for those who are accustomed to living out someone else's script for them, whether societal or parental. For Jung, reclaiming the unconscious is an ongoing task that provides us with endless paths of exploration. As much as we shy away from the "slings and arrows of outrageous fortune," it is in turning toward them that we find meaning in life. Old age offers an exquisite opportunity. Finding purposefulness in our circumstances—no matter what they are—requires the ability to reach beyond the surface, using both the mind and the heart. Each of us must become an explorer, and we must rely on our own authority, since we cannot rely on the tried-and-true verities of the past. This shift is a major task in a culture that does not provide much incentive or direction for exploring the interior world or maximizing the elder years.

Making meaning is such a fundamental part of being human that even when the prefrontal cortex is damaged, as it is in memory loss, elders continue to act meaningfully. In my work with those who have advanced dementia, meaning can be discovered in their behavior; it just takes more effort and attention from the caregiver. We are not randomly acting beings. Rather, we are fundamentally purposeful. In her book *Validation Breakthrough,* social worker Naomi Feil cites numerous examples of elders with advanced memory loss who continue to act out meaningful roles or emotions from their past. Many of these behaviors are efforts to resolve preexisting issues that have not yet reached resolution.

Level 6: Aesthetics

This is the second metaneed Maslow added to his initial hierarchy of needs. He recognized that the appreciation of beauty, balance, color, and form is requisite for a satisfying life. For Plato and his contemporaries, Beauty—both physical and internal—was one of the most important Forms in existence. Plato believed that to know Beauty is to know what all beautiful things have in common. Finding beauty in unfamiliar places or making beauty from what is considered unbeautiful stems directly from the soul's need for aesthetic fulfillment. There are many artists today who collect discarded junk and use it to create art objects. They give us an excellent example of the deep aesthetic need residing in all of us.

The experience of beauty is essential, and humans can be ingenious in discovering it. Sometimes it's obvious: a sunset radiates reds and pinks across the sky, or light filters through the trees. Other times it's more obscure: we notice a flower growing through a crack in an urban sidewalk in a depressed part of town. Nature is a free source of beauty, which is why it is so important for us to have access to it. When we are feeling disconnected, upset, anxious, or depressed, nature can restore balance. In Wendell Berry's poem "The Peace of Wild Things," he says (I'm paraphrasing) that when he's upset, he goes and lies down by the wood drake resting in the water. Just imagining this returns our breath to an easy pace. French photographer Henri Cartier-Bresson was a master of showing beauty in ordinary people's faces. His photographs enable the viewer to see things from a much broader and more tender reference point—the kind that Maslow captured with his self-actualizers. Elders who take up art, music, gardening, flower arranging, or other creative endeavors are unknowingly meeting this need.

However, one doesn't have to create art to gain the benefits of beauty. One person I know with early-stage Alzheimer's disease derives much satisfaction from watching the antics of squirrels and birds in his backyard. Good memory-loss facilities take elders to museums, offer art programs, put an elder's favorite music on an iPod, and offer other innovative activities that touch the sensibility of aesthetics. As a result, these elders are able to engage in ways that have astonishing outcomes. For a wonderful example of this, rent the documentary film *Alive Inside.*

Level 7: Self-Actualization

For Maslow, self-actualization refers to the desire for self-fulfillment, which occurs when a person has realized their potential to the highest degree possible. Self-actualization is the aspiration to become more and more who one is, to become everything one is capable of becoming. This is almost a paraphrase of the definition of individuation given by Jung and of Hillman's acorn theory.

Maslow identified the need for self-actualization as a result of his lifetime interest in peak or mystical experiences, during which our relationship to life perceptually shifts. Our senses are heightened, and we experience a feeling of deep connection both internally and with the world, accompanied by a sense of awe, wonder, and deep happiness. Examples include falling in love, successfully completing a complicated project, being transported out of oneself by nature, the high that comes from athletic accomplishment, and insights that come when writing, reflecting quietly, or meditating. What distinguishes a self-actualizing person is that they tend to have more peak experiences than average and are usually highly creative. Maslow insisted that it is possible to set up our lives so we become more attuned to these experiences. He puts it this way in *The Farther Reaches of Human Nature:* "Recovering the self must, as a sine qua non, include the recovery of the ability to have and to cognize … inner signals, to know what and whom one likes and dislikes, what is enjoyable and what is not, when to eat and when not to, when to sleep" (33).

Usually we think of creativity as tied to the arts; however, creativity is a capacity for thinking outside the box that is available to each of us. In the opening chapter of his book *The Mature Mind,* physician Gene Cohen (1944–2009) tells the story of his in-laws coming to dinner during a snowstorm in Washington, DC. Unable to hail a taxi because of the weather, the couple spotted a pizza place. They went in and ordered a pizza to go, and when the cashier asked where to deliver it, Cohen's father-in-law gave Cohen's address and told the cashier that he and his wife wanted to be delivered with the pizza. Cohen used that story to illustrate the kind of creativity that becomes accessible in older age. Chapter 11 explores more of Cohen's ideas.

Too often older adults' creativity lies buried in the shadow because it was discouraged when they were youngsters. Creative children, and creative people, often challenge the status quo, so they are frequently shamed or admonished. By the time they reach old age, their creativity has been marginalized in the psyche. In situations like this, throwing off the shackles of prior conditioning is necessary if we are to meet this need.

Like the individuating person, self-actualizers are able to successfully integrate life's many opposites into a new synthesis, including making the unconscious conscious. This is one of the tasks of the second half of life, according to Jung. Being able to sustain a connection with what Jung called Self, despite outer circumstances pulling us away from Self, is a hallmark of self-actualization. We are able to take direction from within rather than from the myriad forces without that clamor for attention and allegiance. The specific form self-actualization takes varies from person to person.

The attitude about aging encouraged in this book—to see all that comes to us as purposeful—can go a long way toward fulfilling the deepest part of our being. We can make an ongoing commitment to creativity, coupled with the intention to shift perspective from ordinary consciousness to an extraordinary way of perceiving.

Level 8: Transcendence

The need to dedicate oneself to some higher goal, otherwise known as transcendence, is the last need Maslow added to his hierarchy. In *The Farther Reaches of Human Nature,* he describes it this way: "Transcendence refers to the very highest and most inclusive or holistic levels of human consciousness, behaving and relating, as ends rather than means, to oneself, to significant others, to human beings in general, to other species, to nature, and to the cosmos" (33).

The difference between self-actualizing and self-transcendence is that the former has to do with the personal ego, whereas the latter transcends ego. At this point, Maslow enters the territory of what is usually reserved for religious or spiritual consciousness. Yet these ideas are not as ethereal as they may seem at first glance. Several years ago, social entrepreneur and thought leader Marc Freedman founded Encore, an organization dedicated to helping people in midlife and beyond become human resources to help address societal issues. In 2005 he created the Purpose Prize, which "awards $100,000 annually to older individuals who are creating new ways to solve tough social problems," according to the prize's website. Individuals who have received the prize come from all walks of life and have varied interests. The one thing they have in common is that they look beyond their lives to a broader social context, and they put effort and energy into creating innovative approaches to resolving societal problems. That is an example of self-transcendence.

Experiencing transcendence doesn't require you to have a big idea or to be recognized for your contributions. It is enough to identify something beyond your own needs that inspires your passion and pursue it. A homebound elder writing letters to the editor on social issues, an elder grandparenting neighborhood children, an older adult pinching pennies to save money for his children, and caregivers sacrificing their own desires to be available for their loved ones are all examples of actions that transcend the boundaries of personal concerns (when not motivated by codependency). I know of an older person who writes postcards to help get out the vote irrespective of political party. To offset her costs, she started a GoFundMe site. There are as many ways to experience self-transcendence as there are creative ways to meet the myriad needs of our world. Increasingly, studies are being conducted on the impact of self-transcendence. At least one such study showed a decrease in depression.

The philosopher John G. Messerly says in his "Summary of Maslow on Self-Transcendence" (https://ieet.org/index.php/IEET2/more/Messerly20170204) that Maslow called transcendent states *plateau experiences* because they are "more lasting, serene, and cognitive states, as opposed to peak experiences which tend to be mostly emotional and temporary. Moreover, in plateau experiences one feels not only ecstasy, but the sadness that comes with realizing that others cannot have similar encounters." Maslow's final need dovetails amazingly well with chapter 7's theory of *gerotranscendence,* which suggests that transcendent states are more naturally available as we age when we do so consciously.

As we become familiar with the needs discussed in this chapter and learn to identify them when they arise in life, we are better able to live creatively. Notice when you might be stuck in one of the four deficiency needs—physical, safety, belonging, or esteem. When you encounter an impasse or obstacle, it is useful to ask which need is not being met. Is this need something you can satisfy in the external world, or is it something you need to manage within the psyche? If we can identify what we're missing, we're more likely to come up with a solution that at least partially meets the need. Sometimes the simple recognition of what is driving us in the moment is sufficient. Keeping in mind Maslow's second-order being needs of cognitive, aesthetics, self-actualization, and transcendence is what allows us to experience joy. Of course, we cannot expect to do this all the time; such a desire would come from a lower-order deficiency need. It is surprising how even very small efforts to recognize and meet these needs can lead to shifts that are larger than expected. It is the degree of conscious awareness we bring to our life—coupled with the effort to be present—that can make the difference.

6

The Eriksons and Aging

What is needed [in aging] more than anything else is a turning toward interiority and toward the Self which, for many of us, has been excluded and minimized in our lives.

—MICHAEL CONFORTI, "Intimations in the Night: The Journey toward New Meaning in Aging," in *Jung and Aging: Possibilities and Potentials for the Second Half of Life,* edited by Leslie Sawin, Lionel Corbett, and Michael Carbine (New Orleans: Spring Journal Books, 2014)

The Eriksonian model of the stages of life offers a provocative lens for perceiving and conceptualizing the strengths and weaknesses we are called to encounter and resolve in old age. This model highlights how, as we mature, development proceeds at an uneven pace. We become more competent in skills we are already inclined toward, while we fall behind in skills that challenge us. In this chapter I go through each of the model's stages, give a brief overview of their place in life development, and relate them to how they might reappear as we age. My intention is for you to develop a working knowledge of the stages so that, when they emerge in your life, you will recognize them. Once we can name a thing, we can begin to free ourselves from its grasp.

In his classic 1950 work *Childhood and Society*, psychologist Erik Erikson (1902–1994) outlines eight stages of psychosocial development, starting in infancy and culminating in old age. He conceived of these stages as periods of conflict, each of which must be resolved for development to proceed. In this sense his work is close to Jung's, who also believed that a person individuates through struggle.

Erikson's eight stages are:

- Trust vs. mistrust

- Autonomy vs. shame and doubt

- Initiative vs. guilt

- Industry vs. inferiority

- Identity vs. role confusion

- Intimacy vs. isolation

- Generativity vs. stagnation

- Integrity vs. despair

As you can see, each stage is framed as a polarity, with ego strength on one hand and potential weakness on the other. Mastering a stage means one has sufficiently integrated it to allow the corresponding virtue for that stage to become accessible. These virtues are the strengths we use to negotiate the tasks life gives us. The virtues, listed in order of the stages, are hope, will, purpose, competency, fidelity, love, care, and wisdom. Just reading through the list, you probably already have a sense of which virtues are strongly developed in your personality and which ones you have struggled with over the years. Aging presents us with an opportunity to achieve balance.

In 1997, at the age of ninety-three, Erik's wife and collaborator, Joan (1903–1997), extended his book, *The Life Cycle Completed*, and introduced a ninth stage of development. Commenting on this ninth stage in the film *On Old Age I: A Conversation with Joan Erikson at 90*, she observes that in late life the Eriksons both found themselves in foreign territory. As they lived into their nineties, they realized old age was a more nuanced experience than they had imagined in their fifties when they theorized these stages.

As with prior chapters, I suggest the reader pay attention to any memories, emotions, images, or thoughts that arise as the chapter unfolds.

Stage 1: Trust vs. Mistrust (birth to two years)

This is the stage of infancy. Many researchers believe that it actually starts in the womb. It is one of the most critical stages, and many get snagged on its shoals. If a child is lucky enough to have the right kind of early environment, he or she will gain the ability to hope, the virtue of this stage.

The word *trust* comes from an Old Norse root meaning "confidence" and is intimately connected to hope. Trust is the foundation upon which all the other virtues rest. If lack of trust is an issue in your life currently, as it is for many, now is the time to start to adopt this very valuable stance in small ways. Learning how to take care of ourselves when trust is broken is equally valuable. More important than avoiding having our trust broken is knowing what to do when it happens.

Most of us know that studies of children in orphanages who do not receive love, touch, and attention show that these children fail to thrive. These are extreme cases; yet, when the infant experiences illness, trauma, or abuse at this early stage, or when competent parenting has been absent or inconsistent, the infant cannot establish basic trust. This can lead to an inability or reluctance to presume basic goodness in oneself, the other, or the world. Hopelessness can get deeply buried in the unconscious, leading to isolation, frustration, suspiciousness, and lack of self-esteem.

Infants cannot distinguish between their needs and themselves. When needs consistently are not met, the infant equates this lack with a lack of self-worth. Although thinking has not yet developed, the infant gets the sense that there is something inherently wrong, and that sense of wrongness often lodges deep inside their being. Unless this self-messaging is intercepted in some way by an attentive mentor or relative, it negatively influences the person for the rest of his or her life. Once I heard an NPR interview with a doctor who works in a New York prison who said that in her thirty years of work, she had never met a prisoner who did not experience some kind of abuse as a child. The ability of our early environment to set the pattern for the rest of our life is excruciatingly powerful.

Some degree of mistrust is required for us to discern what is helpful and what is not, who or what is trustworthy and who or what is not. These necessary frustrations help us build psychic muscle. When the early environment does not prolong these disappointments, we build the virtue of hope because we have the experience of our needs being met sufficiently often. For an elder who is grappling with the decision of whether to leave home, that elder's initial experience of trust—coupled with the psychological work they have done (or not done) up to this point—will make the difference between a willing embrace of change or a clinging to what has been.

For elders who are disoriented, words are no longer available, so their main sources of communication are touch and eye contact. The elder's early experience of trust has much to do with how they respond in the caregiving situation. Early trust experiences also have a strong influence on how much trust the caregiver is able to engender. Many problematic behaviors seen in memory care units have to do with a failure at the level of trust. Just as there is a diagnosis called "failure to thrive" in children, "failure to trust" is a problem affecting many old people. Trust and the hope that goes along with it are foundational experiences for all of us. The degrees of trust and hope we have will determine how we respond to the curve balls that come our way.

Stage 2: Autonomy vs. Shame and Doubt (ages two to four)

This stage of life is a time of gathering self-reliance. The virtue or quality we develop as a result of successfully meeting the challenge of autonomy is will. Will allows us to keep going even when what we really want to do is give up or be complacent. Finding the balance between willfulness or the need to control and helplessness is essential.

Toddlers are learning how to toilet, dress, and feed themselves. We can all smile when they say, "I can do it!" Of course, this is also the time of tantrums and willfulness. The issue is learning when to hold on, when to let go, when to be separate, and when to be together. The country song "The Gambler" epitomizes what is learned in this stage: "You've got to know when to hold 'em, know when to fold 'em, know when to walk away, and know when to run." This is an art that often takes a lifetime to learn. It is a lesson we are all confronted with throughout life and especially in old age.

Fiercely independent elders who insist they can do it themselves are reminiscent of that toddler who adamantly insisted the same. There are times when stubbornness is tenacity, a virtue, and other times when stubbornness is obstinacy. The issue in both is willfulness tied to self-esteem; however, there is a world of difference between the two. We all need to feel as if we are in charge. Exercising control over ourselves and our environment is important to civilized society and self-determination. If early parenting is overly protective or controlling, we learn to doubt our abilities. This can lead to hesitancy, fearfulness, and feelings of inferiority later in life. As compensation, these feelings can lead to aggression, excessive self-assertion, or contrariness. As Jung noted, there are always two opposite poles. In this instance, one is contraction (flight/freeze), and the other is animosity (fight).

Among older adults, this stage can manifest by refusing change, lashing out in anger, or insisting on things being our way. What often underlies this response is a feeling of shame or a fear of failure or rejection. When we feel this way, we cannot ask for what we need because our needs are shameful to us, so we act as if we don't have needs. This is what I call the John Wayne mentality, or the "pull yourself up by your own bootstraps" approach to life. This strategy creates a false bravado (persona) that gets us through until it can no longer be sustained in the face of multiple assaults.

An antidote to such a dilemma is to sidestep the dichotomy of autonomy vs. shame by cultivating an appreciation of interdependence. As we age, we most certainly will need the help of others. If we live long enough, we may need help with basic functions of life. Should this occur, we are being offered a final opportunity to negotiate this stage for the sake of our interior development. Another quality we need to cultivate is genuine self-love—not selfish love, but a softness toward the child within who feels so shamed or fearful.

Sadly, the return of this developmental stage in old age usually goes unrecognized by elders and our society; nor is it understood in care settings. The result is that the kind of psychological support elders need—such as strategies for self-care, opportunities to talk about feelings, knowledgeable partners, and friends and facility staff who can respond in caring ways to the elder's anger, tears, and confusion—is often not available. The elder gets entrenched in old habits that increase the painfulness of the situation for all.

For those with memory loss, these early stages can create problems. As cognitive capacities are compromised, forgetful older adults no longer understand what is dangerous. Nor do they feel bound by rules. In facilities especially, but also in the home, efforts to protect the older person conflict with efforts to give them autonomy. It takes a great deal of skill on the part of a caregiver to negotiate these challenges.

Stage 3: Initiative vs. Guilt (ages five to eight)

Stage 3 is the play age, the time when we begin to find a sense of basic purpose, which is the virtue of this stage. Much of our orientation to life and the world are laid down at this time. In our culture, play is not a highly regarded activity. We tend to leap over this phase and go right into the next phase of industriousness.

For elders who have memory loss, I advocate the use of sandplay, a dynamic process in which a person accesses internal states by using a box of sand and small figurines to create a picture depicting some aspect of their life. Unfortunately, a psychologist for the Alzheimer's Association once told me that sandplay is infantilizing. There are two misguided assumptions embedded in this point of view: that there is no value in resurrecting the child within, and that it is infantilizing for an adult to do childlike things. Comments like this always remind me of Jesus saying that unless you become like a child you cannot enter the kingdom of heaven. This is such a profound statement, yet most haven't a clue what it means. For Jung, the child within all of us is the part of us that brings together what is known and what is unknown. When we are in touch with our child, it is easier to reconcile the many opposites that confront us, because the child archetype has a clarity, vision, and pure desire that can light the way through confusion and doubt. I have been able to witness this wholeness-making process unfold for a number of elders as they "play" in the sand with the miniatures. There seems to be something inherently healing when the adult part of us (ego) makes room for the child within.

It is unfortunate that the gift of playfulness is often denigrated. This is true in childhood as well as adulthood. Children who are frequently admonished to be useful, who meet with ongoing reprimand from adults, or who are ridiculed for not being serious enough end up feeling a sense of guilt whenever they make a mistake or take initiative. Since one of the best ways to learn in life is by making mistakes, the child who does not have the freedom to err is hampered by the fear of experiencing guilt or feeling stupid. Underneath, anger and self-hatred simmer. These emotions can often be the source of angry outbursts, depression, anxiety, and indecisiveness later in life.

Play is intimately tied to creativity, which in turn is associated with our ability to respond (response-ability), cooperate, and initiate. As we age and lose certain faculties, we are challenged to find new interests and new ways of understanding old beliefs and values. We need the strengths of stage 3 to allow us to experiment, fail, and test out new ideas, inclinations, and hunches. An ease with this stage is what permits some elders to discover the artist within, allows others to pursue activities that held little interest earlier, and gives permission for some to radically reappraise deeply held beliefs. Not being able to renegotiate this stage can lead to a feeling that the meaning and purpose of life have been lost.

Purpose is perhaps the most elusive quality for the older adult, yet it makes the difference between a life of boredom and a life of engagement.

Finding a cause and using one's energy to advance it is the surest way of living life with purpose. Joining organizations such as the Gray Panthers, the Older Women's League, the National Council of Senior Citizens, or the National Council on Aging is a way to make our voices heard for the betterment of present and future elders.

When play is developed along with purpose, we can be curious, hold things lightly, and develop a sense of humor. These traits can change even the most fearsome internal state or external situation into one that is manageable. When we do this, we increase our capacity to initiate.

Elders who have cognitive loss also grapple with this stage. Their attempts to be purposeful are seen in many of the behaviors they assume: seemingly aimless walking (to work?), folding and unfolding a piece of cloth (doing laundry?), humming (soothing a child?), or trying to get up (having somewhere to go?). There are many ways in which elders try to exercise their sense of purpose through whatever means are at their disposal. Their creativity is often alive and well, but it is not easily recognized as such, leading caregivers to discourage, medicate, or redirect these behaviors.

Stage 4: Industry vs. Inferiority (ages nine to twelve)

The fourth stage deals with issues that are central to United States culture. On the developmental ladder, this is school age, a time of learning both in and out of the formal educational environment. It is the time when we develop the virtue of competence. Conflict emerges at this stage when the child feels wrong or inadequate.

Not all children are interested in competition, external accolades, or even being noticed. Extroverted qualities like these are highly prized in the United States. Those who are outgoing, talk easily, think quickly, and enjoy the limelight are rewarded in this society. Contrast this with a country like Japan, where the predominant orientation is introversion. There the individual is much more comfortable as part of a group, is not anxious about solitude, and is a keen observer. If, as a child, you were more introverted, you may have frequently felt out of step with your peers and the dominant energy of your environment.

The typical type A personality, characterized by always being on the move, is founded during this stage. So too is the inner critic. This is the stage when we try to prove our value to ourselves and those around us. For elders, what they experienced on their first day of school can be replicated when they move into a new environment. If they felt confident and made friends easily, that is more likely to happen now. If that early time was fraught with insecurity, clinging to a parent, or withdrawal—and the adult was never able to overcome this initial hesitancy—then new situations can recapitulate the earlier ones. Whenever we feel useless, worthless, or good for nothing, we are facing another opportunity to rework this crucial stage of childhood. The phrase we hear some old people say too often—"What good am I?"—reveals a deep need to explore the source of this feeling. Unfortunately, in a youth-driven, technologically oriented society, this need is exacerbated rather than explored. A sense of worthlessness arises from living in a culture biased toward productivity. We are often judged— and we often judge others—on the basis of their accomplishments, which are measured in terms of outer success and competence.

Aging, like death, is a great leveler. Status, educational degrees, and financial resources have the advantage of providing multiple care options, but they tend to confer much less power when it comes to living on a daily basis. Answering the question "What good am I?" requires a different orientation, one that is based on internal factors rather than external ones. To have a psychologically healthy old age, it is crucial to be aware of deficiencies in our early environment that influence our present responses and to develop competence in navigating our internal terrain. When we can bring compassion, love, and understanding to the wounded child who still lives within, we can better counter negativity from within or without. Learning to reflect on the many times in life when we have demonstrated competence and felt successful is one of the best compensations for times beset by anxiety, uncertainty, and doubt. Another helpful strategy is recognizing the part of us that keeps these voices alive and substituting kind voices instead. As we do this, we increase our feeling of competency and self-esteem because we are able to meet challenges and negotiate our way through them.

Competency, as it is usually defined, is exactly what an oldster with memory loss is losing. As the disease progresses, even simple tasks become difficult. Yet the need identified in this stage is not absent. Discovering tasks that can be accomplished when sufficiently broken down into sequence is an endless adventure in creativity for those working with this population. The Montessori method has been adopted in working with these older adults, and it is quite successful.

Stage 5: Identity vs. Role Confusion
(ages twelve to nineteen)

The quintessential question of identity—Who am I?—lies at the heart of this stage. It is as relevant for elders as it is for the adolescents progressing through stage 5. This is a time in both youth and old age when values and beliefs are upended and sorted, roles are assumed or abandoned, and personas or personal masks are set in place or relinquished. For young people, the necessary opportunities to try out various possibilities are provided by peer groups, cliques, and special groups of all kinds—even gangs.

The youth counterculture of the 1960s provides a vivid example of stage 5 at work. Many young people of that era rebelled against traditional mores of their day. Young men of that generation abandoned the prep-school look of the starched shirt and every hair being in place in favor of letting their hair grow long and sporting beards. Young women of the era eschewed teased hair and makeup, opting instead for a more natural look. These surface differences had roots in a deeply divergent system of morals and values. Yet whether you were in a traditional group or an avant-garde one, people in both camps derived their identity from their particular group's persona. Fidelity and the ability to commit oneself are the results, which are necessary ingredients for successful adulthood and forging an identity. Usually around midlife, the identities we evolved in youth begin to unravel. Fidelity again becomes important; however, the frame of reference shifts from outer conformity to inner direction.

The question "Who am I?" surfaces for elders when various roles are no longer viable or have been outlived, such as spouse, manager, parent, executive, financier, coach, artist, teacher, sibling … you fill in the blank. Even religious and spiritual guiding principles are often questioned.

Joseph Campbell called the journey that the young person takes the "hero's journey." Jung called the second journey we take individuation, in which we shift focus from ego, with its roles, attitudes, habits, and beliefs, to Self. Both journeys chart new territory. As elders discard what is no longer relevant or suitable, they pave the way for something deeper to come to the fore. The natural process of asking who we are in old age leads to existential and spiritual questions. Both the adolescent and the older adult face these questions from different ends of the continuum. Just as the answers we chose in adolescence set the course for the next several years of life, the answers we find in old age set the course for our final years of blossoming or struggling.

The term "second adolescence" has often been used to describe this journey of reevaluation in old age. When used in a pejorative sense, it describes elders as uncooperative, dependent, recalcitrant, cranky, curmudgeonly, senile, demanding, and impatient. Attitudes like these are reinforced when elders are unable to step out of prior roles and responsibilities. The need to maintain a comfortable identity can be observed when a group of residents in an eldercare facility eat and do things together and are unwilling to include a new resident, especially if that person is perceived to be different in any way. These elders may never have developed a strong sense of self, so they keep their world secure by keeping others out. They are living out of this earlier stage of development where there was safety in "their group," however they defined that. A good facility develops strategies to minimize the effects of this type of behavior and helps elders address issues of identity.

Thankfully, there are those who see value and potential in this emergence of identity issues in old age. One such person, psychiatrist Allan Chinen, uses the term "emancipated innocence" to describe what he sees as a major task in older life: the restoration of innocence. This is achieved by a reevaluation of past goals, values, roles, beliefs, and behaviors to discover the authentic Self. In his book of eldertales, *In the Ever After*, Chinen uses stories from around the world to illustrate how the process of finding oneself returns us to childlike wonder, appreciation, spontaneity, and freedom from convention. This practical rationality, as he calls it, leads to the melding of childlike creativity and trust with maturity. Chinen likens this unification to the development that takes place during Erikson's eighth stage of development: integrity vs. despair.

Elders with memory loss are much less concerned with Erikson's trajectory from this stage onward. Some people look upon this development with horror; however, it is also possible to take the perspective that the elder is now living in a psychic space that is free of these tasks. Identity is a fairly sophisticated concept that includes ego, and ego is one aspect of psyche that goes off-line as dementia advances. More on this is discussed in chapter 9.

Stage 6: Intimacy vs. Isolation (ages twenty to thirty-nine)

Young adulthood is the time when we focus on relationships. If we form relationships easily, both with ourselves and with others, then loving and being loved are comfortable for us. We have developed the ability to overcome the fear that can keep hearts locked. This stage relies on the previous one, in that who I decide I am significantly affects whom I choose as a partner and friends, what projects I take up, and even how I relate to myself. Those who have not been successful in developing a strong sense of self in adolescence tend to struggle during this phase. They may feel lonely or depressed. They are often unable or unwilling to make commitments, whether to another person or a project.

Underlying these problems is a weakness in the person's capacity to care for themselves. Often this comes from an inadequate or downright harmful early environment. Children are good imitators, and those closest to them are their models. If a child's models did not or could not (for reasons stemming from their own brokenness) provide models of love, compassion, understanding, and support, children are left to acquire these on their own. This is a lifetime task. In the book *Healing the Eight Stages of Life*, one of the authors tells the story of a therapist who trains other therapists. As part of the training, each student must get up in front of a group and brag about themselves for five minutes. How many readers would be comfortable with that? Take a minute to reflect on what comes up as you contemplate this. What internal voices start making such a ruckus that you become almost paralayzed? It is only by bringing awareness to these areas of weakness that it is possible to initiate healing.

Many present-day elders, raised with a theology of sin and a condemnation of pride, are presented with a very real obstacle to self-love. Many also were raised to believe that negative emotions are not acceptable, particularly anger. It is difficult to establish intimacy when parts of us must remain hidden. Intimacy demands vulnerability, sharing interior worlds, and disclosing weaknesses, angers, depressions, lack of faith, scars, and unhealed places. If we cannot do this with a deity or ourselves, it is very unlikely we can do it with a partner or friends. If we arrive in old age still trying to appear good, perfect, or whatever value we hold in highest esteem, we will have difficulty with intimacy. Part of the task of older adulthood is to evaluate, understand, and jettison many of the carryovers from an overly harsh theological background.

Isolation, the underlying fear of stage 6, entails two factors that combine to aggravate the situation: a series of losses, and the inability to grieve losses, hurts, disappointments, and betrayals accumulated over a lifetime. In both instances, the heart is locked away in safety. On the outside it may appear that we are being intimate, but on the inside, we recognize that we keep a certain distance from others for protection. The trouble with aging is that many of these well-hidden places have a tendency to seek the surface. Dependency forces us into interdependency. Some elders react to this turn of events with depression or bitterness and refuse to engage with life.

Flexibility in our roles, an ability to accept ourselves and others (even those we do not like), and the willingness to get out of our self-enclosed siloes and make an effort to establish new relationships and new interests are all healthy responses to risk. When we are able to grieve loss, acknowledge needs, and choose the new, we establish the virtue of this stage: love. Love is the heart of aging with grace.

Stage 7: Generativity vs. Stagnation (ages forty to fifty-nine)

Erikson's seventh stage is midlife. When the Eriksons first envisioned these stages, and when Jung talked about midlife, they were referring to someone in their late thirties or early forties. In 1920, the average life expectancy was fifty-three for men and fifty-four for women. According to the Centers for Disease Control and Prevention's 2015 US health report, as of 2014, life expectancy in the US had risen to seventy-six for men and eighty-one for women. Life-span theorists now consider midlife to range from the late forties to the midsixties. In the US, this stage is the epitome of all that can be desired. On the one hand, we have reached the height of our power. On the other hand, the realization that this is as good as it gets sometimes precipitates a crisis that motivates people to make a last attempt to be young in the face of an anticipated downhill slide. Many want to remain in the perceived power of midlife forever. Those who have not "made it" by their own or societal standards often experience depression, physical issues, or some other destabilizing event.

If you've looked through magazines aimed at older adults, you may have noticed that although the models (both men and women) are supposed to be in their seventies or eighties, they actually look like they are in their fifties with grey hair. That is the midlife image: strength, confidence, and well-being—which usually includes being well-heeled, too. We are unwilling to surrender this image and this stage of life. For many, this is the time of greatest productivity, a skill highly lauded in our society. We believe that now is when we leave our mark on the world, although many throughout history have done so before and after this phase. The polarity assigned to midlife is the creativity of generativity versus the sterility of stagnation. In this context generativity means we seek to move beyond ego needs for self-aggrandizement and take an active interest in nurturing others or being a positive influence in the world. In this way the virtue of care is born. When we don't take this up, it's often because we are clinging to our roles or professions in the belief that we are indispensible and that no one can do it (whatever "it" is) as well as we can.

Care, the virtue of this stage, is the root of the desire to leave something valuable behind and contribute to the larger whole. This care includes oneself and is a balance between giving and receiving. The Purpose Prize mentioned in chapter 4 is one example writ large. Other examples include mentoring younger people through work, sports, faith communities, or friendship. Care is also shown in political, environmental, or social activism. Raising grandchildren is a generative act. For me, writing this book is generative because it reflects my contribution to the field I have loved for more than thirty years.

Opportunities for generativity and care are always present in our life. How do we treat the grocery store clerk or the person we ask for directions? What particular abilities or talents do we have that we can share with neighbors, friends, and local organizations? There are as many ways of expressing care as there are opportunities to do it. The need is built into our genes and must be met for us to be healthy.

For those who cannot find a way to pass along what they know, stagnation ensues. Stagnation could be caused by self-absorption, overextension, or feeling disconnected from the community or society. In these cases, one's personality contracts rather than expands. The individual can get mired in critical states of mind, become a martyr, subscribe to a quid pro quo mentality, or remain narcissistic.

From a spiritual perspective, this time of life initiates what I think of as the great shift inward. (Those who have undergone trauma or suffering earlier in life may already have made this shift.) Difficulties often associated with this shift include a crisis of meaning, poor health, deaths of meaningful others, conflicts with family members or friends, work issues, and problems arising from lifetime patterns of productivity and overachievement. For many, facing death and the concomitant question

"What's it all about?" add to the pressure. Previous coping styles no longer work. We often experience frustration, a feeling of being lost, a need to wipe the slate clean, or just plain restlessness. In order for newness (generativity) to take hold, we must turn toward the emptiness, doubt, and confusion we'd rather avoid. Tibetan Buddhist practices that use images of ferocious deities symbolically depict the states of depression and anxiety encountered at midlife. By working with the emotions and thoughts these images represent rather than avoiding them, we paradoxically loosen their hold on us. We see them for the fearsome states they are, not the reality we imagine.

Jung believed midlife is the time to cultivate qualities and abilities previously left behind. The woman who has spent much of her life tending to others now finds an interest in caring for herself in new ways while learning to say no. The man who sacrificed his interests to get ahead in the world of commerce may now take an interest in matters of the home. These changes can be unnerving to the person undergoing them, and to family and friends who may feel they can no longer depend on the person. This is the land of the shadow. Whatever is opposite of our established routine and persona comes to the fore. As Jung was so fond of saying, life seeks wholeness, and for that to occur, we must experience many avenues, not just a few.

Stage 8: Integrity vs. Despair (ages sixty and above)

The last stage of the original eight is directly related to the tasks of later life. By successfully negotiating the terrain of this time, it is possible to attain the gift of wisdom. For the Eriksons, integrity means the acceptance of the life one has had, with all of its successes and its failures. It means bringing together the actual self with the idealized self by realizing that all the pieces of life's jigsaw puzzle form a coherent whole. We enter old age in possession of a few principles gleaned from changing experience. This is, in essence, individuation—that task of discovering one's wholeness and deepest Self. Like life, this stage is a work in progress. We don't one day arrive at integrity. Instead, we spend much of later life spiraling through earlier periods of our lives, salvaging lessons learned and revisiting heartaches we've adapted to. This is the task and value of reminiscence.

I once heard Israeli Jungian analyst Erel Shalit (1950–2018) describe old age as the time of "gathering together what was shattered." It's not simply remembering the past, but integrating past actions and choices into the person we are today. This means we boldly face times when selfishness, meanness, jealousy, and the whole panoply of negative states gained ascendancy within us. We see these times in their unvarnished reality, and we embrace them as part of our journey. At these times, we are vulnerable to the negative pole of integrity: despair. Events in our lives cannot be changed, and many mistakes cannot now be corrected. The affirmation of choices made and actions taken is crucial for this stage. It is a time to work on abandoning judgment, condemnation, or wanting our life to be different from what it was. Instead, we see how each and every misstep, and each and every choice, resulted in who we are today, and we affirm that. When we do this, we exercise wisdom, the virtue of this stage.

Unfortunately, many people arrive at the eighth stage resisting the aging process or totally unprepared to assume its tasks. They may be angry or bitter about infirmity or the inability to find pleasure in previous interests. They may be estranged from family or friends, or they might be unable to make new friends. They could be nursing grievances from the past or trying desperately to hide signs of aging. In *How to Say It to Seniors,* David Solie offers this truly insightful observation: "Because no previous developmental stages were reflective ones, most people don't have the skills to tackle this job" (38). By "this job" he means being able to engage in the life-review process as well as making legal, financial, and medical decisions about the end of life. He sees the struggle at this time as the need for control versus the need to let go. For the most part, life is a process of gaining increasing control, mostly of our outer environment. (For those who chose a contemplative life, such as monks or nuns, the emphasis is more on inner control.) This is considered competence.

In old age, however, life is about understanding, accepting, letting go, and surrendering—the opposite of what went before. We are asked to cultivate qualities exactly opposed to those we have spent decades refining. The situation we find ourselves in is comical; it is also deadly serious. When we cannot accept who we are now, we are unable to understand, accept, and integrate the past. We need to keep working on the puzzle until we can see the warp and woof of our life. It takes time, and it takes courage. If we are not willing to engage in this task, we end up just being old. We do not achieve the wisdom of our years, and we do not feel the consequent gratitude and hope that are part and parcel of wisdom.

The eighth stage also includes legacy. In midlife, we consolidated ourselves on many levels. Leaving a legacy was a dominant thrust of this time, even if that motive didn't rise to conscious awareness. At the eighth stage, legacy continues to be significant. Death no longer feels far off; it could be right around the corner. The need to leave something behind or finish some external or internal task is paramount. Solie says the elders he has worked with have often been resistant to planning and making decisions. When this happens, he attributes their resistance to the fact that they have left something unsaid, undone, or unthought. They needed to understand the legacy they were leaving behind and could not make major decisions until this was resolved.

Legacy is also about values, not just finances and mementoes. Barry Baines, a medical doctor working in end-of-life care, recognizes the need to know who we are and to communicate that information to others before we die. His book *Ethical Wills* walks elders (and all of us at crucial times in our lives) through the process of putting our values on paper. In addition to our financial assets, Baines invites us to consider our ethical assets: What do we see as the purpose of our life? What will we be remembered for? What stories shaped our life? What are the major lessons we've learned from life? What guidance do we have to offer? These and many more questions are the heart of what the eighth stage is about.

More ancient societies recognized the value of elder knowledge and incorporated its transmission into their rituals. Our present culture has no such procedures, yet younger people inevitably feel drawn to elders who have worked or are working with these questions. People intuitively feel they can learn from these elders. One of the tasks I see for the present generation of older adults is to become elders and to map the terrain for those coming behind. Never before have there been so many older people on the planet. The legacy of this generation can be to till the soil of their lives and give those of us following some guidelines and information about the journey.

Stage 9

In the film *On Old Age I: A Conversation with Joan Erikson at 90*, made after the death of her husband, Erik, Joan Erikson explores the meaning of the eighth stage as she sees it at age ninety. For her, integrity came to mean the ability to continue engaging with the world and with people even as circumstances continue to change. While in theory this is similar to what the Eriksons postulated in their midfifties, living out of integrity came to have a very specific meaning for Joan in her late years.

She added a ninth stage to the Eriksonian model that reverses the order of syntonic (normal, healthy) and dystonic (pathological, unhealthy) possibilities for each of the eight stages. For example, the eighth stage is characterized by the struggle between integrity and despair. In the ninth stage, this polarity is reversed. Overcoming despair takes precedence, and integrity is achieved when this process is at least somewhat successful. Joan felt that this slight twist more accurately portrays the nature of the challenges people face at the end of a long life. Based on her experience at the time, she believed that each of the eight stages must be revisited but with their polarities reversed. She attributed this necessity to the challenges brought on by frailty and the temptation to slip into unhealthy patterns. She concludes, "If elders can come to terms with the dystonic [unhealthy] elements in their life experiences in the ninth stage, they may successfully make headway on the path leading to gerotranscendence." By this she means that the aging person who is able to shift beyond the pull of negativity is better able to experience the various positive states of gerotranscendence. (For a full discussion of the meaning of "gerotranscendence," see chapter 7.)

Erikson's stages are circular in nature. Few people ever reach a point where they have fully integrated each of the stages. That is not a bad thing, because it ensures the continuation of growth up to our last days. In order to remain vital, a healthy sense of curiosity is a necessity. We may experience a strong desire to not be bothered, but we have an obligation to be responsible to ourselves and to future generations. Although we cannot see the results of our actions, we are called upon to trust that they matter. Just as teachers rarely know their influence on their students, so too older adults cannot know how their efforts to self-actualize affect the people around them.

Whether we make the effort to cultivate the first eight virtues in our aging process has an impact on whether we face the last phase of life with a sense of integrity or one of despair. If we manage to incorporate these virtues, however imperfectly, we will naturally develop the qualities of gerotranscendence.

7

Gerotranscendence

New life comes small,
insignificant,
calling your name
in the womb of the unexpected:
like a hawk feather fluttering to your feet,
sun shimmer quivering on a wall,
cathedral bells telling the times,
a rag-wrapped woman lying curled in a doorway,
headlines and breadlines shouting war, hunger.
Something in every moment offers birth.

—CLARE MORRIS

Unlike Maslow and the Eriksons, who devised theoretical frameworks for the general populace, Lars Tornstam (1943–2016) did work specific to older adulthood. As a social gerontologist, he was motivated to discover how older adults actually experience their aging, partly to counteract what he saw as a persistent tendency in the research community to describe old age as a time of misery or to project midlife values onto older adults as a way to evaluate successful aging. In the late 1970s and early 1980s, he and his colleagues at Uppsala University in Sweden gathered research data by interviewing older adults. Tornstam combined his research findings with his study of both Jung and the Eriksons to develop a theory he called *gerotranscendence,* which illustrates a shift in consciousness that happens as we age.

Tornstam described his work as a developmental theory of positive aging. He believed that progress toward gerotranscendence is natural; however, as he wrote in his book *Gerotranscendence,* this progress is "obstructed by our value patterns and notions of how life in old age should be" (3). We've spent the previous chapters in this book discussing how to recognize and shift these "value patterns and notions of how life should be." Tornstam's theory suggests the changes that we make occur in three ontological or existential dimensions: cosmic, self, and relationality.

Shifts in the Cosmic Dimension

A primary change in the cosmic dimension is a shift in relationship to time and space. The boundary between past and present seems to merge seamlessly. It's not just that elders live in their memories; their memories come alive in new ways and often inform the present. As a general rule, elders move between the past and present more easily than the rest of us.

In this connection it's useful to know that the ancient Greeks had two words for time: *chronos* means linear time, how we keep track of hours and days, and *kairos* means personal time or the "right" time and is accompanied by a sense of certainty. Elders engaged in soul work may appear to be procrastinating, but instead they may simply be waiting for the right time, when inner forces align with outer ones.

An awareness of these different approaches to time is helpful both for elders and for those who care for them. In facilities that are person-centered, *kairos* time is given preference over *chronos* time. Thus, residents do not all get up at the same time, nor do they have meals or activities at the same time. In daily life, older people do not experience time in the same way that younger people do. If you are a younger person, how many times have you felt the impulse to rush the elder you're with? Whether it's crossing the street, getting ready to go out, using the bathroom, or heating water for tea, an older person can be maddeningly slow from the perspective of a younger person. It's ironic that people who have less projected time on earth tend to take their time, whereas in youth, when time stretches out ahead of us, we seldom feel we have enough of it.

This difference in relationship to time is also common among people with dementia, where it is often attributed to brain dysfunction. Although deteriorated brain cells clearly play a role, gerotranscendence theory offers another perspective. Elders with dementia seem to live in a kind of timelessness where demarcations between past, present, and future collapse. Perhaps they are living in a dimension of time that those of us still caught in the busy-ness of living cannot access. Perhaps for them time has become circular, so that every point in time is equidistant and equally accessible. Thus, when we ask them if they remember something, that particular memory may now be part of a panorama of sensory data that may not be available to them as a distinct experience.

Another manifestation of a shift in time consciousness occurs in relationship to activity. Satisfaction with small, commonplace things, often in the natural world, takes precedence over spectacular events that captivated us when we were younger. In the activity field where I worked for some years, we focused on simple pleasures—the ordinary things we all do in life, such as drinking a good cup of tea or coffee, feeling the sun on our back, taking an afternoon nap, enjoying a leisurely walk, or sitting quietly and watching the world go by. Tornstam offers an excellent example of simple pleasures when quoting one of his subjects in *Gerotranscendence:* "Earlier [in life] it may have been things like a visit to the theater, a dinner, a trip.... My best times [now are] when I sit on the kitchen porch and simply exist, the swallows flying above my head like arrows" (51). Stepping off the fast track of life and allowing ourselves to be more contemplative is not an indication of depression, disinterest, or disengagement but rather tuning into and honoring a different set of priorities.

Along with a different relationship to time, elders develop a broader understanding of how generations are linked. Whereas earlier in life, oldsters might have expressed more concern with what was happening in the present generation, now the future is equally important. There is recognition of the chain of being or the flow of history. That recognition displaces ego concerns in favor of a more expansive viewpoint. Those who work with older adults often see them giving things up so their children or grandchildren can have a better life. When I worked as a case manager, I was often frustrated because my client made decisions that lessened her present well-being so her progeny could have more. I learned it is futile to use the logic of the mind in these situations because the mind is no longer in charge. The heart has taken the lead, and values have shifted accordingly. The political tug-of-war for resources that pits younger generations against the old is generated not by old people but by those in midlife who have not yet entered into this more altruistic mindset.

Also in the cosmic dimension, Tornstam noted an acceptance of the mystery of life and a decreased fear of death. These two seem to be linked. The need to know is a youthful endeavor. As we age, wisdom shows us that we cannot even know ourselves in a lifetime. Elders who are wise tend to be less reactive and more philosophical about things—even topics that are undeniably upsetting. It takes years to see how phenomena are intertwined, how solutions create problems of their own, and how delicate the balance is between seemingly competing values in life. This willingness to withhold judgment and accept not knowing extends to how Tornstam's elders approached death. Although his research subjects expressed anxiety about the possibility of a protracted illness prior to death, death itself was no longer something they feared. They accepted both life and death on their own terms, in contrast to earlier demands for how things must be.

Shifts in the Dimension of Self

Tornstam used the term "self confrontation" to refer to the process elders naturally undergo of welcoming both the positive and the negative sides of themselves. The elder who always prided herself on her intellectual acumen may find that she now has more difficulty grasping or retaining information. She may previously have disdained those who were not as smart as she, although not consciously. Now that unwelcome trait comes to the fore within her and asks to be integrated into her understanding of herself. Conversely, a man who was a jock all his life now finds that climbing stairs is an exertion. Perhaps his self-worth was tied to his agility and the frequency with which women sought his company. Confronting his feelings and thoughts about living with limitations forces him to balance his previous views with a more human and humane one.

Tornstam's research also demonstrates that elders return to the past and childhood in order to do reparative shadow work. In reaching this conclusion, Tornstam follows the lead of Jung, who maintained that one of the primary tasks in the second half of life is to integrate those aspects of ego that we have previously repressed or denied. This is precisely what occurs with memory loss, according to retired social worker Naomi Feil. Perhaps there was a school bully who always picked on you, and as a result, you have carried a latent fear of large men your whole life. Or maybe you once had a boss who treated you unfairly and didn't recommend you for a promotion, or you took a dislike to a coworker and spread gossip about her. Maybe you fought in a war and have never been able to talk about those experiences. Few of us reach old age without at least a few broken relationships and unaddressed matters. In all these cases, the past comes up for a reason. When we allow memories to arise and explore them from this distance of years, we are releasing trapped energy. These kinds of memories bring with them hurts and wounds that need the light of day to heal.

Such memories also resurrect past yearnings, talents, and interests. For example, perhaps as a child you wanted to please your parents, so as an adult you chose a career or a mate that they approved of rather than what you really wanted. Now, as a widow or widower, you might decide to try to find that original love or enroll in a writing class to finally work on that novel that's been tucked in a drawer for years. Sometimes interests change and we discover a passion that surprises us. I have a friend who is eighty-seven who always loved the life of the mind and didn't have much respect for sports. Now, to her amazement, she finds herself enthralled with basketball. What has been concealed now comes unbidden to those who have slowed down and are willing to receive. As a result of this self-exploration, ego boundaries loosen, and elders broaden their definition of who they are. Ego concerns no longer occupy center stage, and the older person's boundaries expand to include more and more.

Elders who have shifted into gerotranscendence no longer try to be the center of attention. They do not vie for power or flaunt their knowledge. When we encounter older adults who continue to need ego gratification, we often label them as pompous, arrogant, or needy. These elders need assistance with negotiating their ongoing need to be recognized. They are still holding onto something tightly, and that something is vital to that elder's identity. Unless and until it is named and brought forth from the unconscious, elders remain stymied in their development.

The body itself is included in this reappraisal. Keeping healthy is still a goal, but the bodily obsession many of us experience falls away. For younger people, it may be hard to imagine not being concerned about weight, skin tone, muscle mass, and sleekness. A lessened concern with how one looks is in direct contrast to the antiaging, Botox-oriented culture of the United States today. One of Tornstam's gerotranscendent elders describes her shift in this dimension: "I'm not the slightest bit worried about my belly or bad skin or the wrinkles in my face. It means nothing to me, nothing at all" (52). It might be worthwhile for the reader to imagine what it would be like to experience such freedom.

In my experience, lessened attention to appearances also manifests in decreased attention to the upkeep of one's home. Poor eyesight and lessened energy most likely contribute to this as well; however, I think there is also a reevaluation of what's important. It is not uncommon for an older person to refuse to make home repairs unless they are absolutely necessary. Sometimes this is for economic reasons, but if money is not an issue, something else is happening. Many older people have told me they can "live with whatever" and will be dead before a given issue becomes a real problem. In their younger years, these same people would not have been able to tolerate such circumstances. If their personality had allowed them to let things slide, they would have been concerned with what the neighbors might think. In gerotranscendence, this mandate is no longer operative. Sometimes this signifies the older person's liberation, but it can be problematic when it causes safety to be compromised.

As with the loosening of generational boundaries in the cosmic dimension, heightened concern for others coupled with less concern for self leads to more generosity. Yet for some older people self-transcendence can be a double-edged sword. The urge to help others has the potential to diminish an older person's quality of life. Sometimes they impoverish themselves to make sure their children have money after they die. Sometimes they lend a child money they need for themselves, even when they know the child will never be able to pay it back. Other times they share their home with a child who is addicted to drugs or alcohol, or they move out of their home to a less desirable location in order to give their children a larger inheritance.

One of the most compelling findings Tornstam made in the dimension of self concerns rediscovery of the child within. This kind of rediscovery is evoked in a lovely Japanese story from Chinen's book of eldertales, *In the Ever After*. The story tells of a kind old man and his wife who were very poor. On one cold, wintry day, as the man was returning home from the market having failed to sell any of the hats he and his wife had made, he noticed six statues of gods standing in the snow. Concerned that they were cold, he placed a hat on each one and continued on his way home. That night, their door flew open, and a bag of rice cakes landed in their hut. When they went out to see what had happened, they saw the six statues bowing to them. This tale illustrates the type of generosity and childlike care it is possible to retrieve in our older years, as ego takes a back seat to Jung's Self.

To those of us not in this stage of life, the old man's behavior seems irrational. I had exactly this response many times in my younger years as I worked with elders who made decisions that I considered not to be in their best interests. At the same time, the story depicts a quality of trust and wonder that can reawaken a longing within us, if we are not too jaded. Chinen suggests that dispensing with pragmatic considerations and social conventions in favor of spontaneously honoring the heart is emancipating for the older adult. He says the old man's attitude toward the statues is comparable to what theologian Martin Buber (1878–1965) called the "thou" attitude of love, as opposed to an objective "it" attitude.

The final capacity Tornstam described in the self dimension is taken from the Eriksons' final stage: integrity. In Tornstam's study, elders were able to put the parts of their lives together into a whole that made sense to them. They were able to see that their lives could not have been any other way than what they had been. Integrity arose from accepting all the twists and turns that had brought them to the present moment. The shadow work they'd done, a lower level of self-interest, greater altruism, and a return to innocence all contributed to these elders' ability to achieve coherence.

This lessening of self-interest can also be seen when an elder's cognitive ability collapses. While the process is different for these elders, some of the results are similar. Elders with memory loss are indifferent to ego concerns of any kind. They have a remarkable ability to manifest the inner child in all her vicissitudes. It seems that dissolution of ego control is the key to allowing a deeper part within to emerge. Unfortunately, most people usually don't take such a perspective toward these elders. When an elder with cognitive deficits cries, states a desire to go home, expresses anger, or demonstrates any strong emotion, caregivers and family members often treat such behavior as aberrant. Care partners' attitudes make the difference between whether the elder can move through the emotion in a way that releases energy or further binds it.

On the other hand, these elders also display tenderness, playfulness, and even joy. Thankfully, these behaviors are not labeled aberrant.

Shifts in the Relational Dimension

The third and final dimension Tornstam observed in his research has to do with the relational and social aspects of life. First and foremost among these is a lessening of emphasis on social roles. Throughout the first half of life, most of us are identified with our masks (personas) or roles. With retirement, we no longer have to function in those capacities.

Freed from our confines, we begin to see how tightly we were held by the demands of our roles.

As we discover our authentic self, there is a lessening of interest in superficial relationships. Perhaps because we know time is no longer endless and our energy is not what it was, we tend to become more parsimonious with our time. If you are sixty-five or older, consider whether you have experienced a winnowing of friends. Some of us, particularly women, have a history of being there for others who drain us of energy or who are not able or willing to share equally in the friendship. As we begin to know ourselves more intimately, we often begin to value time with ourselves and a few reciprocating others. We are less willing to squander time, especially since doing the reflective work essential to this part of life requires solitude.

For those still in midlife or younger, an elder's day can look like nothing was accomplished. As an experiment, stop reading for a minute, close your eyes, and see what thoughts arise.

What predominates in your mind when you do this? Engaged as we are in the rough-and-tumble of life, we're often preoccupied with thoughts of work, plans we're making, or conversations we've had or expect to have. Older people don't have most of these pressures. They can allow the mind to find its own ground. They can spend time in reverie. To younger people, the quietude of some elders may look like lethargy or passivity. However, like the duck who seems to sail so effortlessly across the lake yet is constantly flapping its feet below the surface, that elder is allowing the interior landscape to unfold at a natural pace. Solitude becomes an essential and fundamental necessity to meet the unknown—and sometimes the unknowable—at this time. If we do not know how to use our alone time, loneliness ensues; if we do know how, solitude opens the door to a barely charted world within.

Solitude leads naturally to what Tornstam suggests is modern asceticism. Elders begin to see the underside of the consumer culture, and they understand that owning things can be burdensome. They naturally sympathize with the counterculture that says less is better. This can manifest in simplicity of choices, fewer relationships, limited goals, and culling of possessions. This process, while natural, does not occur for all elders. It requires a commitment to live the reflective life.

Jane Thibault, clinical gerontologist emerita at the University of Louisville's School of Medicine, offered a very compelling perspective at an American Society on Aging conference in the early 1990s. Ever since then I have kept the handout from her workshop. In the workshop, she suggested that aging constitutes a natural monastery. Her workshop took participants through a step-by-step process of letting go that monastics undertake and that elders encounter on the aging journey. The main difference between the monastic and the elder is that the monastic chooses to undergo this process, whereas the elder does not. Thibault's presentation challenges the predominant orientation of our culture and opens the way for what she calls a "radical reframing" of this time in life.

Beldon Lane demonstrates an understanding of this perspective in his book *The Solace of Fierce Landscapes,* where he describes the end of his mother's life in a nursing home: "My mother's acceptance of the cell [the small room she was assigned in the facility] gave her for the first time in her life, a quiet space for the healing of memories. She was able to pour a lifetime of anxieties and compulsions into that suffocatingly quiet room. It received everything. As a place she could not leave, it became ironically a source of the highest freedom she ever attained" (206).

What if we actually were to choose what comes? What if we were to look at whatever shows up as an opportunity to explore life from a different perspective? We are so attached to how things have always been and how we have always been. In older age, options and distractions are more limited. Change becomes an almost daily companion. In this situation, our attitude and approach become critical. Incorporating Chinen's quality of "emancipated innocence" into our reframing gives us the capacity to deliberately ignore the tried and true, the practical and socially acceptable, in favor of a deeper movement from within.

The final capacity Tornstam identified in the relational dimension is overcoming duality. Thinking that focuses on dichotomies of good/bad, right/wrong, or black/white tends to recede. A sterling example of this stance was recently given by Pope Francis, current leader of the Roman

Catholic Church. Amid the controversy over same-sex marriage, when self-righteous individuals openly attack and denounce gay people, Pope Francis was asked what he thought about the issue. In true emancipated style, and with great wisdom, he responded: "Who am I to judge?"

Franciscan priest and author Richard Rohr insists either/or thinking stems from ego. Its opposite is nondual or contemplative awareness. In his daily reflection piece for September 3, 2014, he says: "Nondual consciousness is about receiving and being present to the moment and to the now exactly as it is, without judgment, without analysis, without critique, without your ego deciding whether you like it or whether you don't like it." Those who divest themselves of ego priorities, choose humility over prowess, and approach life with an attitude of wonder live in a state akin to the liberation described in the teachings of most spiritual traditions.

Progression through the relational dimension can also be seen in elders with cognitive loss. In the early stages, elders are aware of losing abilities and capacities that once defined them. This is a time of grief and loss, and maintaining roles to the extent possible is a best practice. However, as the egoic self dissolves, preserving social convention ultimately gives way to presence without the need to appear a certain way or do certain things. The abandonment of roles, a return to innocence, the relinquishing of material wants and desires, and the acceptance of self are all experiences these elders go through. In the latter stages, simply being is enough. What seems to last throughout this time is the desire for close relationships. When family and friends do not withdraw from the elder and when care needs are skillfully met, quality of life can be maintained.

We have thus far spent time familiarizing ourselves with a few maps for the terrain of old age when our cognition is intact. Like Lewis and Clark, the authors we've explored have given directions for those interested in going on a pilgrimage. Seeing life as a developmental process and linking one's personal journey to the greater journey makes aging an adventure. As more and more people take up the call to be pioneers of this stage of life, maps will become more detailed and diverse. My hope is that what you have learned in these chapters will start you on a journey of exploration and that you will leave some notes about the terrain for those who follow after.

The next several chapters focus on memory loss and ways to approach it that support psychological health and a soul-work perspective.

8

A Primer on Memory Loss

I can let go and love at the same time.
May I let love in.

—OLIVIA AMES Hoblitzelle, *Ten Thousand Joys and Ten Thousand Sorrows* (New York: Jeremy Tarcher/Penguin, 2010)

Receiving a diagnosis of Alzheimer's disease rocks the very foundation of everything we hold precious. Yet forgetfulness is one of the fastest-growing illnesses in the world. The Alzheimer's Association reports that someone develops Alzheimer's every sixty-six seconds in America. As soon as we reach a certain age and start misplacing items or forgetting names and words, a low-grade anxiety sets in. Underlying that anxiety is the question: do I have Alzheimer's? Almost everyone knows someone—a loved one, friend, or neighbor—who has this diagnosis. Rather than face the attendant grief, vulnerability, helplessness, and loss, we distance ourselves, either internally or physically. We may want to be helpful, and we may feel guilty because anxiety frequently prevents us. It's too close to home. We could be looking at a version of our future selves.

This chapter covers the basics of memory loss and how it presents for many people living with it. As you read, I encourage you to pay attention to the parts where you find yourself holding your breath, where your mind has left the material and you are thinking about something else, or where you feel a weight descend. These moments are invitations to explore aspects of yourself that are often pushed aside. The more we know about what lies at the base of our reactions, the more freedom we can exercise in choosing our response.

Memory and Memory Loss

The word *dementia*, which first appeared in the early 1800s, does not refer to a specific disease. Rather, like an umbrella that has many spokes, dementia refers to a group of symptoms associated with a variety of diseases that involve the disintegration of mental abilities. This disintegration begins with consistent short-term memory loss—for example, the frequent inability to recall where you parked your car—and can progress in the later stages to an inability to remember the names of one's children or oneself. Aging itself does not cause memory loss, although most people begin to lose some recall as they age.

Current research shows that two areas of memory are usually affected by age: selective attention (the ability to distinguish relevant and irrelevant information) and divided attention (the ability to do more than two things at once). This is why concentrating and multitasking become more challenging with age. Perception is another component of cognition that undergoes change, primarily through a decline in sensory input. Lessened acuity of sight, hearing, smell, and taste affects how we experience our world. For instance, we may find our taste in foods changing as our taste buds become less sensitive, or we may have a hard time hearing in a movie theater or in a large group because the ability to differentiate sounds is compromised.

Working memory (which allows us to hold onto new information) declines with age due to its relationship with attention. For instance, if we are trying to remember a phone number someone just gave us but someone else clamors for our attention at that moment, chances are that the distraction will precipitate a loss of that number. I once heard a wonderful metaphor for this. Zalman Schachter-Shalomi (1924–2014), a rabbi, writer, and teacher in the field of aging, likened the brain to a computer. By the time we have reached old age, we have accumulated a lot of files, and there's not enough room for more unless we purge what's no longer needed. Instead of seeing loss as deficit, Zalman reframes what is happening. The ability to reframe is a skill we all need to develop in response to the changes brought on by aging.

The other part of memory that tends to be affected by age is called episodic memory, which has to do with specific events or experiences from the past. What is interesting about episodic memory is that it is not necessarily factual. Over the course of many years, we are exposed to a variety of perceptions and ideas. We bring these multiple perspectives and experiences to our memories, which can have an effect on how we understand and perceive what happened in the past. It can seem as if we are rewriting history when instead we are recontextualizing it. The mind's natural ability to align the past with the present in a healthy way—an ability that comes on line with age—allows us to integrate past and present in a new synthesis.

Causes of Memory Loss

Conditions such as delirium, vitamin deficiency, alcoholism, and depression can cause symptoms that mimic cognitive loss, especially in elders; however, once these conditions are treated, the symptoms vanish. Early signs of genuine cognitive loss resulting from damage to the prefrontal cortex involve the loss of executive decision-making skills such as planning, decision-making, organizing, and self-monitoring. So far there is no proven effective treatment or cure for this type of cognitive loss. Medications intended to slow the progress of some dementias have been developed; however, these drugs are only palliative. Clinical studies do not consistently bear out their effectiveness for everyone.

In recent years the diagnosis of mild cognitive impairment (MCI) has come into usage. It is estimated that 10–20 percent of people ages sixty-five and older are affected. The Mayo Clinic considers MCI an intermediate stage between the expected cognitive decline of normal aging and the more serious decline of dementia. MCI does not necessarily lead to other dementias, and for this reason, some professionals question using the label because it can create undue anxiety.

Some people prefer to believe that symptoms will naturally go away if not given attention and energy. Others feel empowered by knowing what to expect and plan for it. This chapter is written for those who want information they can use to make more informed choices about memory loss.

There are eight main types of memory loss:

1. Alzheimer's disease is the most common form of memory loss among older people. The term was first coined in 1910 by Emil Kraeplin (1856–1926), a noted German psychiatrist, who was supervising physician Alois Alzheimer (1864–1915) at the medical school in Munich. While working in Frankfurt, Alzheimer treated a fifty-one-year-old woman who showed symptoms of an unrecognized disorder. When she died in 1906, he obtained her brain and did an autopsy. He described the irregularities he discovered in her brain at a conference in 1907, and the disease was named after him. The cause of Alzheimer's remains unknown. It is considered a cortical dementia because it primarily affects the cerebral cortex, the most recently evolved outer layer of the brain that controls language and thinking. Alzheimer's also affects parts of the limbic memory system (the hippocampus) and the connectors that facilitate communication between various centers in the brain.

2. Cerebrovascular disease is the second-most-common cause of memory loss in the elderly. In this disease, brain damage is caused by a clot that blocks the flow of blood for a period of time (stroke) or briefly interrupts the flow of blood (transient ischemic attack,

also called a mini-stroke). In the case of a stroke, damage is usually noticeable during the recovery period. Brain damage from mini-strokes is often not detected until a sufficient number of incidents have occurred, causing cumulative damage that eventually becomes noticeable. When the number of mini-strokes reaches a tipping point, the elder's abilities decline, seemingly overnight. The elder with cerebrovascular disease displays memory loss symptoms that are similar to those seen in Alzheimer's; however, the illness's progress is stepwise rather than linear. This means that the elder alternates between stable periods and sudden declines in ability.

3. Parkinson's disease is a neurological disorder that affects the motor system. Its primary symptoms include tremors in the hands or feet, stiffness, slow movement, and impaired balance. Unlike Alzheimer's, Parkinson's stems from subcortical regions of the brain. Thus, language problems are not always present, but movement problems are.

4. Frontotemporal disease (also known as Pick's disease) affects the frontal lobes of the brain and causes speech and personality changes. Symptoms can include an apparent loss of caring, disinhibition, obsessive behavior, and aggression. Pick's disease is often confused with Alzheimer's because it affects memory and has an early onset; however, it is fairly rare, and behavioral changes manifest first rather than memory loss.

5. Lewy body dementia (LBD), currently being classified as a type of Alzheimer's, is named for Frederic Lewy (1885–1950), a German neurologist who discovered abnormal protein deposits (named Lewy bodies) in the brain in 1912. LBD is an umbrella term for two related illnesses: dementia with Lewy bodies and Parkinson's dementia. LBD is progressive, highly variable, and often accompanied by visual hallucinations, fluctuating body temperature, movement and attention problems, and sleep disturbances.

6. Korsakoff's cognitive impairment is often associated with alcohol abuse, although it can also come about from a severe vitamin B1 deficiency. Symptoms include short-term memory loss, confabulation, and some long-term memory problems.

7. Creutzfeldt-Jakob disease (CJD) is a rare disorder with an early onset and short duration. Most elders who contract CJD die within six months to a year. CJD is a type of encephalopathy in which the brain comes to resemble a sponge filled with holes. Some forms are hereditary.

8. Huntington's disease usually manifests between ages thirty and fifty. It is caused by a genetic defect. Symptoms are often characterized by involuntary muscle movement and cognitive loss.

Each of these illnesses manifests somewhat differently, yet all significantly alter an elder's cognitive and emotional landscapes. As these diseases advance, impairment of abilities increases. Since Alzheimer's is the most well-known of these diseases and tends to cause the greatest anxiety, we'll examine its development in more detail.

The progression of Alzheimer's takes almost as many forms as the people who live with it. For this reason, some professionals are increasingly reluctant to assign a stage in the process. Nevertheless, it can be helpful to have a general idea of what to expect, with the caveat that each individual has a unique history, psychology, and life trajectory. Personality and other factors strongly affect the way forgetfulness presents. With the loss of cognitive dominance, some may struggle with childhood losses or abuse; others may mourn present-day losses; some may return to earlier life situations where there is still an emotional charge; and others do not seem to have psychological issues that are constellated by the disease.

Little is known about the causes of Alzheimer's other than that when onset occurs in the midfifties to early sixties, it seems to be hereditary. Until very recently a postmortem of the brain was the only conclusive method of diagnosis. Recent advances in neuropsychological testing, blood work, and brain imaging are now able to diagnose Alzheimer's with 80–90 percent accuracy.

Alzheimer's is progressive and can loosely be divided into three major stages—early, middle, and late—although there are many variations of the stages, and some clinicians use seven or even twelve stages to account for the many gradations both within and between the major stages. Despite distinctive variations, for most people what starts out as forgetting of names, places, words, and the locations of familiar objects ends as loss of categorical thinking and naming—and, if the person lives long enough, a total dependence on others for self-care.

Stage 1: Early. In this stage, a person gets easily confused and has difficulty with time and place. Medically, a person's orientation to their environment is measured with regard to whether they're aware of their own name, the date, the place, and the current situation. In early-stage Alzheimer's, most elders will be "oriented x3," meaning they can recall three out of these four items. For the most part, these elders live at home. They have a sense of the season but often don't know what day it is. The Mini–Mental State Examination (MMSE), originally developed for use in facilities, was until very recently the main screening tool for assessing cognitive status both in the community and in nursing homes. The MMSE is a set of ten questions that provide a score reflecting a person's general level of impairment. The questions fall into five categories: orientation; memory retention (three objects are named, and the testee is asked to repeat them back); attention (e.g., spell "world" backward); recall (recall the three items from the second question); and language (a combination of repeating phrases and following commands). The maximum score is 30. Elders in stage 1 usually score in the mild impairment range of 20–23, while those experiencing moderate impairment score in the 11–20 range.

The MMSE is a controversial indicator of the extent of memory loss, and it has many critics. Its strength is that it has fairly good reliability regarding the need for further testing. Weaknesses I see in the MMSE stem from assumptions about what is important to know and the situation of testing itself. For example, while we're on vacation, many of us lose track of the day of the week and often the date. We consider this an indicator of relaxation. Older people who no longer have a work environment to provide orientation and therefore have a more casual relationship to time are evaluated against the standards of younger people.

In addition, the testing situation itself is stressful. The requirement to repeat three words (e.g., apple, table, hat) and then, several questions later, to remember and repeat these back is a task that many so-called normal minds might be challenged to negotiate successfully under pressure. When used in nursing homes after admission, MMSE results can be very misleading. These elders have lost their habitual orientation because of a disruption to routine and environment. They are often under significant duress. Usually the move is the last stop in a series of changes, sometimes over weeks or months, that have eroded the elder's sense of belonging and their emotional and psychological moorings. No test is a reliable tool under such circumstances, and results need to be used with caution. (As of this writing, the Montreal Cognitive Assessment is gaining in popularity. It is similar to the MMSE but looks more in depth at the specifics of loss.)

In this early stage of loss, signs of dementia can include making up words; repeating questions in the same conversation; not being able to remember recent history; difficulty with planning, organizing, and making decisions; trouble concentrating; and misplacing objects and then forgetting where they are. Some elders tend to wander at this stage; others have problems with eating and sleeping. The ability to express what one wants to say can be compromised, as can the ability to read and comprehend material. Emotionally, some elders are anxious; others are easily agitated. Some seem insensitive to other's feelings, some are easily angered, and some are quite content. No one person will have all of these behaviors; some will have more, and some will have fewer. The degree of impairment is dependent on that particular elder's specific losses, personality, and environmental factors.

Stage 2: Middle. Perhaps the most significant marker of this stage is the loss of practical everyday skills. Most elders in stage 2 require someone to be with them for a good portion of each day. If the elder is living at home or with family and has financial resources, he or she attends a social day program or has an in-home caregiver. Elders who qualify for Medicaid are eligible for in-home support services, where a caregiver is paid to be with the elder. Another possibility is for the elder to move to a board-and-care facility or a skilled nursing facility. The challenge with this option is finding a facility that takes Medicaid. Unfortunately, memory care facilities do not take Medicaid, so this choice is only available to families with financial means.

Elders at this stage will often start a task but be unable to complete it because they do not have the cognitive sequencing ability to follow through. For instance, let's say the elder and an attendant are cooking together. The attendant asks the elder to cut vegetables and demonstrates how to do that. The elder makes a start, but after a few cuts, she stops. Confusion has arisen, interfering with the process. If the caregiver has a task-oriented personality, this kind of deficit can generate friction with the elder. These situations are wonderful opportunities to slow down, have fun, and relax. A chance to explore the imagination presents itself when the elder has trouble remembering the correct word for what she wants to express. She will often creatively substitute other words; like a sleuth, the caregiver needs to figure out what is being said. Some elders are still able to read and comprehend at this stage, while others no longer have the interest or ability.

One situation that often places stress upon caregivers is when an elder repeats the same question, often related to time or destination, over and over because they cannot retain the answer and are experiencing anxiety as a result. This is a time for the caregiver to step back and take a few deep breaths. Next, consider what need might be driving the question, and address that. If the question persists, it could be arising out of boredom, so finding a distracting activity can help. If anxiety is at the question's base, talking with the person to ascertain what the source of the anxiety is can be helpful to both parties. Adopting a stance of humor almost always changes the dynamic for the better. Since previous interests are usually abandoned at this stage because the elder loses the ability to pursue them, finding new interests and new ways to thrive is an ongoing opportunity to develop creativity.

Some elders experience auditory or visual hallucinations at this stage. Others can become quite angry and belligerent, especially when they feel thwarted by their environment, which is often the case in an institutional setting. In his 1997 paper "The Experience of Dementia," Thomas Kitwood (1937–1998), a psychologist and advocate for personalized care of elders, references a 1988 study in the UK that identifies six main temperamental differences in memory loss among elders: the dependent, the independent, those with paranoid tendencies, the obsessional, the hysterical, and the psychopathic. It is likely that one or more of these styles—affected by individual temperament, genetics, and habitual coping skills—will manifest as the older person responds to living with disorientation. Caregivers who are able to identify which style is dominant at a given time are more successful in meeting the person's need than those who have a blanket response.

Disorientation to space and time is common. The elder in stage 2 often is not able to tell a questioner the year, month, or season and has difficulty finding their way in familiar surroundings. They also confuse the present with the past. Disoriented older people can talk about a parent as if the person is still alive, and they often insist they have to go home. This happens even with those who are still living at home, which indicates a need for a sense of home or the nurturance of a parent. If, at this point, the elder is living in a facility or attending a day program, attempts to leave are called "elopement," and staff are required to prevent such behaviors. Unfortunately, if staff do not have appropriate training, incidents can take place that are greatly upsetting for the elder and staff alike.

At this stage family members will frequently comment on unaccustomed behaviors, saying that their parent was "never this way." Elders who have been prim and proper their entire lives can be given to bouts of temper and cursing, while those who have been difficult in earlier life can be models of graciousness and politeness. From a psychological perspective, this seemingly uncharacteristic behavior is not necessarily random. In keeping with Jung's idea of wholeness, the arising of opposite tendencies may be psyche's way of moving toward balance and integration.

Stage 3: Late. If the elder does not succumb to pneumonia, an infection, or other disease conditions common among this population, he or she arrives at this final stage of Alzheimer's, which can last for quite a few years. By now the elder is often in a wheelchair. If they are ambulatory, it is with a walker because their gait is unsteady. Some elders move to facilities at this point because their care requirements are so great. They need significant help with grooming, bathing, dressing, and eating. They often do not recognize family members on a consistent basis. Speech, if maintained, is often what is called "word salad," a combination of unrelated words or sounds. Actually, the words and sounds may seem unrelated, but they likely are meaningful on a symbolic level. The caregiver skill required at this time is to be able to enter the elder's world deeply enough so that it is possible to understand emotively what they are communicating. This requires a looser grip on reality as we know it and a willingness to cultivate fluidity.

Some elders in stage 3 forget how to swallow, which makes choking when eating or drinking an issue. Incontinence is common. In addition, contractures (a shortening of the muscles) develop in the hands or feet because independent movement does not occur. A good case can be made for ongoing physical therapy with elders so contractures can be minimized.

These are the elders many of us fear becoming. They can be seen in the hallways and open areas of facilities, drooling or staring vacantly. These are the elders who are often described as being "only a shell" of themselves. We almost universally deny personhood to elders in this stage because they lack social responsiveness. Lethargy of spirit or inertia seems to dominate. What caregivers need now is a working understanding of Self or soul. Without a conceptual framework that includes the elder in the mutuality of experience, caregivers can only relate to the old person as a body, or worse, as a sack of flesh to be turned, hauled, pushed, and maneuvered until death. Providing compassionate care at this stage of loss requires caregivers to have an appreciation for the sacred and for mystery. Without such an understanding, it is difficult to find value in the life you are charged with caring for.

While it may have been alarming to read this chapter, it is helpful to remember that our projections are just that. We never really know how dementia is going to manifest in someone we love or in ourselves. We do not know what changes may come about. We do not know how our hearts might be opened as a result of encountering this disease. The intense onus of fear attendant upon memory loss in our culture increases the burden exponentially for those who have the disease and for those who care for them. Yes, it is hard. Yes, it is something we do not welcome. There is much in life that falls into this category. If we could cultivate an attitude toward memory loss that is less loaded with our worst fears, perhaps we might experience it differently.

9

Perspectives on Memory Loss

When someone deeply listens to you,
your bare feet are on the earth
and a beloved land that seemed distant
is now at home within you.

—JOHN FOX, "When Someone Deeply
Listens to You," in *Finding What You Didn't*
Lose: Expressing Your Truth and Creativity
through Poem-Making (New York: Jeremy P.
Tarcher/Putnam, 1995)

The poem above sets the tone for a perspective on memory loss and a
way of being with our fears about it that this chapter will advocate. For
most people, the possibility of memory loss is one of the most frightening prospects about aging. Unlike heart problems or cancer—where
there is loss of function but the personality remains intact—cognitive
loss causes us to undergo significant changes in who we think we are.
Our core self is threatened, and because we are identified with our brain,
the threat is intolerable. Even though we know that suffering is a part of

life and that life isn't fair, that knowledge is tucked into the recesses of our minds, and it borders on the unthinkable. When illness of any kind arrives on our doorstep, it is almost always unexpected, and it is rarely invited in. This is all the more true with memory loss.

When it comes to memory loss, there are no easy answers, no pill to take to assuage our discomfort, no methods guaranteed to prevent this turn of events. As with any situation in life that knocks us off course and stymies our plans, hopes, and expectations, memory loss leaves us limited choices. As psychoanalyst Karen Horney (1885–1952) noted years ago, when conflicts arise we tend to defend ourselves in one of three ways: moving toward the situation or person to align ourselves with them and thus escape bad consequences; backing away by using denial; or fighting against by becoming aggressive, argumentative, or aversive. The Buddhist meditative tradition presents an alternative: it suggests we turn toward what is unknown, fearsome, and unpleasant with kindness and curiosity. Responding in this way does not make everything return to the way we want it to be. However, it does allow us to discover things about life and ourselves, find value and meaning that were previously hidden, and most importantly, connect with something that lies deeper than the turbulence on the surface of our lives.

This chapter is written for those who do not yet have a diagnosis of memory loss, for those in the early stages of their memory-loss process, and for those who care in any capacity for an older person who is living with dementia. Although we cannot reverse a diagnosis, we can change our attitude toward it. Even a slight shift makes a tremendous difference in how we feel about the loss of this supposedly indispensable component of our identity. To aid in that process, this chapter introduces conceptual resources that can help us shift our perspective on memory loss. My hope is that these resources will spark a light for those who need it, especially those caring for a forgetful old person. Although this chapter does not explore books written by those in early stages of memory loss, there are quite a few that give us a glimpse into their world and educate us without expressing doom and gloom (see appendix B). Some memory-impaired people and their caregivers have been able to find deeper lives as the experience of Alzheimer's unfolds. As with aging (and life) in general, it is always the attitude we take toward something that makes the difference.

Naomi Feil and Validation

Naomi Feil came of age at a time when Sigmund Freud's thought dominated the mental health field in the United States. Freud was intensely interested in what goes on in the mind. He believed we all unknowingly deceive ourselves about ourselves and our lives, because we have all experienced traumatic events that our minds have closed off from daily awareness. In his therapy sessions, Freud always made a couch available for patients to lie upon and talk about whatever thoughts or feelings presented themselves. He would then offer interpretations of these free associations, linking them to incidents in the patient's life. In this way he discovered memories that the mind had repressed and excavated them from the unconscious. Like a pressure cooker whose lid has been removed, the patient's symptoms sometimes disappeared after these sessions took place.

While psychodynamic psychology has evolved significantly in both theory and practice since these early years, a focus on self and one's relationship with significant others remains. Within eldercare, the psychodynamic viewpoint emphasizes exploring the history of an elder's life to discover clues to present behavior. Feil believes that those with disorientation are attempting to resolve unfinished business before the end of life. This corresponds with Jung's insight that Self is purposeful and has its own trajectory that is not always in accord with our egoic or conscious desires.

Feil grew up in a nursing home where her father was the administrator and her mother the social worker, giving her ample exposure to older adults at a young age. In 1963, when it came time for her to choose a career, she too became a social worker in "old age homes," as they were called. During Feil's early working years, care in nursing homes was still in its infancy, and specific positive methods of working with old people (particularly those with severe disorientation) were nonexistent. Elders who were disruptive were physically restrained, just as disruptive people in mental institutions were.

As noted in chapter 2, it wasn't until 1954 that public nursing homes were constructed and regulations implemented. The predominant therapeutic method used at the time was called "reality orientation," which focused on keeping the elder in the present and reinforcing "normal" behaviors. For example, if someone with memory loss wanted to see their mother (a frequent request from disoriented old people), they were told their mother was dead. At the time, the value of maintaining the elder's grip on consensual reality overrode other considerations, no matter how much sadness or anxiety this strategy provoked. Remnants of reality orientation can still be found on facility bulletin boards with the day, date, and season posted on them.

In response to this method, Feil developed validation therapy, an approach that validates the reality of the older person, even when that reality is clearly not the consensual version. Staying with the example of an elder who keeps asking for his mother, a validation-trained caregiver acknowledges, with empathy, that the man misses his mother. She might say, "You miss your mother, don't you? When was the last time you saw her? What do you like about her?" Using open questions that begin with who, what, when, where, and how, the validation-trained worker explores the experience of mother with the elder.

While validation has been around for a long time, it is not widely practiced in families, where there has been little or no exposure to the kind of communication training that facility staff receive. Unfortunately, although facility staff are aware of the rudiments of validation, they too have often not had the kind of training necessary to use more than its very basic techniques. Validating provides an opportunity for those who are disoriented to reexperience early feelings of nurturance, and it is comforting for most elders in the moment. It also works quite well in the normal course of daily communication with everyone. We all want to be seen and heard—and to know that we are. The communication techniques learned through validation go beyond helping cognitively challenged elders. At the core of validation lies recognition of the individual and his or her value as a person.

Many people go through life without a great deal of self-exploration. As we lurch from experience to experience—some painful, others joyful, many neutral—we don't take time to reflect on how these experiences are influencing our attitudes, opinions, habits, choices, and judgments. In the US, the dominant culture values extroversion and the outer life. Time is not devoted to investigating experience, and there is virtually no support or modeling for how to go about it. For many oldsters currently in their eighties and nineties, stigma was attached to any kind of psychotherapy or even introspection; thus, they arrived in old age without the tools needed to process their internal world. It is not surprising, then, that this material shows up when they are most vulnerable. Now, as boomers are becoming elders, this perspective is shifting. There is increased interest in the interior world, along with greatly reduced shame about asking for help with thorny psychological dilemmas from the past that impede healthy relationships and perspectives in the present.

The key to the effectiveness of validation techniques is the recognition that all behavior has a reason behind it. On the face of it, this conclusion seems obvious; however, somehow this maxim seems to be forgotten when we're dealing with an elder who has memory loss. Too often we dismiss their wants and needs, or we ignore or silence them, because we do not understand their intent and we see them as "mindless," which means they can't possibly know what they want. Returning to the example of the man asking for his mother, a validation approach sees this as an expression of need. Creativity comes into play as we try to discern what the need is: Reassurance? Companionship? Relief from boredom? We may never know for sure, but our efforts will eventually pay off.

Older adults with memory loss are much more aware than we give them credit for. They seem to develop a greater sensitivity to others and the environment. Even when our efforts to figure out what they need go awry, the effort to understand them does not go unnoticed at a deeper level. Frustration may still be present, but the message of care has gotten through. This can be seen in situations where an elder who has been treated compassionately and respectfully has fewer episodes of distress than others who have not.

Feil distinguishes between those who experience late-life disorientation and those who develop Alzheimer's. She believes that those who develop early-onset Alzheimer's follow a typical disease process, while those who develop memory loss later in life are responding to physical deterioration and an inability to cope with accumulated psychological and social losses. Elders who grow old without having developed good coping strategies do not age well. They are unprepared to face the many losses and changes that are a natural part of aging. In addition, they may never have resolved sundered relationships, loss, trauma, or other painful issues. These are the elders who retreat into the past so they can get their interior house in order, in preparation for a peaceful death. Some might question the notion that this kind of retreat can be purposeful or meaningful. It is true that we cannot know this with certainty; however, those who have skillfully observed old people over time have told many anecdotes indicating the presence of some kind of purposeful, ongoing process.

Feil's work is in keeping with Jung's notion of Self and the work it requires in later life. Because of physical and social losses, the personality is pushed beyond its comfort zone. When this happens, the many boundaries we have fabricated to keep us safe dissolve. This is especially true in old age, when time is running out and the forces of age are weakening the ability to control ourselves or the events in our lives. Elders without memory loss who shift perspective from denial and withdrawal to seeing the changes of age as opportunities for growth in consciousness have taken a step toward Self. For elders with cognitive loss who can no longer consciously attend to what arises, attempts to heal earlier wounds seems to arise without conscious intent. When layers of cultural, familial, and personal compulsions are released, a measure of meaning and healing can be brought to life, no matter what circumstances prevail.

Thomas Kitwood on Person-Centered Care

In the early 1990s, psychologist Thomas Kitwood, a leading proponent of compassionate eldercare, founded the Bradford Dementia Group, an educational and research hub at the University of Bradford in the UK.

Kitwood was a deep thinker and prolific writer. His commitment to re-visioning how elders with memory loss are seen and treated is unwavering and conceptually well developed.

The question "What is self?" is foundational when we face loss of our cognitive capacity, and indeed when we face aging itself. If we give the question room to ferment in our minds and hearts instead of rushing to close the door on it, we end up with a greater sense of aliveness. For Kitwood, one of the key determinants of the self was the social context. In *On Being a Person,* he places great emphasis on what he termed "personhood": "a standing or a status that is bestowed on one human being, by others, in the context of relationship and social being. It implies recognition, respect and trust" (246). His concern was to retain personhood under all circumstances. As it says in *Tom Kitwood on Dementia,* "As the sense of self sustained by internal processing begins to fragment, it is the environment of others that can alone give continuity" (63). In other words, when we, because of incapacity, can no longer sustain our narrative and history, the way in which our environment meets or fails to meet our need for confirmation and emotional validation is crucial.

How the caregiver (whether a family member or a professional) sees or "positions" the elder, what aspects of the person's self are affirmed or denied, and what beliefs are maintained about the elder make the difference between supporting life or simply supporting existence. Unfortunately, mere existence is too often the goal because supporting life requires time, commitment, ingenuity, and good support for ourselves. These are hard to come by in a fast-paced, hypercognitive, youth-oriented, production-focused, consumerist culture. To age well and to provide good care to someone with memory loss requires us to step off this conveyor belt.

Alzheimer's threatens the very foundations of modern notions of selfhood because society has built its definition of self primarily on cognition. Advancing a personhood approach to memory care, therefore, has positive consequences for society. In *Tom Kitwood on Dementia,* he delineates personhood's three guiding principles: the uniqueness of each person, each person's subjectivity, and the need for relatedness (229).

Valuing the uniqueness of each person is an act of care because it affirms diversity by recognizing the different ways in which each of us interacts with the world. As we age, we become more of who we are. This means our particular foibles and strengths stand out in greater relief. When we value our own peculiarities, it is much easier to support the eccentricities of another. It's helpful to know some facts about the disoriented older person, but what is even more important from Kitwood's perspective is the caregiver's openness to the elder's uniqueness.

The second guiding principle of personhood, subjectivity, is intimately linked with the first. It arises from our history, our experience, and our reactions to both. No two people respond the same way to events in life. This is clearly seen when two siblings or a couple recall an event from the past or when witnesses describe what happened at the scene of an accident. Sometimes there is so much variation in what they say that one might wonder if they were really at the same event. Yet, there is a positive side to this variation, because the differences in perspective enlarge the field of awareness. I have often been surprised by a comment made by someone with memory loss who is seeing the same thing I am but is experiencing it in a very different way. It is hard for those of us imbued with the values of modernity to affirm our subjectivity. We tend to look outside ourselves for affirmation and confirmation. We need to see the deleterious effect this tendency has in our lives before we can adequately and skillfully allow the full range of subjectivity in the forgetful elder.

Relatedness, the third guiding principle of personhood, is at the heart of care for disoriented elders, and it is too often heartbreakingly absent. It is hard for many of us to comfortably relate to someone when we don't understand them and feel inadequate around them. It is harder still when that person seems to manifest our innermost fears of disability and death. We shy away and stay away. This is a natural defensive response, but we need to go against the grain of what is easiest. As noted in the discussion of the Eriksonian trust vs. mistrust stage in chapter 6, both babies and old people who do not receive enough contact and attention are susceptible to a diagnosis of failure to thrive. A sense of belonging—being a part of something, being connected with a group or another person—is crucial to well-being. The elder with forgetfulness needs more contact, affection, and interaction because it is difficult for her to initiate.

Kitwood's work has been a source of unending encouragement for me because his approach provides a solid foundation for research I conducted with disoriented elders in 2010. In that project, I invited elders with and without memory loss to explore sandplay with me. Sandplay is a therapeutic medium used predominantly with children to help them express feelings and thoughts without the need for words. It uses a box of sand and numerous miniature figures depicting various aspects of life, such as people, animals, houses, nature, and transportation. The sandplayer creates a sand picture using whatever items they want. The resulting picture, when viewed symbolically, is often quite revealing about how the person is feeling and what concerns are present. It is an excellent tool for facilitating communication with elders who no longer have access to language. The closeness and attentiveness required of the facilitator and the one-to-one time spent with the elder allows genuine relating to take place. This in and of itself has a salutary effect.

If we take Kitwood's definition of personhood—uniqueness, subjectivity, and relatedness—seriously, we join him in nothing less than a complete revitalization of the meaning of personhood in modern society, with profound ramifications for the care of disoriented elders. As Kitwood says in *Tom Kitwood on Dementia*: "Dementia care is one of the richest areas of human work. It requires very high levels of ability, creativity and insight. In our involvement with those who have dementia we are pushing our humanity to its outer limits" (223).

Dementia care is always a learning environment because each person's personality, history, and disease process is unique. It requires the ability to leave one's world of rational thought and enter into the other's world as best we can. We must give up objective notions of "truth" or "reality" when we're with someone who has cognitive loss. This in turn can make us question what we so tightly cling to, opening up the possibility of experiencing altered states. Sometimes these states are pleasant, as when the older person says things that are funny or wise. Sometimes they are a hell realm, as when the older person accuses us of stealing or insists that we leave the home immediately. These altered states are actually invitations to enlarge our capacity to be. In this sense, these states call us to a more spiritual experience of life.

A good example of encountering and entering into an altered reality took place for me when I agreed to be with an elder on Mother's Day while her daughter worked. For days ahead of time, I had an uneasy feeling about the day, but I figured my experience would carry me through. This was a very angry elder. She had not accepted her diagnosis and did not believe she needed to be "babysat," as she put it. To exacerbate matters, she was stuck with a stranger instead of her daughter on Mother's Day. As expected, the day was hellish for both of us. This elder was holding onto her anger as a protective device. She rightly perceived me as trying to take her anger away from her with my validation responses, which just escalated her outrage. At one point—unfortunately much later than would have been optimal—I told her I was both hurt and angry about our day so far, I was trying my best, and she was not helping. This gave her pause. While she didn't stop being abrupt or angry, she did modify her responses and began treating me with a greater degree of respect. Upon reflection, I realized that admission of my own feelings of disappointment and frustration allowed me to enter into her world. She was then able to connect with me, however tenuously. When I allowed myself to own and express my feelings, she didn't feel so alone in hers.

Although our time together was highly unpleasant, it helped me see the importance of being genuine with someone who has memory loss. Exploding in anger at the person is not helpful, but being able to authentically and directly express one's feelings actually honors the older person. This experience is a good example of the kind of learning that can take place when we open ourselves to someone with memory loss. It also flies in the face of those who say the person with cognitive loss is an empty shell or not there anymore. From my perspective, this elder knew what she was doing at a noncognitive level. She needed to express her rage at her daughter, and I was the stand-in. At the same time, she also needed to be met in that interior place. Thankfully, I was finally able to meet her.

Alternative Visions for Eldercare

In the 1990s a number of new models of care sharing similar philosophies arose to address the care needs of elders living in facilities in this country and the UK. These models promote quality of life in the later years and oppose giving biological and medical needs priority over other needs, especially emotional and spiritual. The biomedicalization of care recognizes only the first two levels of Maslow's hierarchy: physical and safety needs. That approach results in old people being treated as things rather than persons in care environments. While the care concepts advocated by these models were initially directed at nursing homes, they have since expanded to any setting that houses elders, including the elder's home. In the last few years, recommendations from these models have been incorporated into federal guidelines for skilled nursing facilities that take Medicare or Medicaid.

This new approach to care goes by various names, including person-centered, resident-directed, patient-directed, and individualized care. Here is one of the most succinct definitions of person-centered care, from Karen Love and Jackie Pinkowitz: "Person-centered care focuses on the individual needs of a person rather than on efficiencies of the care provider; builds upon the strengths of a person; and honors their values, choices, and preferences. A person-centered model of care reorients the medical disease–dominated model of care that can be impersonal for those oriented to holistic well-being and that encompasses all four human dimensions: bio-psycho-social-spiritual" ("Person-Centered Care for People with Dementia: A Theoretical and Perceptual Framework," at www.asaging.org/blog/person-centered-care-people-dementia -theoretical-and-conceptual-framework).

One of the pioneering models of this philosophy of care is the Eden Alternative, developed by geriatrician Bill Thomas. In *What Are Old People For?* Thomas says, "The Eden Alternative shows people how to integrate knowing and being into the daily rhythms of life in long-term care settings" (181). The movement has affected most facilities in some way in the US through federal mandates.

Following graduation from Harvard, Thomas took a job as medical director at a nursing home in upstate New York while he decided what he wanted to do. As he tells his story, one day while making rounds in the nursing home, as he was leaving the room of a bedbound elder, she called out to him. He stopped and returned to her beside. This simple act might seem insignificant, but if you have ever spent time in a care environment, you will know how staff often simply do not stop for the elder. They either become inured to the perceived neediness all around them, or they are too compelled by the next task to feel able to take time to respond. Thomas did respond, and that response changed his life, the life of many elders living in care environments, the staff in many of these environments, and the environments themselves.

Thomas discovered what he calls the three plagues of old age in an institution: loneliness, helplessness, and boredom. His antidote for these is companionship, opportunities to give, and spontaneity. The three plagues do not only exist in institutions, although they are more readily found in these environments. There are many elders living in their own homes or apartments who feel equally alienated. Often their primary caregiver is exhausted by daily chores and can't provide the kind of attention that is needed (an excellent reason for family caregivers to use day care, respite, and paid relief on an ongoing basis). Alternately, the elder has paid help but that help is not well trained, is from a different culture, or for some other reason cannot meet the psychological, social, or spiritual needs for the intimacy that is such an important part of a healthy lifestyle.

In the world of facilities, the Eden Alternative is mostly known for its innovative practice of bringing plants, children, and pets into these environments. The nature of care itself is much harder to modify. Changing the way care is provided involves moving decision-making from top management to the elders and the line staff who work most closely with them. To implement such a tsunami of change requires management commitment, staff empowerment, and ongoing, consistent training. Many facilities call themselves Eden Alternatives but never manage to do the hard work of implementing this fundamental change. One of the major stumbling blocks is the necessity for training that is difficult to schedule because facilities have high staff turnover, and staff often go from one job to the next in order to make ends meet.

But the core problem is one of power and trust. Most administrators do not trust staff or elders to make good choices. Fearful of litigation and conscious of the bottom line, most facilities do only what is expedient and required. Bringing in plants, pets, and children is very visible and sends the right message, so these measures are considered sufficient. While these changes do improve the lives of elders, the alterations are cosmetic and do not touch the core issues confronting long-term care. Only a few places have wholeheartedly embraced the Eden model, yet they demonstrate that it is possible to change how care is provided and the physical environment of that care. Many of the intractable problems faced by facilities, such as high staff turnover, become a thing of the past in Eden communities.

Thomas also worked to create alternative environments that he calls Green Houses, which replace the large nursing home with small houses where residents actively engage in decisions about their care and their daily lives. Caregiving staff in the Green House are no longer specialized by function; instead, they all perform the various tasks but for fewer elders. There is no rigid schedule and therefore more time to accommodate individualized preferences for waking, dressing, bathing, eating, and socializing. Residents are encouraged to participate in the running of the house as they are able.

As of this writing, Thomas has expanded his vision from changing facilities to changing how society perceives aging. To that end he has created a traveling road show that includes music, poetry, skits, and discussions in the hopes of changing aging attitudes across America. His latest project, Minka, involves providing small, prefabricated modular homes for elders and anyone else interested in thinking small and living communally.

Another pioneering voice in the field of eldercare is physician Al Power, who, like Thomas, ended up working in long-term care through a series of coincidences. As a frontline physician at St. John's Home in

Rochester, New York, he has become an inspired and inspiring advocate for innovative care. While Thomas's efforts are focused on elderhood, Power emphasizes care for those with memory loss. In his book *Dementia beyond Disease,* he outlines seven domains of well-being for elders (and all of us): identity, connectedness, security, autonomy, meaning, growth, and joy. Power illustrates through example after example how these basic needs manifest in the lives of forgetful elders and how attention to them allows elders to live a life of dignity and quality.

Power's work is inspiring because it demonstrates beyond any doubt that elders with memory loss have much in common with people who do not have memory loss, and they can enjoy life when they are supported appropriately. His experience with nonpharmacological intervention for memory-impaired elders shows unequivocally that humane care is not a pie-in-the-sky approach. Even though his examples come from facility living, the home caregiver can gain much from reading his books and applying the principles to their own situation.

In 1997, a number of innovators, including Eden Alternative, banded together to create the Pioneer Network, an umbrella organization for all those concerned with culture change in long-term care. The Pioneer Network comprises individuals and facilities committed to grounding theory in practice. Also located in Rochester, the Pioneer Network describes its work this way: "Pioneer Network supports models where elders live in open, diverse, caring communities. In-depth change in systems requires change in governmental policy and regulation; change in the individual's and society's attitudes toward aging and elders; change in elders' attitudes towards themselves and their aging; and change in the attitudes and behavior of caregivers toward those for whom they care. We refer to this work as culture change. Our aim is nothing less than transforming the culture of aging in America" (www.pioneernetwork .net/about-us/mission-vision-values).

A similar model of care is process-oriented care, developed by psychologist and businessperson Nader Shabahangi and used by several of his facilities in the San Francisco Bay area. Process-oriented care seeks to change perceptions about memory care by using an existential process approach. According to Shabahangi, process work developed in the 1970s when Arnold Mindell, a Jungian analyst in Zurich, began researching illness as a meaningful expression of the unconscious mind. This model sees physical symptoms, relationship problems, group conflict, and social tensions as opportunities vital for personal and collective growth.

In essence, a process perspective offers new ways of understanding and working with aspects of life experienced as problematic or painful. Most notable for memory care is this model's claim that the solution to a problem is contained within the disturbance itself. For instance, wandering, one of the symptoms of memory loss, is reinterpreted as indicative of feeling lost; hiding possessions is seen as a way to keep them safe; weeping is a response to immense loss. In the example of the angry elder discussed above, her anger can be seen as an attempt to preserve a sense of self and keep terror at bay. Shabahangi refuses to call the losses associated with aging "dementia." Instead he advocates using the term *forgetfulness*. He understands that well-being of the body is only one important aspect of a person's care. The inner journey is equally important, and it requires the help of others. As with person-centered practitioners, a process approach humanizes memory care. Shabahangi has recently teamed with a woman from India, Ami Champaneri, to revamp an assisted living facility in Oakland, California, into an ashram community called Elder Ashram. The philosophy behind their vision is truly revolutionary for eldercare.

A colleague of Shabahangi's—Bogna Szymkiewicz-Kowalska, a psychotherapist and lecturer at the University of Warsaw—expands beyond memory care to include the attitude society takes toward aging in general. She describes aging as an awareness practice, like meditation, and she calls our attention to the potential inner growth available as we age. Using the term *eldership* to portray a state of mind that is present and free from expectations, she advocates curiosity and purposefulness to counter fear and dread. Eldership has the potential to reveal glimpses of the timeless self, or essence, a perspective supported by this work.

Whenever I am asked to give presentations on aging, I like to use the following statement from nursing practitioners and researchers Barbro

Wadensten and Marianne Carlsson: "Our views on ageing [sic] affect how we address and treat older people, and which needs in the caring situation we think must be satisfied. What one considers important in the care of older people actually depends largely on one's theoretical perspective" ("The Theory of Gerotranscendence in Practice: Guidelines for Nursing—Part II," *International Journal of Older People Nursing* 2 [2007]: 295).

Their view succinctly sums up the essential attitude advocated by all the thought leaders this chapter has covered. Feil's validation, Kitwood's emphasis on personhood, and the alternative visions of Bill Thomas, Al Power, the Pioneer Network, and Nader Shabahangi all have at their core this deep appreciation for the hidden values that inform our thought and spill over into our actions. It is crucial that we make the implicit explicit if we are to have any hope at all of changing how old people and people with memory loss are perceived and treated. My hope is that the early chapters in this book have alerted the reader to this need and that these last two chapters have opened a mental clearing, however small, that will be the beginning of a new path.

10

Meditation, Aging, and Caregiving

Sitting and waiting without having made every effort of which the conscious personality is capable would be merely a matter of sloth or evasion.... Always ... we must remember that in the end the answer will be given, not earned. The real goal of all our efforts is to arrive at the capacity for this goalless waiting.

—HELEN LUKE, *The Way of Women*
(New York: Doubleday, 1995)

On the surface, old age looks like a series of losses. For the caregiver, it looks like a series of unending tasks with little time left for oneself. If we limit our view of life primarily to externals, then these perceptions are indeed correct. How we cope or fail to cope with loss or duty becomes the focus, and we often feel as if we bounce from one diminishment or task to another. If we're lucky, we'll have short periods of respite in between. However, there is another viewpoint we can adopt: aging and caregiving provide a unique opportunity to finally heed the clarion call of Self. Hillman named this summons *daimon*, the spiritual companion and guide that helps us find our path (see chapter 4).

After an initial "Oh no!" in response to a particular change or loss, we can look a little deeper. We can ask ourselves: how might this change push me in a beneficial direction? Even though we prefer the status quo, relinquishing habitual responses often provides an opportunity to "polish the mirror," as the Sufis say. By this phrase, they mean clearing away the fog and scratches that have kept the heart safe and blocked from recognizing gerotranscendence. Jung's understanding of the "teleological Self" is similar. Self, he maintains, is a natural thrust toward expansion in the universe. Through humans it manifests as an increase in consciousness. This impulse becomes compelling in the second half of life.

Regardless of whether your sensibility is religious or secular, the use of elder time to explore the inner world, become acquainted with unconscious parts of Self, and revisit experiences that were overlooked or denied earlier is one of aging's greatest benefits. Caregivers, on the other hand, can learn to balance care for the other with care for themselves, develop the capacity to accept reality while not succumbing to its overwhelming aspects, and find relatedness in the midst of so much that mitigates against it. These are the foundations of wisdom.

Most of us equate the word *wisdom* with having extensive knowledge of things out there in the world. That is one form of wisdom, which we can also call practical knowledge. It's the kind of wisdom we get from the *Farmers' Almanac* or through any of the myriad ways of doing things that are passed down through the generations. There is another kind of wisdom, however, that is based on a set of internal qualities. We often think this kind of wisdom is reserved for saints or spiritual teachers, and most religious and spiritual traditions do have their own language to describe this state. When I ask elders or caregivers if they are wise, very few say "yes." Their response may be due to humility or to an overblown sense of what constitutes wisdom. I have met uneducated elders living in deplorable circumstances who are wise. I have met caregivers who, while acknowledging the difficulties of managing so many tasks, are still able to appreciate the daily gifts of life. These elders and caregivers have inner sight, the ability to look deeply within to understand the world without. The gift of a hard life (if it doesn't make us bitter) yields the resiliency that makes us inclined to focus on the positive instead of the negative. This is true for both elders and caregivers.

The ancient Greeks held the maxim "Know thyself" in such high esteem that it was inscribed on the entrance to the temple of Apollo at Delphi. For Socrates and his student, Plato, philosophy was literally the love of wisdom (philosophy = *philia,* love + *sophia,* wisdom). While we can get along without using the traditional tools of introspection, if we truly want to embrace this time of life, some proven methods are helpful, regardless of our religious, spiritual, or philosophical persuasion. If, as suggested, the essence of wisdom is to know oneself, knowing how to be present to the interior world that is always affecting our thoughts, emotions, perceptions, attitudes, beliefs, and relationships is indispensable. Meditation is a practice designed for just this purpose. It is by far the most powerful method of exploring the inner life.

Meditation: An Overview

Thanks to the counterculture movement of the sixties, meditation and its companion, yoga, are household words today. If we see meditation as a state of mind that facilitates creative, contemplative states, then we can say that meditation in some form has been a mainstay of spiritual traditions since the Paleolithic era, when humans created cave paintings.

Unfortunately, in most religious traditions, the practice of meditation is not taught to the average participant unless they seek it out. It is considered too powerful for dissemination among the people, and it encourages individuals to develop their own authority, which counters the agency of the institution. In the three Abrahamic traditions of Judaism, Christianity, and Islam, specialized groups practiced meditation. People in these groups were interested in going deeper than they could in the context of weekly or daily services. In Judaism, it is the Kabbalists who meditate; in Christianity, the monastics; in Islam the Sufis. In Buddhist cultures, despite the Buddha's last injunction to "be a light unto yourself," laypeople believe meditation can make you unstable, so they leave meditation to the monastics, whom they support and revere. Within Hinduism, meditation is called *dhyana*. One must be initiated into *dhyana* by a guru or teacher, and the average person practices devotion more than meditation.

The word "meditate" comes from Latin *mederi*, "to heal." This etymology is particularly relevant to old age, when the primary task is to revisit people, experiences, and situations from the past, heal old wounds and misperceptions, and put the puzzle of life together into a meaningful whole. Although meditation has traditionally been tied to religious traditions, it is not necessary to subscribe to a particular set of beliefs in order to practice it or experience its benefits. Meditative techniques are increasingly readily accessible in our secular society. In the last twenty years, scientists have been studying the brain functions of long-term meditators, particularly Buddhist monks. Among other things, they have found that meditation increases attentional skills and can even reorganize the brain to enhance feelings of well-being.

Jon Kabat-Zinn, a longtime meditator and a psychologist at the University of Massachusetts, has done much to bring meditation into the mainstream with his creation of the Mindfulness-Based Stress Reduction (MBSR) program. MBSR is an eight-week course, taught either online or in many medical and nonmedical communities. It systematically teaches participants how to be aware of their thoughts and feelings by observing what is taking place in the present moment. This is precisely the work of coming to know oneself.

Let's take the example of living with chronic arthritis. The mind seems to naturally gravitate to the experience of pain. It can get easily trapped there, resulting in a life that is focused on pain. Instead of sinking in and letting the pain suffuse our being or trying to buck up and ignore it, there is a middle way: exploration. This would involve asking questions like these: Exactly how does the pain feel? Where is it located? What thoughts and emotions accompany it? How is it influencing me? What does it remind me of? These and many more questions help us get to the root of what is moving within us. Going through this type of inquiry with a group supports us in seeing that we are not alone with our disquiet. This adds a critical element to self-understanding.

Communities using MBSR are now located throughout the United States and much of Europe, particularly since it has a good success rate with people who live with chronic pain, anxiety, or depression. In some cases, the cost of the class is even covered by Medicare and private insurance. MBSR has taken meditation from being an exotic religious practice and has firmly ensconced it as a secular healing method that uses awareness to promote recovery or relief from symptoms.

From a complementary perspective, Dan Siegel, a neuropsychiatrist and mindfulness researcher at UCLA, founded Mindsight, an organization dedicated to exploring the interface between brain, mind, and relationships. In *The Mindful Brain,* Siegel distinguishes between the brain, the physical matter with its neurons and dendrites inside our head, and the mind, which he defines as "a process that regulates the flow of energy and information" (5). For Siegel, the mindfulness we cultivate in meditation helps us integrate the brain. A more interconnected brain is an indication of overall well-being. The work of Kabat-Zinn and Siegel demonstrates the benefits of meditation for coping with illness and unwanted emotional states and for enhancing well-being. It also points to the usefulness of teaching people how to be aware of, and relate to, inner states.

One of the most compelling outcomes of meditation is an awareness of the multiple levels inside us. There are many different forms of meditation, yet many people shy away from it because they believe they can't meditate. I have come to see this response not as inability but as misinformation about meditation. Sometimes it is as simple as not recognizing that what we are doing in daily life can be a form of meditation if we approach it with this intention. At other times the impediment comes from having a fixed idea about what one should do or experience when meditating. It may also be the case that individuals are working with a practice that is not suited to their temperament. Contemplative states can and do happen spontaneously when one is simply being present, perhaps while taking a walk, drinking a cup of coffee in a quiet place, washing the floor, digging in the garden, or even while driving a car.

As I see it, there are five broad approaches to meditation: concentration, reflection, mindfulness, heart centered, and visualization. Each cultivates a different aspect within. I once saw Bede Griffiths (1906–1993)—a Benedictine monk who lived in India for years and was deeply immersed in Hinduism—explain the differences between religions by holding up his hand and pointing to his palm. Each of the fingers, he said, is like a different religion. However, they all meet in the middle, at the palm. This is also an excellent analogy for various types of meditation. Each is a boat that carries us into our interior. No one boat is better than any other. Each type has within it aspects of the others. As with so much else in life, each approach has its strengths and weaknesses. The task is finding a practice that fits your personality and has a special harmony for you.

Whatever form of meditation we use, ultimately meditation teaches us to befriend death, and that includes loss. Meditation requires letting go of what we value, what torments us, and what we're engaged with. It entails facing the darkness, emptiness, and fullness—in short, the mystery inside. Each time we sit, we are invited to leave the world as we know it. This is no small matter. Noticing the degree of struggle we undergo gives us some idea of how seductive our thoughts and beliefs are and how unwilling we are to let them go. This awareness is an excellent starting point. It's only through awareness of what is so for us right now that we can incorporate a more expansive consciousness that includes, and even welcomes, the unknown vastness. The rest of this chapter is devoted to exploring various types of meditation with the hope that readers will experiment with a few and find one that resonates with them.

Concentration

Concentration is the form of meditation most people think of when they think of meditation. It is also the one people find most challenging. When we sit down intending to find a place of stillness within, we find instead that the mind races from one thought to another, one feeling to another, one memory to another, one plan to another. The result is that we give up in frustration at our inability to control what is often referred to in meditation circles as "monkey mind." Indeed, in concentration, the intention is to hold the mind on one object for a designated period of time. Anything other than that object is considered a distraction. This means the elder or caregiver must develop the skill of retraining the attention away from all that is not the chosen object. The chosen object can be something external, such as a candle flame, or it can be an internal thought or bodily experience, such as a word, a phrase, or the breath.

Zen meditation in Buddhism, transcendental meditation in Hinduism, and Centering Prayer in Catholicism are some well-known examples of concentration meditation, as is Vipassana (a form of Buddhist mindfulness) in its early stages. These forms build our ability to focus on one thing. Concentration practices tend to change our state of consciousness. Over time, the ordinary mind, with its abundant chatter and multiple directions, recedes, and a calmer, more centered awareness takes its place. Figure and ground shift from busyness to calmness. Learning to achieve this state takes many failures, often lasting years. When thoughts and feelings leak through despite our best efforts to maintain one-pointed attention, we return the mind to the meditation object, over and over and over.

Let's say you have a persistent worry. Perhaps you are going in for a second test to determine if you have cancer. You sit to meditate and at once you find yourself assailed by anxiety. What if the test is positive? Will you need surgery? Who can take care of your dog? Who can you count on to be there for you? Is your will in order? Pretty soon you're spinning in a world of "what ifs," and you haven't even noticed you're a body. Since there is nothing to distract the mind, it gallops along and takes you with it. Using a concentration practice, with great effort you would continually turn attention away from your questions and anxiety to focus on the meditation object. After the meditation period, you may well feel as if it was a waste of time because you spent most of the time in anxiety, with brief interruptions of returning to the intended focus.

Actually, this is not wasted effort. Training the mind in this way strengthens the ability to focus over time. Like learning to stay balanced on a bike, it takes practice, which builds "muscle memory." Remember, researchers found that meditators have better attentional skills, and we know from research on aging that aspects of attention weaken with age. This is also true with caregivers who find themselves easily distracted and often feel either scattered or tightly controlled. With perseverance, it is possible to enhance the ability to concentrate no matter what age we are. Concentration meditation is also a good way to practice renunciation or letting go. This is where building "muscle" may prove useful for the time when we may have to let go of abilities, interests, and eventually life itself.

One rudimentary form of concentration practice that older adults and caregivers can engage in with some degree of success is allowing attention to sink into something that holds interest. This could be creating a piece of art, listening to music, writing a memoir or poetry, or putting a puzzle together. Whenever we devote our attention to an object and sustain it, we experience the benefits of one-pointedness. This can be particularly helpful when dealing with chronic pain, as so often happens with aging. It is also salutary for coping with stress.

Strengths and weaknesses are often a Janus-faced coin. Flipped one way, they're positive; flipped the other, they're negative. The drawback to concentration practice is that we engage in it at the cost of blocking out thoughts, memories, or emotions that may carry bits of information and unfinished business that need attention. By viewing anything outside the meditative object as a distraction, people can—and often do—avoid dealing with troubling thoughts or working with psychic material that needs healing. Bay Area psychologist John Welwood coined the term "spiritual bypass" to describe how many meditators fail to address problematic areas of their lives by cultivating peaceful states. Despite its ability to heighten attentional skills or distract the mind from physical pain, concentration practice is less optimal for elders because this time of life is exactly the time to notice what is surfacing in the mind and use what is revealed to better understand one's self and life.

The most essential ingredient in all forms of meditation is kindness. Unfortunately, it often takes years to realize how important this quality is to practice. How we perceive or interpret what arises in meditation, and in life, has everything to do with whether or not we get stuck in an unfortunate event or learn and grow from it. When we can notice the critical voices within and respond with kindness, we are exchanging the ingrained habit of judgment for compassion. When an unwanted emotional state is present during a meditation session, the most beneficial approach is to imagine your child within experiencing this state. What attitude do you take? Do you admonish the child, or do you wrap your arms around her and let her know she is loved? Noticing these states and your responses to them is one of the most powerful outcomes of meditation practice.

Reflective Meditation

Reflective meditation, often called analytical meditation, refers to disciplined thinking. You choose a question, theme, or topic and focus thought on it. This is a form of concentration practice, but its scope is broader, and it is aimed at engaging the mind. A good example is *lectio divina,* or divine reading, used by Christian monastics. In this practice, the meditator slowly reads a Bible passage several times, paying attention to where the mind naturally stops and what questions or comments arise. These then become the focal area as the person reflects on the feelings, thoughts, and images evoked by their reading. Usually this type of contemplation will bring up memories or thoughts about one's life, and these are brought into the context of the believer's relationship to God.

Those interested in exploring this type of practice can use a word, a phrase from poetry, a passage from a spiritual tradition, or a passage from an inspiring author that is especially provocative and follow what is evoked as the words sink deeply within. The point of the practice is to access what lies beyond ego consciousness. In Jungian terms, this form of meditation is designed to help you enter the personal unconscious, that storehouse of both joy and sorrow.

An alternative practice is to introduce basic questions as a focus of thought. You might ask yourself: What is that feeling that's been dogging me these last days? Should I move out of my house or stay put? What strengths can I call on to help me with my increasing memory loss? What is holding me back from hiring someone to be with my loved one so I can have time off? As you ask these questions, make no effort to answer them. Rather, simply allow them to hang in the silence. When ego races for an answer, as it most surely will, pose the question again. What you are doing in this kind of practice is creating internal space for deeper aspects within to surface. It is hard to recognize these aspects amid the usual clamor of ego managing everything.

On a more profound level, you can use this method to explore questions such as: "Who am I?" "What is the purpose of my life?" "What happens after death?" and "How can I accept suffering?" Once again, the point is not to find the answer, but to invite the unconscious into consciousness. Often we find dispositions or attitudes surfacing that have not previously been in awareness. Sometimes this kind of reflection arouses a memory, emotion, or insight that has relevance to our present situation.

Reflective meditation is particularly helpful when we are facing decisions and are unsure of what direction to take, or when we are in a life quandary and don't know how to respond. Since elderhood is about change—in social and familial relationships, physical well-being, finances, and housing, to name just a few areas—this type of meditation can be especially accessible and useful. For caregivers it can offer a refreshing break from the inner turmoil of doing too much while creating space for something other than ego to come to the fore. Priorities can be allowed to surface from a deeper place, often resulting in greater clarity about what is really important. A caveat here is that meditative practices do not provide quick fixes or answers. What they do is expand our awareness of the factors involved and help us see where we might be stuck, thus loosening the tight grip of ego and offering us a broader, deeper vision with which to contemplate our questions.

Mindfulness Meditation

Mindfulness meditation seeks to help us become aware of our experience in the present. In the beginning, it generally starts with a concentration practice that helps stabilize attention, such as breath awareness.

Once a degree of constancy is established, practitioners go on to use whatever thought or sensation arises as the object of meditation. The intention is not to get involved with what arises or judge it. Mindfulness is not directed toward changing our perceptions; rather, it is intended to help us see more clearly what our perceptions are and to recognize their fleeting nature.

For instance, imagine that when you start to meditate, you immediately feel discomfort in the body where previously there did not seem to be any. You notice where the discomfort is and what it feels like, such as tightness, throbbing, or stabbing. You might notice any thoughts or emotions alongside the discomfort, like worries about the pain or not wanting the pain to be there. It is at this point that mindfulness becomes challenging. Our natural tendency is to think in stories. We're constantly telling ourselves stories about today, yesterday, and tomorrow. These stories have a way of snowballing. When this happens, we forget we're meditating, and we get lost in the story. We forget our intent is to simply observe. Eventually, through many failures, we develop the skill of observing the physical sensations, along with their accompanying thoughts, feelings, and stories without being pulled into them so strongly.

With a little practice, most of us can learn to identify physical sensations—sound, taste, touch, smell, sight—when we meditate. We can also fairly easily learn how to describe these sensory experiences while remaining aware of them. Once we move into thoughts or emotions, however, the mind goes off in a thousand directions, the emotions follow suit, and it often feels like havoc inside. As with concentration practice, it is at this point that many people feel they cannot meditate. Alternately, the mind can feel as if it is in dense fog; sluggishness and sleepiness can take over, counteracting our best intention. This can be discouraging. The chaos and lethargy are not separate from the meditative experience. If we are willing to persist, we eventually learn the habits of our mind, and we develop better methods for not getting sidetracked in our observations.

A side benefit of perseverance is that we begin to see how much of our discomfort is temporary. What felt excruciating, sad, uncomfortable, or boring one minute can dissolve into some other state without any attempt on our part to cause a change. Seeing this can be incredibly freeing. It teaches us not to take everything that's going on in the mind so seriously. When we don't take our thoughts, feelings, or beliefs as fact or truth but are simply able to watch them unfold, we find we are not so pushed and pulled by them. It is easy to see how beneficial this can be for older adults and caregivers. As we age, there are more occasions to get pulled into worry, regret, uncertainty, and melancholy. Learning to name these states, tolerate them without caving into them, and witness their ephemeral nature can shift our entire orientation.

Caregivers have other sets of conditions that tend to arise. Guilt, grief, confusion, and lethargy are the most common. For caregivers and elders receiving care, meditation helps us identify and acknowledge what is happening. Amazingly, this awareness can lead to noticing the sun is out, this flower is beautiful, and I am safe. In effect, a natural rebalancing can take place.

Vipassana, meaning "insight," is a form of Buddhist meditation from Southeast Asia. Insight into oneself and the nature of life comes as we master the ability to observe the mind without getting caught up in the story that is constantly being spun. Neuropsychiatrist Dan Siegel describes the calmer states that result as "egolessness," because the grip of "I" or "me" is lessened. When this happens, we gain access to our subjective inner life, which increases our emotional intelligence. Interestingly, this is what Freud encouraged his patients to do when he asked them to free associate. There is much value in what the unconscious generates when the grip of ego is lessened.

Perhaps one of the most significant and helpful changes that occur over time with meditation practice is a lessening of the need to control. This change can be quite revolutionary, and it can be particularly helpful for older adults and caregivers. Ordinarily we tend to take misfortune personally, as when someone ignores us, cuts us off on the freeway, criticizes us, forgets our birthday, or doesn't return our calls. It is so very hard for us to enlarge our scope of vision to include the other person's possible perspective. Frequently, the incidents we get upset about have nothing to do with us personally and everything to do with the other person. This is where it is crucial to understand how projection operates (as discussed in chapter 4).

The caregiver who is certain she will be judged as an inadequate partner, friend, or child if she puts her loved one in day care is unable to meet her need for self-care because she is projecting her own unexamined values onto others. What she thinks, feels, and believes is what she thinks others think, feel, and believe. There may in fact be a few people who will judge her; however, the vast majority may be either supportive or indifferent. Her attachment personalizes the situation and traps her. Conversely, the older woman who, in her fear, insists that her children take care of her because she took care of her mother (under entirely different circumstances) is foisting her value system onto her progeny. Not only is this an unrealistic expectation; she is also tying their love for her to their ability to care for her. She cannot or will not see the larger picture. We do not need to take everything that happens to us personally. We don't need to hold on to misfortune to the extent that we do; we can relax a lot more than we think.

Many years ago when I lived and worked in a meditation center, I had a great deal of anger toward another staff person. Staffers had regular interviews with a teacher, and during one interview I talked about my anger. The teacher tried to get me to see that the anger was impersonal. It was not necessarily mine; it had simply arisen. I was so attached to "my" anger that it took me almost our entire session to force my mouth to say "there is anger" instead of "I am angry." This was a profound lesson for me. While a shift didn't happen overnight, I look back on that teaching as nothing less than a conversion experience. Now I see how closely this experience is related to archetypes.

When we are vulnerable in any way—and anger is certainly a vulnerability—we open ourselves to the added energy of the archetypal field, which is impersonal and universal. If we think that energy is ours, we can be consumed by it. When we adopt a perspective that includes a measure of detachment, we are in a much stronger position to resist being overcome by it. For Siegel, relationships—including our relationship with ourselves—shape the way brain and mind integrate as we become more mindful. A byproduct of this integration is that empathy for others arises, breaking down the sense of "me." When I saw anger as present without claiming it as mine, I created space to explore what might be going on with the person who was the target of my anger. It also gave me space to look at the beliefs I held that triggered the anger in the first place. Sometimes seeing the roots of these experiences leads us to let go of outdated values. It can also help us reaffirm values and figure out constructive ways to effect change.

Several years ago I discovered an offshoot of Vipassana meditation called Recollective Awareness (RA), which opened the doors of meditation for me in a way I had not experienced previously. I believe this form is well suited to exploring the inner world in older age. In RA, the goal is simply to come to know how the mind works. There is no attempt to corral it or focus it on any one point. Everything is acceptable, including mental wandering, falling asleep, getting into mental arguments with oneself or others—in short the whole gamut of what most forms of meditation call distraction. With time, we come to know our thoughts, feelings, reactions, proclivities, lacunae, perceptions, and mental habits without the need to bypass them. We become more attuned to the processes of our internal life; because of this, we are less at the mercy of the thoughts and emotions that compel us to indulge in unwanted actions and engage in undesirable states of mind. In short, we come to know ourselves, and along with that knowing, we develop a trust in ourselves, the mind, and the unfolding of life within us. Within the Jungian framework, we are coming to terms with the unconscious.

A unique aspect of RA is that, directly after the sitting period, practitioners write down whatever they can remember about the thoughts, images, moods, and emotions they experienced within the sitting. They then share this material in a group or with a teacher. The act of describing the meditative experience, answering questions about it, and hearing the experiences of others enlarges our understanding. In time, greater self-insight develops as a result of witnessing the many ways in which mind operates and seeing the similarities we have with each other—a direct experience of the nonpersonal aspect of mind. Since everything is acceptable in this type of practice and there are no rules to follow other than seeing what happens, this form is ideally suited to the project of coming to know oneself. Without dogmas to adhere to or instructions to struggle with, meditators are free to interpret their experience in light of their own religious or philosophical orientation.

The final two styles of meditation shift attention from the mind to the heart as a vehicle for awareness. They are powerful methods for accessing states that help us cultivate qualities of well-being and acceptance.

Heart-Centered Meditation

Heart-centered meditations combine concentration practice with a focus on opening the heart. Because many of us experienced loss or trauma at an age when we did not have the resources to integrate the experience, we have erected a protective covering around the heart. Using a practice to slowly, methodically loosen the bindings helps us be comfortable in situations where we feel threatened. Negotiating the uncertainty of older age and the stress of caregiving with heart-opening practices can school us in the art of humility and receptivity.

Some form of heart-centered meditation is found in all major religious traditions. Examples include the Jesus Prayer or Prayer of the Heart in Eastern Orthodox Christianity, the Islamic practice of *zikr*, the Hindu tradition of *japa*, the Roman Catholic rosary, the Tibetan practice of using a mantra such as *om mani padme om*, and the Vipassana practice of the Brahma Viharas ("divine abodes"). Each of these consists of repeating a word or phrase meant to engage the emotions by activating a feeling-state of openness and care. The actual words are less important than the state of mind that the sound and feeling are meant to invoke. The goal is to shift energy from our usual place of contraction and tightness to one of fluidity.

Growing old and becoming a caregiver are two situations in life that require us, as the line in *A Chorus Line* says, to dig right down to the bottom of our soul. We require specialized tools to do this because there are so many opportunities to tighten rather than expand. Heart-centered practices can lift the spirit beyond the tragedy or adverse narrative of the moment. They can help us gain some distance from whatever is causing difficulty by stabilizing psyche enough to allow us to return to the vexing situation with renewed energy, perspective, and wisdom.

The similarities of these methods from diverse traditions over the course of millennia are remarkable. All are designed to help the practitioner develop a lived relationship with the interior, however one defines it. By generating open-hearted states that foster kindness, trust, and acceptance, we invite these presences into daily life. We then find, often to our surprise, that we have become less rigid, fearful, or distrustful. Over thousands of years different religious traditions have recognized our capacity to achieve states of consciousness beyond the ordinary. Each has developed a language and rituals to facilitate this process, even as they have become encrusted with outdated and constrictive doctrines. Still, the practices themselves have survived because of their effectiveness in loosening ego, opening to the unexplainable, and helping followers achieve self-awareness.

Visualization

Visualization meditation is often used for healing. As the word implies, it typically asks the meditator to use their imagination to create images. A guide often leads visualization meditation, either in person or by video or audio recording, so this form works well for those whose style is more auditory than visual. People who have a tactile orientation can benefit by assembling physical items related to whatever theme is used for the meditation. For instance, if the visualization focuses on a natural location, such as a beach, mountain, garden, or desert, items reminiscent of these places can be made available beforehand to enhance the psyche's readiness to engage.

Religious worshippers use images of saints or holy people (icons in Eastern Christianity; *thangkas* in Tibetan Buddhism) to invite their presence or the quality they represent into the practitioner's mind and heart. Other people visualize colors (imagining oneself bathed in white light for healing) or nature (taking a walk in a favorite place). Some practitioners use chakra meditation from the Hindu tradition to open up energy centers in the body. People undergoing cancer treatment use guided imagery to facilitate healing and strengthen positive mental states. Frequently the patient imagines healing entities entering the body to destroy invading malignant cells.

People also use visualization to help them open to unacceptable emotions such as grief, fear, loss, and anger. Visualization can be a powerful method for accessing inner states because, when we fully surrender to the imagery, sound, or sensation of visualization, we activate deeper levels of psyche, including archetypes. When we are in a state of reverie, meditation, or heightened emotion, images often arise of their own accord. When Jung was going through his "confrontation with the unconscious," as he called it, he was deluged by images that he faithfully drew and painted. He would often converse with them, and a few of them became lifelong companions. (We will discuss inner dialogue with images in chapter 11.) His *Red Book* contains depictions of the many images that came to him during this time.

Here's a powerful visualization: imagine a beautiful spot in nature, and allow it to come alive in all your senses. Take your time and feel your way into it. Once you are mentally and emotionally situated in your spot, invite a wisdom figure to join you there. This could be any person of any age, or even an animal. See who shows up. When the figure appears, spend time just being together. Maybe you have a question you'd like some help with; perhaps you'd like to hear what the figure has to say to you. If you notice yourself trying to make something happen, relax and let go of that urge. This is a time to just be. When you feel ready, thank the being who appeared. Slowly return to ordinary consciousness and savor the experience. This type of visualization is closely aligned with the practice of active imagination (see chapter 11). The appendixes in this book also present a guided meditation and other resources to help you explore the inner world.

Meditation practices are like fingers pointing to the moon. We make a mistake when we confuse the finger with the moon it's pointing toward. We may not know exactly what propels life, and we may not know for sure if there is a purpose and meaning to life's movement; however, we at least know that we don't know. Meditation practices help us touch the unknown, and this touching gives us some indefinable capacity to see life and the world with new eyes. It's as if we are able to stand on top of a mountain and survey the length and breadth of our life. This seeing lifts us beyond the challenges of our daily routine and gives us the power and wisdom to live this mysterious life more fully, compassionately, and passionately. The methods described in the next chapter offer additional paths to the interior.

11

Inner-Life Practices

Outside: the freezing desert night.
This other night inside grows warm, kindling.
Let the landscape be covered with thorny crust.
We have a soft garden in here.
The continents blasted,
cities and little towns, everything
become a scorched, blackened ball.
The news we hear is full of grief for that future,
but the real news inside here
is there's no news at all.

—RUMI, "The Tent"

In addition to meditation, there are many avenues for making the unconscious conscious. This chapter introduces some methods I have found useful both personally and professionally in my work with older adults. Books and websites for the various practices mentioned here can be found in the resource guide in appendix B. The chapter starts with active imagination, the method Jung discovered as he grappled with eruptions from his psyche. Then we'll discuss how to work with dreams, which come from deep levels within and attempt to balance the conscious mind. Discussion groups and various creative endeavors that invite us to give voice to the forces and characters within round out the chapter.

For different reasons, both oldsters and caregivers can find themselves in ideal predicaments to realize the benefits of this chapter. Changing circumstances are like an initiation. To thrive amid these changes, something new is needed. This book suggests that the newness we need comes from within rather than outside. Each of the practices described below has been used for this purpose by many people over long periods of time. They have been tested, and if we take them up, they can change how we experience the parts of life that most people find meaningless or distressing.

Active Imagination

Active imagination is a way of interacting with the spontaneous images and internal voices that we all experience, although we do not necessarily give them credence. As noted in chapter 10, Jung used active imagination when undergoing experiences he later recorded in the *Red Book*. He never developed guidelines for how to use active imagination; regardless, many who follow his psychology use this technique as a tool for self-inquiry. Active imagination relies on integrating the symbolic into conscious awareness.

We live in a society that values objectivity over subjectivity and that doesn't take symbolic life seriously. We say things are "just" subjective or "just" anecdotal and then dismiss them as not real or not relevant. This is unfortunate, because this approach can ultimately victimize us. A glaring example of this is how most people feel toward someone with Alzheimer's, especially when that disease is in its later stages. Many people no longer see the person who has the disease. Because we do not value subjectivity, we do not value the subject, either. From here it is a short step to treating someone with memory loss as an object.

The subjectivity/objectivity divide affects how we view symptoms of any kind. If we have a stomachache, suffer a heart attack, or are in an accident, looked at objectively these are just random occurrences, the luck of the draw. Looked at subjectively, however, they may in fact be symbolic. A stomachache can be a response to learning bad news, a heart attack can happen when we have been emotionally injured in some way, and an accident can occur when we are on our way to do something we really don't want to do. Is this symbolic layer of meaning true in all instances? Probably not; sometimes things do just happen. In many instances, however, there are antecedents we have not recognized that now show up. Hillman describes this as "infolding" and suggests that many of the symptoms we experience in old age have to do with our particular psychology. These symptoms can be seen as a helpful guide to encourage us to turn inward and retrieve or acknowledge some aspect of psyche previously neglected.

For Jung, a symbol is something that points beyond itself. A symbol is different from a sign, which has an objective meaning, e.g., a "stop" sign. Symbols come from the archetypal level of psyche. When an archetype shows up in consciousness, it shows up as a symbol that is subjective to that individual, and it may not be meaningful for another. In *Ego and Archetype,* Edinger says: "The ultimate goal of Jungian psychotherapy is to make the symbolic process conscious" (113). Symbols are powerful carriers of meaning. Active imagination, dreams, and some types of creative work are ways to become acquainted with them and harness their energy for growth.

Unlike visualization, which has a script we follow to help us enter into the internal world, active imagination has no set formula or agenda. Instead, we work with images that appear spontaneously, such as those that occur during periods of reverie or in dreams. Images also arise during meditation or at other times when we are least expecting them. The point is to notice them, take them seriously as messengers from below, and work with them to discover how they relate to our present life. Drawing an image, however childlike the drawing may be, or conversing with it is to begin engaging it. Active imagination is usually done alone because it requires the spaciousness of being able to focus entirely on the internal image. It can, however, be shared with a trusted friend or therapist—someone who will not interject themselves into the process but will be a supporting presence.

The task with this method is to switch off the conscious mind, not unlike meditation. We need Erikson's first stage of basic trust in order to let go of control. Once we are quiet and attentive, we bring in an image, or we wait for one—or a feeling or a strong thought—to emerge. When it does, we pull it out of the unconscious into consciousness by some act. This could be through bodily movement, drawing, painting, or naming it and initiating a conversation. Since I am comfortable in the world of words, I use words to talk with whatever has emerged.

Let's say I am aware that I have been feeling emotional discomfort for a few days. I have reflected on how this discomfort may have come about, but it persists. Using active imagination, I sit quietly and invite the mood out of the background and into full consciousness. As it begins to fill up my inner space, an image emerges: a red ball located in the middle of my chest. Now I can begin a dialogue with that image. I can do this internally or with pen and paper. I often use the computer because it is easier for me to stay focused by keeping my eyes closed while using the keyboard. I might open the dialogue by asking the image first if it has a name and then what it wants. There is no specific timeline or direction for this type of conversation. It tends to come to a natural conclusion. Since I have a typed record, I can go back and reflect on it later, or I can do another active imagination based on images that arose during my review. The point of this process is to develop a relationship with the mood and its attendant image.

On December 19, 2016, NPR's *The Takeaway* interviewed Anthony Ray Hinton, a man who spent thirty years in a small cell awaiting execution for a crime he did not commit. What I found most compelling about the interview was his description of what he did while in prison. He said he spent his first three years ruminating on escaping so he could get back at those who had put him there. By year four he realized he couldn't escape physically, but he could get out mentally. Without any coaching or prior knowledge, he used active imagination to leave his cell. The first place he imagined going was the UK to visit Queen Elizabeth. In great detail he described how he got there, what they discussed, the tea they had together, and her loneliness. From that point on, Hinton used active imagination to take him all over the world. He spontaneously discovered the power of using imagination to create images and converse with them. He says these imaginings were what allowed him to remain sane in his cell for all those years until justice was finally delivered. Hinton's use of his imagination was different from traditional uses of active imagination, yet his case offers a profound example of the power inherent in each of us to engage with forces or energies inside ourselves.

When you first start doing active imagination, you may feel awkward and even foolish. Jung certainly felt that way. He initially questioned and doubted his inclination, but he persisted. Many people feel this way when using this technique. However, if you make a regular practice of using active imagination to be with yourself, an interesting thing happens. It's as if the unconscious begins to trust you, and it becomes easier to enter into these discussions. There are several variations on this type of exploration. One is "focusing," a practice based on research conducted at the University of Chicago by philosopher/psychologist Eugene Gendlin (1926–2017). Another is "feeding your demons," a Tibetan Buddhist practice updated for our times by Lama Tsultrim Allione, a spiritual teacher based in Colorado.

Dream Work

Sigmund Freud said dreams are the royal road to the unconscious. Since, as Jung said, the second half of life is about making the unconscious conscious, dreams are a wonderful entryway into this work. Those who regularly work with their dreams testify to how compelling they can be in many different ways.

Unfortunately for many, the major stumbling block to working with dreams is catching them. Dreams are known for their elusiveness—not only with regard to their meaning, but also in trying to remember them.

This is indeed a challenge. The method I've found for making it easier to remember dreams has two parts. First is to set an intention in the mind and desire in the heart to remember your dreams when going to bed. The second part is to keep a notebook, pen, and flashlight within reach by the bed. When, as is often the case with older people, we awaken in the middle of the night, there is frequently a dream we can capture before it scuttles to the outer recesses of the mind. When you awaken, keep physical movement to a minimum. Slowly reach for your writing paraphernalia, bring it into the bed with you, and begin to record whatever images, words, thoughts, or feelings are still intact. At first you may not be able to capture a complete dream. Most likely, however, you will be able to recall a mood, emotion, image, or thought. That's enough. With sufficient steady effort, over time you will be able to remember more of your dreams.

The next challenge is to interpret your dreams. Even Jung struggled with understanding his own dreams. Early on, following his split with Freud, he lamented that he had no one to go to with his dreams. Sometimes it took him years to understand a dream. When working on a dream with a patient, some helpful questions he would ask, according to *Memories, Dreams, Reflections,* are: "What occurs to you in connection with that? How do you mean that? Where does that come from? What do you think about that?" These are also excellent starting questions for us.

Once we are awake, maybe over morning coffee or tea, we can decipher what we have scribbled in the night and let it sink in. It is helpful to make notes of our responses to Jung's questions, as these usually lead us in a fruitful direction. One caveat is not to wander too far afield from the original dream images. If you dreamed about being locked out of the house, for instance, you can ask yourself: Whose house? What does it look like? Does it remind me of any houses I have known or seen? What did it feel like in the dream to be locked out? What does it mean to be locked out of a house? Usually the mind will offer all kinds of possibilities. It is not helpful to go too deeply into too many responses. This just generates more associations and takes you away from the initial images.

It's best to pay attention to where the energy and feelings are as you explore the dream and the questions. As your reflections on the dream generate thoughts, sensations, feelings, images, and moods, keep connecting that material back to the dream itself. Do this until you feel you have exhausted the dream's meaning for now. If you are recording your reflections, you can always return at a later date. Sometimes we can continue to be perplexed about a dream even after having spent considerable time with it. Then, a few weeks or months later, its deeper significance will become apparent. Tending to the internal life is necessary for it to blossom, begin trusting us, and inform us in new ways.

There is an enormous array of helpful books and websites on how to approach dream work, and there are many different ways of working with dreams. Earlier I suggested that you can use active imagination with a dream image, mood, feeling, character, or scene. This is how people have traditionally used active imagination. The most helpful way to work with dreams is to be part of a dream group. It is notoriously difficult to interpret our own dreams because, by their very nature, dreams arise to tell us something about ourselves that we do not already know. In addition, dreams communicate indirectly through symbolic language. These factors make it challenging, but not impossible, to understand what the unconscious is saying. Fellow dreamers can help you interpret your dreams by presenting different perspectives. This can help open up the dream's meaning and relevance for your life. As when we are generating our own associations, it is important to stick close to the emotion of a dream and not get sidetracked by possibilities that are intellectually interesting but do not hold any emotional valance. A dream group does not necessarily have to be led by an expert; however, it's useful to have at least one person in the group who has some familiarity with dream work and group process. The work of Jeremy Taylor (1943–2018), a noted expert on dreams, is very accessible for a group format.

Dreams are like friends that come in the night and want to wake us from our slumber. They are wonderful companions for the aging because they can help us get off our usual track and step onto another that can lead us somewhere magical. When we regularly follow our dreams and spend time deciphering their meaning, we begin to know that, despite appearances to the contrary, we are not alone. There is a kind of guidance we can access if we but turn toward it. This is subjectivity at its best because it brings meaning to our life.

Discussion Groups

For many years I have been leading discussion groups that focus on the challenges of aging, spiritual possibilities, and recent research or thought in the field of gerontology. Most of the groups are in care facilities or faith-based communities. Every community that serves elders would do well to offer at least one weekly discussion group that focuses on the aging experience itself. There are certainly groups of every stripe to serve many different needs in the larger community, such as those devoted to particular illnesses (Parkinson's, cancer, Alzheimer's); groups that target inner growth or unique experiences (new mothers, entrepreneurs, men, women, gays and lesbians); and others that focus on psychological issues (anger, depression, self-esteem). But when growing old probably has more challenges than any other period of life—and more potential for insight—why are these groups lacking for aging people?

From my perspective, the answer is that aging is still in the closet and that we take aging for granted. All of our focus on elders seems to be about "caring for" them rather than offering programs that might support their inner development. We'll all grow old if we're lucky (or not, depending on your point of view), so what's the big deal? When people died right after retirement, that perspective was almost defensible, but now that people are regularly living into their eighth and ninth decades, it no longer suffices. Negotiating the physical, psychological, social, and spiritual changes attendant upon aging is the new norm. Most of us at least need companionship to give us diverse perspectives. To exacerbate matters, few people are willing to acknowledge that they are old; few see aging as anything more than decline and decrepitude; few understand that aging offers the possibility of a whole new area awaiting exploration.

We need to mount a huge education campaign to change these perspectives, and an educational support group is one of the best ways.

In groups, elders are finally able to talk about what it's like to be old, explore the feelings and anxieties that arise when facing an unknown future, discuss the nature of changing familial relations and long-term friendships, and investigate the new internal movements that are pressing for acknowledgment. Together, elders in groups discover the many permutations of this time in life and their impact. They identify and share resources, and they talk about death. Groups have demonstrated time and time again that you can teach an old dog new tricks and that the process of learning, developing, and maturing is ultimately deeply satisfying, enriching, and indispensable for a robust elderhood. I encourage those reading this book to urge your local senior or community center, faith community, or facility to start such a group.

If you are living in your own home and are still mobile, you might consider gathering a group of friends for a weekly discussion group. Pick a theme relevant to your life to discuss the first week, and have group members take turns choosing a theme for subsequent weeks. There are many good books listed in the bibliography that can help with this. You could start with this book or with the works of gerontologist Jane Thibault, author and Catholic priest Richard Rohr, professor Drew Leder, psychiatrist Allan Chinen, or psychologist Susan Stewart. If you are living in your own home and are not mobile, consider Well Connected, the virtual senior center mentioned in chapter 5. As with any senior center, Well Connected publishes a quarterly catalog that offers a wide range of activities to choose from. When you sign up for a program, you will be given a code for your phone and a toll-free number you can call that will connect you to others who signed up for that program from your area and beyond. For elders who are tech-savvy, the program has recently introduced video conferencing. There is a wide range of programs available, and most of them encourage participant interaction.

In January 2018 a group launched an elder salon in Oakland, California, with the express purpose of providing an ongoing forum for those aged sixty-five and older to gather and discuss issues of aging. The salon is modeled after a long-term elder group in Sebastopol, California. The leaders of that group published a book, *The Age of Actualization*, that offers guidelines and topics for others interested in starting these kinds of groups. The Oakland group meets twice a month in the early afternoon and usually has twenty-five to thirty people in attendance at any given meeting. The salon's robust attendance demonstrates the community's desire for such a forum.

One of the most important ingredients in successful aging is maintaining connections. This often proves to be difficult to achieve. During my years of working with older adults, I have noticed that those who enjoy their aging have two things in common: a rich inner life and an ability to continue making friends. Groups, whether virtual or face to face, are essential to that effort.

Creative Endeavors

Creativity comes in many guises and can be harnessed to help us with our inner explorations. In chapter 9, I talked about the value of sandplay to help us bypass the cognitive mind and enter into the symbolic world. While most people do not have access to a collection of miniatures, we all have access to the symbolic. Whether through our dreams, reveries, books we read, movies, photographs, or even images on the TV screen, we can pay attention to what stands out for us.

As you may have noticed, I enjoy looking at the etymology of words. The word *exist* means "to stand out, emerge, appear." Each day offers us untold aspects that stand out for us: a conversation, feeling, sight, thought, smell, touch. In our daily round of existence we have become inured to these kinds of messages between psyche and our environment. When we are older and freed from many have-tos and shoulds, we can take the time to pay attention, notice what is moving both within and outside ourselves, and most of all, stop and question. What stands out for me will be different from what stands out for you. To become curious about the things that "exist" for us is to become curious about the promptings of our inner world.

Perhaps no one has explored the area of aging and creativity as thoroughly as psychiatrist and researcher Gene Cohen (1944–2009). His work and perspective live on in his books and the many lives he touched. Cohen re-visioned the elder years from a slow slide into senescence into what he called "developmental intelligence." He describes developmental intelligence in *Sky above Clouds:* "In the second half of life ... all of the major qualities of the mind are reaching their highest level of maturity—cognitive functioning with the development of postformal thought, social intelligence benefiting from accruing life experience, emotional intelligence, judgment, and consciousness including spiritual awareness" (174).

Cohen effectively argues that there are positive developmental changes that accompany aging and that these actually give older people advantages over their younger selves. The mature mind moves to what Cohen calls "all-wheel drive," meaning that the two hemispheres of the brain—the left, primarily concerned with cognition, and the right, which is more intuitive—begin working equally well and together. This means older adults use their brains more holistically and efficiently, enhancing the brain's creative capacity to engage in challenging situations. Another of Cohen's concepts, the "inner push," reminds me of what Jung called Self. In *The Mature Mind,* Cohen describes the inner push as a "life force composed of many individual forces." It includes our urges, desires, longing, and seeking. To recognize this force we must be able to creatively listen and receive.

Art, collage, clay, journaling, memoir, drama groups, sandplay, and reading or writing poetry are like highways into the internal terrain. When I was in graduate school, a teacher gave each of us a ball of modeling clay and suggested that we simply manipulate it during class. The point was to engage in the usual class discussion and not pay attention to what our hands were doing. At the end, we were all invited to see what we had created. I still have the pair of lungs that spontaneously sculpted themselves from my unconscious. Two years later, when I was diagnosed with early-stage lung cancer, I immediately remembered this intuitive creation still sitting on my windowsill.

Artwork is an avenue for self-expression that can facilitate the inner life. Like many people, I shy away from artistic endeavors. When offered a paintbrush or drawing pencil, I freeze, no matter how tenderly someone encourages me. Many people (including me) were never exposed to opportunities to create art as children, or perhaps they received negative feedback as a young person. The type of art I am talking about does not need to be seen by anyone other than the person who made it. The point is not to create a thing of beauty; rather, it is to allow what is inside to come out.

As artist and psychotherapist Wendy Miller writes in *Sky above Clouds*, "Art expression affords an opportunity to draw upon and integrate even more the different capacities associated with right- and left-brain manifestations" (179). I discovered that an antidote to my reluctance is to simply close my eyes, pay attention to my breath, and allow my hand to do what it wants. Using the nondominant hand is an excellent way of facilitating this. It is imperative to bring kindness and playfulness to the endeavor. At first, not much may happen, because it is hard to surmount years of resistance and beliefs that we can't or don't "do" art. However, when we are persistent, the effort frequently pays off in pieces of work that are stunningly symbolic and evocative. Even if nothing "meaningful" emerges, the effort, focus, and loosening of self-restraint that's required have their own benefits.

Many long-term care facilities recognize the benefit of art programs and hire artists to work with their residents. In the Bay Area there is a program called Art with Elders in which artists work for nine months with individual residents on a particular piece. At the end of the project, pieces are submitted to the program and juried for exhibition. Final selections are shown in a gala event, and the pieces travel the region on exhibit in different venues for a year. Art therapist Elizabeth Cockey cites the benefits of creating art: "Researchers have seen an amelioration of depressive symptoms, improved cognition, and increased sociability among those participating in these programs" (www.soundoptions.com/blog/art-as-a-mechanism-of-expression -for-individuals-with-alzheimers).

Like sandplay, art seems to have particular efficacy for those with memory loss because it offers the forgetful elder an avenue for self-expression. The drawback of art for this population is that as cognitive decline increases, the ability to manipulate a brush and paints decreases. In both sandplay and art, effectiveness is based on a nonverbal connection with another person who is present to and with the elder as they work.

A colleague of mine, Dorene Mahoney, uses the medium of collage. When Dorene finds herself emotionally grappling with something, she makes a collage. It can take her months to carefully select the appropriate photographs from magazines, cut them out, and arrange them on posterboard. The result always provides an external snapshot of an internal state that could not be accessed directly but only symbolically. Dorene says she always feels a sense of relief and internal connectedness when she completes a collage. Collage works on the same principle as sandplay. By making the unconscious conscious, Dorene broadens her understanding of her current situation. This gives her the momentum she needs to move forward in a way that brings life rather than avoiding or stalling it. Her instructions for collage are given in appendix A.

Poetry is another art form that is close to soul. As with art, most of us feel inadequate when asked to write a poem; yet in times of intense emotion, poetry can spring out of the most begrudging among us. Good poetry is like a key that unlocks the door to unknown bits and pieces inside. We recognize the truth of a poem not with the mind but with the heart.

One of my favorite poets is songwriter Leonard Cohen (1934–2016). For years I listened to his songs and read his poems, yet there are very few that I can explain. Most of them remain an enigma to my mind, yet my heart is drawn again and again to his songs, particularly when I am feeling lost, alone, inadequate, or uncertain. Poetry is paradoxical in that way. When our mood is low, instead of reading something upbeat, reading a poem that directly addresses the mood is mysteriously soothing and comforting. The same can be said about writing poetry, memoir, or journal entries during intense moments. The planning, fixing, organizing mind recedes, creating space that honors what is and allows deeper voices and forces to express themselves.

Poet and author John Fox has a wonderful method for making poetry writing accessible to even the most faint of heart. With his method there is no effort to rhyme or any structure at all. When I participated in a group he led, he selected a provocative poem and, after reading it through several times, invited us to choose a word or line that resonated with us. What each person chose became the first word or line of a poem he or she wrote. Every person in that group successfully created a meaningful piece. In facilities where I use his method, participants find themselves expressing memories long forgotten and emotions longing for a voice, and they bond with other participants in a way that is difficult to replicate. Being willing to experiment by allowing what is inside to come out takes some courage. In my experience the reward is always worth the initial discomfort.

Journaling also offers an entry point to the inner life. One of the easiest approaches to journaling is to simply sit with a notebook and start writing about whatever you're seeing or feeling for at least ten minutes each day without censorship. It is not uncommon to surprise yourself through this practice. The point is not to write well, but simply to write. It can almost feel as if we are channeling someone else. In the 1960s, Ira Progoff (1921–1998), a psychotherapist and student of Jungian psychology, developed the "intensive journal" method to help the general populace attain the same kind of insight that is achieved in individual psychotherapy. Dialogue House continues his work.

In many communities that serve older adults, there are life story, life review, or reminiscence groups that give seniors a set of questions and ask them to write about their memories and experiences. This offers an excellent opportunity to revisit different periods of life and reflect on what happened and how it has contributed to one's journey. It is also a way of preserving for posterity some of the history, knowledge, and perspectives that formed entire generations. The nonprofit organization Story Corps is dedicated to recording the voices of older adults telling their stories for future generations. This is an important project because as older people die, their memories of history die with them. The world is changing rapidly, and if older adults don't preserve the past for us in their voices, the job will be left to historians, who do not always produce neutral results.

Barry K. Baines, a physician who specializes in end-of-life care, takes a different approach, as mentioned in chapter 6. He recommends identifying and writing down the core values that have guided our lives and the legacy we hope to leave through them. For people who have memory loss and their care partners, journaling is an excellent way of tracking both journeys. Books written by those with memory loss also give us a much-needed and valuable window into their world, which is shrouded in mystery.

All of these are proven methods for accessing the interior world. Start with practices that initially pique your interest, but don't stop there. Remember, older age is about becoming an explorer. To that end, also notice which practices make you feel uncomfortable. Explore your reluctance and what might be causing it, and then give the practice a try. Be open to surprise. After all, aging is about learning to live with surprise.

12

Living Environments

Revelation sometimes comes to us in spite of ourselves, whether we can make good use of it or not. But it seems that we are most open to it when we don't "know" the answers. It takes courage to trust the unknown—Mystery itself—out of which revelation comes. I think of it as learning not to be afraid of the dark, even to love the dark, and to be loved by it.

—DOROTHEA BLOM, *The Journey of a Quaker Artist*, Pendle Hill Pamphlet #232 (Wallingford, PA: Pendle Hill, 1980)

This chapter and the next diverge from the rest of this book, which has focused on the inner life. These sections thrust the reader into one of the biggest decisions older adults face: where to live. This material is written not only for the older adult but also for the children and friends who will most likely help with the decision-making and possible move.

Along with medical conditions, housing arrangements offer the most distressing disruptions to life as usual. In the past, most older people stayed on the farm, in the town where they grew up, or in the place where they got married. Families, including extended family, lived closer together, and neighbors knew each other. There was a degree of safety and security in this arrangement. This is no longer the case, especially in urban areas. Old people are living much longer than they used to, and in many cases, their children live far away. Oldsters may not know their neighbors well, since people move so often, and friends are scattered in other areas. Deciding what an optimal living environment would be is a daunting decision—one that tests our mettle, creativity, equilibrium, and ability to include the unknown as meaningful.

Whether or not we intend to stay in our home or move out, it is important to have some basic information on the types of living arrangements available and their advantages and disadvantages before we require new housing. Equally important is having some idea about what kind of living situation is optimal for oneself or a loved one.

This chapter explores living options—home, board and care facilities, continuing care communities, assisted living, memory units, and nursing homes—as we age, with regard to both outer and inner considerations. In addition to providing resources for and salient questions about remaining at home, the chapter discusses options for living in various congregate settings. More information about the organizations mentioned in this chapter can be found in the resource guide in appendix B.

Very few older adults want to live in care environments. There are multiple reasons for this, primary among them the fact that care environments are not perceived as caring. At their worst, they provide what Kitwood famously labeled "uncare"; at their finest, they have dedicated staff who try their best—despite cumbersome regulations, understaffing, and the requirements of the corporate bottom line—to promote quality of life. Most facilities fall somewhere in between these two poles.

The fundamental problem with facilities is that their scope of vision is limited. Rather than embracing a holistic model of personhood, they see their primary mission as meeting needs that fall within Maslow's first two levels of hierarchy: food, temperature regulation, housing, medicine, and safety. Secondary are Maslow's third-tier needs for love and belonging, which are addressed through activities meant to engage the elder. But even here there is a lack of understanding and vision. Activities in and of themselves do not address belonging needs. That comes through intentional building of community, which must fall to staff because many who come to live in a facility have lost the motivation and energy to do that for themselves. The notion that the point of our elder years is to individuate or blossom into our deepest self, as espoused by this book, is not even on the radar of most care environments. It's no wonder few elders willingly choose facilities.

Unfortunately, according to 2015 data from the Family Caregiver Alliance and American Senior Communities, 35 percent of those sixty-five and older will eventually enter a nursing home, while 50 percent of those ninety-five and older will do so. It is difficult to obtain exact percentages for elders in assisted living, but according to one source, around one million Americans currently live in some type of senior living community.

Living at Home

About 90 percent of people intend to stay in their own home as they age, and that makes sense. Aging in place, as it is called in gerontology, has the primary advantage of giving the elder a familiar environment that offers a degree of privacy, lessens disruption of routine, and provides a semblance of autonomy. Essentially, there is a greater degree of perceived control within the boundaries of the known. Remaining at home optimizes personal choice: when to get up, when and what to eat, and what activities to perform in a day. Depending on one's physical capacity, a sense of usefulness and meaning can be maintained by carrying on with errands and familiar chores such as washing the dishes, doing light cooking and cleaning, gardening, handling finances, or tinkering with repairs.

When the elder does not need a significant amount of help, it's usually possible to rely on a spouse, family member, or friend to help out. There is currently a movement for those who have large homes to open their home to peers so costs can be shared, along with home maintenance tasks. As of this writing, there are several organizations starting to provide home-matching services. They are not robust at the moment, but they hold promise for the future. To find out about possibilities in your area, contact your local AAA. Home-matching services operate a bit like a dating service, except the purpose is to find housing. This kind of arrangement can be extended to an exchange where renters enjoy reduced monthly rent in exchange for performing some services. Another innovative option is the village model, mentioned in chapter 2, which has sprung up to help elders remain in their own homes and communities by providing companionship and services from local volunteers while also offering social and educational programs nearby. The village model works well when there is not significant physical impairment or memory loss.

As long as one is able to drive or otherwise find transportation and can take basic care of self and home, aging in place is an agreeable choice. When frailty or physical or cognitive impairment sets in, significant modification needs to take place. It is common knowledge that aging brings physical diminishments with it. Chief among these are chronic illness, mobility challenges, memory loss, and limitations to vision and hearing. These changes provide endless opportunities for exercising creativity and developing aspects of self that have been dormant. Sometimes, however, no matter how well one adjusts, additional support is needed to live fully. When the time comes to move from independence to some measure of interdependence, one has arrived at a new threshold in life.

Let's say one has reached a level of frailty that requires assistance with at least two of the following tasks: meal preparation, cleaning, laundry, and getting out of the house for appointments and social events. At this point the need for greater help is obvious, and the dilemma arises of whether to get that help or to move from one's home. Most people initially consider bringing help to the home. In this case, the first question is: What do I need in order to continue living a full life in my home? Take some time to reflect on this. Discuss your thoughts with family and friends. Consider the cost of care and your ability to pay for it over time. Any kind of care involves substantial costs, and some can be anticipated, while others cannot.

Elders with children or grandchildren living nearby may choose to assess whether these relatives can help. Perhaps a family member can move into the home, or an accessory dwelling (also known as a granny unit) can be built on the property to house a caregiver; or perhaps the elder can move to that unit and a family member can move into the main house. This arrangement can draw you closer together. It can also exacerbate any differences between you. Many older adults don't want to burden a family member. If you're in this position and you feel this way, spend time with those feelings. A frank talk with family members in which everyone speaks honestly about their feelings and limitations can be very helpful in devising a solution that works for all. On the one hand, when a parent depends on a child, old material that never was addressed can now seek the light of day, giving you both an opportunity to clean the slate. On the other hand, the elder's vulnerability may turn a challenge into a threat. Given all the factors, what is the most life-giving decision for all? It is easy to get sidetracked by fantasies about how things can be ideally. A healthy dose of realism and practicality is needed.

As mentioned earlier, across the country many older adults with large homes are now renting rooms as a source of income and companionship. If you are lucky enough to have a large house, you can consider an "energy exchange"; for example, offer room and board to someone in exchange for assistance. Some cities have referral services that screen potential candidates looking for just this type of situation and that match candidates with older adults seeking help with specific tasks. Your local AAA can put you in touch with this service if it is available in your area. To find your local agency, visit Eldercare Locator at http://eldercare.acl.gov.

In addition to the possibility of family members moving in, other options include hiring caregivers to live in your home with you or having someone come into your home for a specified number of hours a day. These caregivers can come from a faith community or from a home care agency—a company that screens, hires, trains, and places workers with older adults. When choosing to bring a stranger into the home, the gain is the ability to remain at home with a modicum of compromise. Sometimes these matches are good. A care partner can become a congenial companion who makes it possible for the elder's accustomed lifestyle to sustain minimal disruption. Sometimes the match is disagreeable, as when there is a language or cultural barrier. Securing and managing reliable, steady, affordable help can be exhausting. There can also be problems of continuity. The regular care partner can become unavailable, and your home can become a revolving door for a variety of short-term helpers. Issues of trust and privacy can precipitate paranoia if your personality has that inclination.

If you find yourself considering hiring someone, here are some helpful questions to ask yourself: How easy is it for you to get along with others who are different from you? How comfortable are you with asking for what you need and want? How demanding is your personality? How much do you value privacy? What is your relationship with money? Do you tend to be more shy, or more gregarious? For this option to work, the elder needs to have a flexible personality that can adjust when confronted with differences and that can see differences as opportunities rather than threats. Success hinges on the quality of the relationship you are able to establish with the paid caregivers. If you are someone who has to have things your way, this is probably not an optimal choice for you, and you may be better off in a congregate facility environment. In the end, the reality is that you need help, which will entail some degree of change. Your primary task is to know yourself well enough to assess whether remaining at home or moving to a facility holds the most promise of living a satisfying life. This is a difficult question, and when trying to answer it, you can feel as if you are groping in the dark. Sometimes, as the quote at the beginning of the chapter suggests, learning not to be afraid of the dark is our best option.

Beyond the practical need for interdependence with a care provider, the greatest impediment to maintaining quality of life in one's home is isolation. When we lose the ability to drive, bike, use public transportation, or even walk to where we want to go, we risk becoming housebound. This might not sound like a problem at first, but consider: much of our gratification in life comes from having a variety of stimuli, including interactions with others. Although we still have the telephone, and some elders are comfortable with the internet, for the most part when we cannot easily leave our home we stop exercising our social "muscle"—and like any muscle that is not used frequently, it begins to atrophy. For extroverts, being at home for extended periods may make life feel like a prison.

One of the most important questions to ask when choosing to remain home is: do I have sufficient interests to occupy my mind and heart when my physical or cognitive ability is compromised? Although this is a difficult question to answer at any time of life, it is especially important to keep in mind as circumstances and abilities change due to age. It is crucial to be honest. This requires knowing oneself—one's patterns, foibles, and strengths. Those who have been probing their inner world before they get to this point are in a better position to answer these questions.

If you feel you can trust family to listen objectively and help you think things through, then that would be a good option at this time. Consider talking with a therapist who works with older adults. Your local AAA can give you therapist referrals, and you may even be able to get the cost of the therapy sessions covered through Medicare. A few sessions may be all you need to get clarity about what is right for you. You can also talk with others who are facing or will face these questions. Consider creating a support group with friends or church members, or find one organized by an eldercare agency. For those savvy with a computer, there is Meetup.com, which lists countless groups for a wide variety of needs and interests. If you don't find one that's compatible, consider starting one. Group members can help each other flesh out multiple concerns and personal predilections to arrive at the best choice for each member.

Too often I have seen older adults put off unwanted decisions until they had few social and physical resources left. Then they moved to a facility, but they had become so acclimated to watching TV all day and having limited social interaction that they simply perpetuated this pattern in their new environment. Thus the isolation they experienced at home was replicated in the facility, despite the availability of peers and activities.

Moving Out of Your Home

Choosing to move out of your home has both pluses and minuses. While the minuses may stand out more prominently, there are times when a group living situation is a better option, especially if impairment is minimal. One of the benefits is relief from trying to maintain one's home and oneself within the home. Another is the increase in opportunities for physical, social, and mental engagement. To be sure, one must be open and willing to use the available resources in a facility, especially because a facility's primary commitment is housing and safety, not community building. Another significant gain for many elders who move to facilities is that they feel like less of a burden on their spouse or children. From the perspective of family members, there is also a sense of relief. Family members who were providing care are now freed to enjoy time with their own families or friends instead of being stressed about trying to meet the needs of a parent. There's also the relief that comes with the knowledge that their loved one is safe and secure. The remainder of this chapter focuses on points to consider when home is no longer the answer.

There are a plethora of terms used when referring to long-term care options, including congregate living, eldercare facility, eldercare community, board and care (B&C) homes, continuing care retirement communities (CCRCs), memory units, skilled nursing facilities (SNFs), care centers (CCs), and assisted living facilities (ALFs), also called residential care facilities for the elderly (RCFEs). Each term refers to a distinct type of situation, and the particularities of each will be described and explained below.

Unless you are adamant about remaining in your own home and you have the resources to do that, I cannot stress enough the importance of being proactive rather than reactive when it comes to choosing a congregate living situation. Many people put off these decisions, thinking or hoping they won't ever have to make them. When a crisis occurs and a facility needs to be chosen, there is often insufficient time to be thorough in exploring options. In such situations, elders and family members often make a choice that is less than optimal. This has ramifications for the rest of the elder's life, so it is important to take the possibility seriously and be prepared.

There are several ways of starting your search. Begin by checking with your local ombudsman and your AAA, both of which are programs of the Older Americans Act of 1965 and are funded by federal, state, and county dollars. An ombudsman is a trained advocate for older adults living in long-term care facilities. Their role in facilities is to educate older adults, family members, and staff on resident rights and to investigate and attempt to resolve any issues or complaints that arise in facilities, including B&Cs, CCRCs, ALFs, SNFs, and CCs. Because ombudsmen frequent these facilities, they are very knowledgeable about the conditions in them and what kind of record the facilities have.

The AAA is also a good resource because they are the umbrella organization for eldercare services in the county. Staff are experts in the field and can direct you to services and other organizations that can assist you in your search. Eldercare Locator (https://eldercare.acl.gov) is a free service of the US Administration on Aging that helps identify resources for older adults anywhere in the United States. It does not, however, evaluate resources; it is up to individuals to do that. Each county is mandated to have an AAA chapter and an ombudsman. Information provided by the AAA and ombudsman services are free of charge and are available by contacting your local AAA.

For readers living in California, California Advocates for Nursing Home Reform, a nonprofit advocacy organization for long-term-care services, and the California Registry, a free public senior referral service, are excellent ways to obtain information about the services, quality, and costs of different places. You can use the internet to find similar programs in other states.

Those who have the financial resources to get an in-depth assessment of need can obtain the services of a geriatric care manager, a professional in the field who is familiar with services and options. This expert will come to your home, work with you to draw up a plan tailored to your needs and desires, and monitor its implementation. Eldercare navigators, a burgeoning sector in gerontology, are fee-for-service professionals who help elders and family members steer through complex choices and resources in their community. Residential care placement specialists are experts specializing in local facilities. These consultants are knowledgeable about the size, type, cost, and ambience of various living options. They can match an elder's needs and interests with available facilities. One caveat here is that placement specialists are paid by the facility when an elder they recommend moves in. This obviously can be a conflict of interest, so you must do your homework.

Many people think Medicare pays for long-term care; however, this is not the case. Medicare pays for temporary stays in nursing homes for rehabilitation services, but once a person "plateaus," or reaches their presumed maximum level of functional ability, funding is discontinued. Medicare does cover some in-home care, but only a minimal amount that is deemed medically necessary. The types of living arrangements discussed in this chapter are mostly private pay, with exceptions noted below.

As of this writing, Medicaid, the federal program that helps cover medical costs for low-income individuals, does pay for stays in SNFs, some B&Cs, and in some states, ALFs. To qualify, however, an elder cannot have assets of more than $2,000, nor a monthly income that exceeds $2,313. This has spawned a cadre of lawyers to help those with financial means hide their assets in order to qualify. Because Medicaid rates of pay are lower than private pay, many SNFs will only take a person if they can prove they have sufficient money to fund at least six months of care at the private-pay rate. At the end of the six months, the resident transfers to Medicaid. The good news is that once a facility agrees to accept an elder, they cannot turn the elder out for lack of funds. Please note that this is only true for an SNF, not an ALF/RCFE or a B&C. Currently, a pilot project in some counties of California and some other states is using Medicaid to fund ALFs. As with nursing homes, reimbursement is below the market rate, but this trend will likely expand as more elders age, require oversight of their care needs, and cannot pay market rates.

What follows is an overview of the most common types of living arrangements available at this time. Remember, however, that "the times, they are a-changin'." It is highly likely there will be other models in the years ahead. Drawbacks for each option are discussed in the next chapter.

Board and Care Home (B&C)

Historically, B&Cs were called boarding homes, rest homes, care homes, convalescent homes, or domiciliary care. They grew out of the public's outcry against almshouses during the rise of the nursing home. Today, B&Cs offer the most intimate form of congregate life. Most are limited to four to six beds, although there are a few that have more. They are often residential houses that have been converted into accessible units under the Americans with Disability Act. B&Cs provide a room (sometimes a single; frequently a double), meals, someone on staff 24-7, personal care (bathing and dressing assistance), medication management, and, if it's a good facility, interesting activities on a daily basis, occasional excursions, and transport to medical appointments. A B&C is like a small-scale ALF/RCFE. Each house has its own criteria for accepting residents based on the degree of physical or mental impairment it can manage. In urban areas, many will not accept Medicaid as payment, which means there is an out-of-pocket cost of between $2,000 and $4,000 a month, depending on what part of the country you live in. Sometimes these homes can be found in your neighborhood or near your current home, giving you more continuity.

The first consideration when looking at B&Cs is who the owners are. On one end of the continuum are proprietors who run the home as a family. They make an effort to have interesting things to do during the day, provide transportation assistance, and hire staff who foster an environment of care. On the other end of the continuum are B&Cs that offer the service primarily as a business. They usually offer minimal stimulation other than TV, staff are often not very attentive to the clients, and meals can be from the staffers' or owners' country of origin, rather than food the elder enjoys.

Regardless of what type of out-of-home option you choose, the following suggestions can be a guide. Obtain several recommendations and then visit the places with a family member or friend. Visit at different times of the day and on different days of the week. Pay attention during your visits. Who are the other residents? What types and degrees of impairment do they have? Can you imagine yourself being friends with any of them? What activities are provided? Do they interest you? Is transportation offered? Can you imagine yourself living there? How responsive is the staff? What is the weekly menu? Will you have to share a room? Is there easy access to the outdoors? These considerations are the basics that can get you started. Don't be afraid to ask questions. This is a time when the more information you have up front, the better off you are.

Continuing Care Residential Community (CCRC)

If you prefer living in an environment with more people, one option is the CCRC model. CCRCs, also known as life care, have their origins in the early nineteenth century, through the initiative of religious groups and fraternal organizations. Today the majority are owned by large corporations, although there are a few that are nonprofit, mostly affiliated with a religious organization. CCRCs provide all levels of care: independent apartments, assisted living, memory care, and skilled nursing. Some are as small as two hundred older adults, while others are situated on large campuses that can accommodate a thousand elders. They are designed to provide a continuum of care allowing oldsters to enter while they are still active and then move through various levels of care as the need for assistance grows. The concept is that in a CCRC, older people will have a place to live until they die, with appropriate care at each stage. The advantage of these communities is that they provide lifelong care and thus some measure of security. Once you move in, you will not have to move off campus, although if and when your needs change you may have to move to a different floor or building. Many people live in dread of this possibility because when frailty or memory loss sets in, personal choice is compromised. The decision for a resident to move to a higher level of care is made by the on-site medical community based on safety concerns that limit their liability.

Since everyone in these communities is there for the long term and most move in before impairment sets in, residents age together and can form bonds. CCRCs have significant entry and monthly fees to ensure that costs are covered. Originally, when an elder moved into a CCRC, she paid a large sum of money, in addition to monthly rent, which ensured care for the duration of her life. Now that people are living longer, many CCRCs have exchanged those early "life contracts," as they were called, for more limited contracts. The new arrangement requires residents to pay for many services that previously were covered by the initial entry fee and the life contract's fees. There are many variations on what is and is not covered in the different CCRCs, so it is important to fully discover for yourself what these are ahead of time. For those with good financial resources, these communities can be like living in a high-quality hotel for the rest of your life, with the added advantage of familiarity over time.

Assisted Living Facility (ALF); Residential Care Facility for the Elderly (RCFE)

By far the most common purveyor of eldercare is the stand-alone assisted living facility (ALF), also called a residential care facility for the elderly (RCFE). In theory, both the B&C and the ALF are designed for those who require minimal assistance: meals, housekeeping, laundry, and some help with medications. In practice, both house elders that qualify for, and may need, more comprehensive nursing home care, but neither the elder nor their family member wants a move to a nursing home because it is much more expensive, and care is perceived as being of lower quality.

The origins of "assisted living" seem lost to history. One of the pioneers of the movement in the early 1980s, Keren Wilson, founder and senior advisor of Concepts in Community Living in Oregon, maintains that ALFs grew up in reaction to nursing homes. Motivated by the desire to find her mother a suitable place to live, Wilson sought the help of researchers in the fields of disability and psychology to conceptualize a new model, the ALF, that provides services, health care, autonomy, and daily activities.

Assisted living was originally intended for those who no longer relished the responsibility of maintaining a home and wanted to enjoy their leisure time in the company of others. Freed of the burdens of home repair and maintenance, cooking, cleaning, and laundry, ALFs allowed elders to maximize their social interests. Over the years, however, the ALF has changed. In the 1990s most ALF residents were in their seventies; however, since around 2015 most people moving into ALFs have been in their mideighties and nineties. People are able to—and are choosing to—remain at home for longer periods, because health and community services have improved significantly. Many people who currently move into an ALF wait until they are fairly physically frail or have some level of cognitive impairment to do so. If home is no longer the answer for a variety of reasons, then an ALF is an option, and the sale of your home (if you are fortunate enough to own one) allows you to pay the substantial monthly fees, which range from $4,000 to $8,000 or more per month.

The ALF and the RCFE both operate under the same kind of license; however, the RCFE is typically smaller and has shared rooms, whereas the ALF usually offers single rooms and is corporately owned. RCFEs also tend to be more limited in the complexity of mental or physical conditions they take. Many ALFs include a separate section for memory care.

Assisted living means you are provided a bedroom with a bathroom, meals, housekeeping services, and sometimes laundry for a set monthly fee. If you need medication management or any kind of physical assistance, there are additional charges. RCFEs and ALFs do not provide nursing care (other than medication management and minimal medical oversight). They are run under a hospitality model of care as opposed to a medical model. That means there is less emphasis on bodily concerns, more emphasis on social engagement, and less infantilizing of the older adult (at least in theory). This is why most of them look like hotels, and their dining rooms resemble fine restaurants.

When you are considering moving into an ALF, as with B&Cs, spend time in the ones that seem the best for you. Look beyond the physical attractiveness of the facility, and observe staff/resident and resident/resident interactions. Once you have ascertained the basics (e.g., rooms, garden, community room, etc.), ask about having lunch or dinner on the premises. Most places will be happy to accommodate you. Notice the other diners. Are people talking to each other or mostly just eating? What do people do after the meal is over? Does everyone head to their room and not emerge again until the next meal?

Many ALFs are even willing to have prospective residents stay there for a week or two, allowing you to observe much more about the facility. Regardless of whether you stay there overnight, ask yourself: Is there an outdoor space for residents to use that is accommodating and pleasant? Do residents use the public spaces? What kinds of activities are available? Ask if the facility has a plan to identify desirable activities for new residents and help the resident get to them. A good activity program has variety, takes different cognitive abilities into account, allows for spontaneity, builds community, offers opportunities for off-site excursions, and emphasizes programs that require active rather than simply passive participation (e.g., discussion or creativity groups vs. documentary or lecture). Meaningful activities mitigate Bill Thomas's three plagues of institutional life—boredom, loneliness, and helplessness.

Another very important thing to notice is how care staff interact with the residents. Do care staff treat older people as equals, or do they talk down to them? Do they greet residents by name when they pass by? Do staff seem rushed or at ease? Ask what the staff-to-resident ratio is; i.e., how many residents does one staff person assist? Ask about staff turnover, and ask staff directly how long they have been at the facility. Ask other residents what they see as the pros and cons of living there. See if you can imagine yourself making friends in this environment and going to activities. Visit at different times of day, especially in the evening when daytime staff have gone home and on the weekend when management is off. You can obtain a very accurate sense of what it is like to live in a facility after hours. Observe, observe, observe. It's possible to take in a lot of pertinent information by simply watching the interactions between residents, staff, and management. Take time. Needless to say, it is highly important to find a place that's good enough.

If you are looking for a memory care place, you are most likely a caregiver in some capacity. In addition to the considerations mentioned above and the caveats offered in the next chapter, there are a few special factors to consider. First is odor, either from residents or from cleaning supplies. Another is the attire of the residents. Are they put together any old way? Is their clothing soiled or wrinkled? Are their nails trimmed? Is their hair combed? Are they sitting around staring at a TV that has an irrelevant program on it, or are they just sitting and staring? How do staff interact with residents? Are they gentle? Do they make an effort to engage them, or do staff congregate in a group and talk among themselves while keeping an eye out? Do you hear the word "no"? How accessible is the outdoors? Can residents access the outdoors at will, or must they be accompanied? This is especially relevant if your loved one loves nature. Do staff pull residents around, or do they match their gait to that of the elder? These are just some of the many factors to notice as you tour the facility and pay attention.

Care Center (CC)

If a higher level of care than that offered by an ALF is needed, you might be able to find a CC. These are medical facilities that are attached to an ALF and operate under the same licensing body. CCs afford a level of care that is between an ALF and an SNF. A CC is sometimes called intermediate care because it provides some medical care but does not support the high level of care available in an SNF. Because of the medical care involved, the atmosphere of a CC is more like an SNF than an ALF. Care is focused on the body, and other needs have a lower priority. A CC employs registered nurses and licensed vocational nurses who dispense medication and treat the ongoing medical maintenance needs of elders living there. Hands-on nursing care such as bathing, dressing, toileting, walking, and feeding residents is provided by certified nursing assistants (CNAs), as is the case in an SNF. Unlike SNFs, CCs do not provide tube feedings, bedsore wound care, or other more complicated medical procedures. Many CCs apply for a waiver that allows them to provide hospice services.

Skilled Nursing Facility (SNF)

When care needs go beyond what can be accommodated at home or in a B&C or ALF, the next and last option is an SNF. The defining characteristics of an SNF are that it must have a doctor on staff, and licensed nurses must be available 24-7. Most people living in skilled care either have medical conditions that require full-time monitoring, or they are unable to transfer from bed to standing or wheelchair with the assistance of only one person. SNFs also have people with memory loss. It is statistically likely that most people aged sixty-five or older will end up in an SNF for rehabilitation services following a significant medical event, such as a surgery or fracture. Unlike the social environment of an ALF, SNFs operate from a medical model. Advice for how to assess an SNF is the same as that for an ALF and a memory care unit.

This chapter has endeavored to lay out various options for end-of-life living situations. More importantly, it has attempted to present basic questions that need to be considered when investigating housing. Whether older adults remain at home or move to some other living arrangement, it is crucial to be informed. This book has emphasized the interior life and how to cultivate it so that when challenges come our way, we can find meaning in the circumstances. This ability is never needed more than when leaving one's home. In an ideal world, we can access the deeper levels within us under all conditions. The reality is that when our housing does not meet our needs, it is easy to be overwhelmed. Making matters worse, we often move out of our home because of impairment that means we are in a weakened state. We must rely on the habits we have developed ahead of time to carry us through, and we must rely on those who love us to be our advocates and our voice.

While this chapter has presented a lot of questions and may have caused you some anxiety, the information is meant to empower you. Good options for quality eldercare are hard to come by in the US, where health care is seen as a business. For this reason, it is not helpful to take an ostrich approach; instead, we need to do due diligence and be prepared. An informed approach may help us address some of the more problematic areas through creativity, forethought, and planning. The field of eldercare needs advocates to change the nature of care delivery. This cannot happen until a significant portion of the population is willing and able to look reality in the eye and mobilize. My hope is that the energy generated in this chapter can be directed toward this life-giving change.

The next chapter discusses the limitations of facilities, the reasons for those limitations, and how advocacy can help.

13

A Cautionary Tale

We must pass our days and nights under the auspice of the impla-
cable god who rules last years and wants sacrifice. The neglect of
that god is reflected in the neglect of the aged, and in the old-age
home with its routines in place of rituals, a secular sanctuary with
no transcendent vision, no archetypal footing.

—JAMES HILLMAN, *The Force of Character*
and the Lasting Life (New York: Random
House, 1999)

When this book was in its nascent stage, I had a dream that insisted
I write a chapter about facilities. At the time I had no such intention
because I didn't see how facilities fit into the overall thrust of what I
wanted to write about. On top of that, I have a great deal of ambivalence about facilities. As discussed in the previous chapter, as long as an
older adult is independent and does not require care (either physical or
cognitive), good-enough facilities can offer a healthy, invigorating, and
sometimes even meaningful path to live out the elder years. The situation changes when assistance of any kind is needed. I totally support

community living in old age, and I wholeheartedly wish facilities were actually communities. In reality, few qualify for that designation. This chapter is about the major obstacles that handicap the creation of life-giving environments for older adults.

Aging is big business in America. In the last twenty years, large profit-making corporations have gotten into the eldercare business, especially assisted living and memory care. On the plus side, there are now more facilities to choose from; on the minus side, because making a profit is the bottom line, once you peel back the carefully crafted persona, the eldercare landscape hasn't changed as much as it might seem.

When I look at facilities, I see them dominated by three main archetypes. One is the archetype of the mother in her devouring aspect. This archetype seeks to control those in her power. She is the overly protective mother who suffocates her children for their own good. The second is the king archetype. It manifests as the authority who cannot be questioned, challenged, or criticized. It demands obedience and allegiance. The third archetype is that of King Midas, the mythological Greek king who turned everything he touched into gold. The well-known author on human consciousness, Caroline Myss, aptly describes this archetype as it manifests in facilities: "That Midas was a king symbolically implies the Midas figure has the power to generate wealth for an entire kingdom, yet is interested only in his personal aggrandizement" (www.myss .com/free-resources/sacred-contracts-and-your-archetypes/appendix-a -gallery-of-archtypes/). Facilities have the power to make life meaningful and precious during the later years, but their concern with profit and the bottom line frequently negates that possibility.

The types of limitations that exist are endemic to both ALFs and SNFs in varying degrees. This chapter emphasizes the most egregious practices that restrict quality of life in each venue. The content is arranged by areas of concern, with ALFs first, followed by SNFs. At the end of the chapter, there is a section called "Planning Ahead" that discusses particular documents designed to maximize choice, and another segment on "Advocacy," which is crucial whenever we move into any facility.

Certification of Administrators

Various certification bodies churn out administrators for both ALFs and SNFs. The problems with care facilities start with the values deemed most important in the training of administrators. As with many training programs, there is no screening to determine whether potential administrators have the temperament, sensitivity, and commitment required to do the job well. Too often, individuals attracted to the "industry," as it is called (and that itself is a very telling statement), go into the business because it is financially lucrative. Many, especially in ALFs, have not had much exposure to old people, and they lack the passion and vision that can turn a facility into a community. Certification bodies, like most education and testing centers, certify people based on their ability to do well on a test. Remembering what temperature the refrigerator needs to be maintained at is more testable than knowing how to make elders feel like a part of where they live. This might work for structural engineers, but it is hardly a wise approach for a cadre of individuals who are going to oversee the well-being and end-of-life care of older adults.

Since January 2016, a bachelor's degree and an eighty-hour training are required to become an ALF administrator in California, along with passing a background check and a one-hundred-question state exam. Prior to 2016, only forty hours of training were required, so this is a move in a positive direction. Out of those eighty hours, approximately twenty focus on resident services, which sounds good on the surface. However, this rubric includes such areas as corporate policies, procedures, compliance, and documentation. The upshot is that minimal education is devoted to the developmental, psychosocial, and spiritual needs of older adults. Yet it is these very needs that make the difference between quality of life in old age and just doing time. Since the administrator is focused on managing rules and regulations, and the company is focused on the bottom line of corporate profit, it is hard to imagine how they can create vibrant communities.

I once knew of a newly minted administrator who received letters from residents requesting that a particular program continue but who never even acknowledged receipt of the letters. While this is certainly indicative of a poor hiring decision, it also demonstrates how inadequate training exacerbates the situation. Other factors also influenced this novice administrator and others like her in "care" environments. Ageist attitudes view old people who need care as enfeebled. This easily allows younger people to ignore oldsters' ideas and requests, and to deem them unimportant. Additionally, from an institutional standpoint, the residents' requests were out of bounds. The adminstrator's training did not include an emphasis on empowering residents to make decisions about their lives. Flexibility and creativity in thought and action are not conducive to uniformity and ease of management, so these traits are not encouraged.

Listening to residents, seeking their opinions, and creating community is simply not part of a training curriculum whose focus is efficiency. To exacerbate matters, most of the current cohort of elders are not good at speaking up for themselves. They grew up in an era where following authority was the norm, and most have not developed the ability to advocate for themselves. My hope is that the boomer generation will turn things around by not accepting the status quo and questioning authority.

SNF administrators go through a more rigorous training program than their ALF counterparts; however, there is still minimal emphasis on the psychosocial and spiritual dimensions of the person. Depending on the state, they often must have an advanced degree or a substantial amount of experience in health care. In California, they must also undergo a pretest assessment that, like the ALF test, focuses on compliance matters rather than psychosocial concerns, as well as a one-thousand-hour training with an on-site preceptor. They also must complete additional paperwork. They are then eligible to sit for the state licensing exam, which consists of 150 questions in five domains: quality of life, human resources, finance, environment, and management.

Despite quality of life leading the list, the focus is primarily on running a facility rather than building a community. Nonprofits are generally more likely to go beyond lip service in trying to meet the needs of the populations they serve. They have boards of directors that occasionally include at least some relatives of residents, and others who are interested in residents' quality of life. The burden of regulations, however, is challenging. Because so many egregious acts have been perpetrated in nursing homes, the set of rules intended to prevent further infractions has become almost unmanageable. Unfortunately, the world has its share of unscrupulous people who only too willingly take advantage of the vulnerable. The problem with regulations, however, is that they always appeal to the lowest common denominator, and then everyone is held hostage. The result is that facilities focus on regulations to the detriment of community building.

An SNF is much more challenging to manage than an ALF. Many SNF administrators gain experience as ALF administrators first. Because SNFs are so much more complex than ALFs, the problems generated are also more complex. This will become clear as we proceed.

Staff Training

Most ALF direct-care staff have minimal training about the specific needs of the people they serve. A high school diploma or GED is the basic requirement. As of this writing, forty hours of training, ten of which must happen in the first month, is now mandatory in California. This is also true for the memory care units attached to many ALFs, where additional training is now required. Unfortunately, there are no directives governing the quality of the training.

Facilities comply with the letter of the law by giving a two-part training. The first part involves hands-on experience, interpreted as following another staff member around. However, there is no guarantee that the staff person doing the training has the requisite skill set for quality; only that the person has been through a similar training and has been at the facility for a bit of time. The second part of training requires the recruit to watch a series of twenty-, thirty-, or forty-minute educational videos. This is cost-effective, but it is not person-effective. Working with elders, especially those with memory loss, requires not only a compassionate nature but also a rich grasp of what is happening cognitively, emotionally, and spiritually in older age. When cognitive impairment is present, certain techniques of communication need to be so familiar that staffers can automatically respond skillfully in the moment of need. This type of discipline only comes about through person-to-person training, repeated role-playing, observation, patience, practice, and diligence.

In SNFs, direct care staff must have a CNA certificate. This consists of seventy-five to eighty-five hours of instruction (depending on the state) and passing an examination that is part multiple choice and part manual skills. Every twenty-four months thereafter, CNAs must take forty-eight hours of continuing education units. CNA training programs are available at many community colleges and nursing schools. As with so much else in eldercare, the focus is on the body, so recruits are trained in the medical model rather than a social model of care. This has implications on the job because bodily needs always trump the person's other needs. Additionally, because these other needs are not emphasized in training, CNAs do not see it as part of their job description to help with activities or to help residents socialize. When I worked in a nursing home, it was an ongoing struggle trying to get CNAs to get residents up in time for the activities they enjoyed. At least in theory, there is a move in some SNFs to cross-train staff so that this problem is ameliorated. That is a good thing; however, unless and until nonbodily needs are given equal emphasis in training programs, this problem will persist.

Staffing Concerns

Staffing ratios for those who provide direct hands-on care, as opposed to dispensing medicines, are tightly controlled in both ALFs and SNFs. While researching ratios for ALFs across the country, I discovered there are no minimum ratios in most states. This means the ratio is left up to the facility, which is like letting the fox watch the henhouse. One state, Colorado, does provide some guidelines: one staffer to sixteen residents in ALFs, and one staffer to six residents in memory care. Neither of these numbers is very workable in practice. A better ratio would be 1:10 in ALFs and 1:4 in memory care.

The ideal ratio for an SNF is one staff member to six or seven residents. Unfortunately, actual levels are a far cry from this. In California—and I'm sure this holds true for other states as well—the requirement for an SNF is one staff person to eleven residents. Given the requirements of most residents (and this is true for CCs also), it is impossible for staff to meet the elders' needs. Consider the difficulty of getting eleven different residents with different needs up in time for breakfast at eight a.m. Staff shifts begin, as they do in hospitals, at seven a.m. Even if the staff person is extremely diligent and focused, that leaves a little more than five minutes for each resident. To make matters worse, even that minimal ratio is often not achieved. When a staff person "calls off" (does not come in to work due to illness or some other reason), often no one is called in to replace them. This is sometimes the result of having no other staff to call because of the lack of people wanting these jobs.

Another staffing issue is consistent assignment, meaning the same staff person is assigned to the same residents in each shift. ALFs do not practice consistent assignment. SNFs have been working toward it ever since the person-centered care movement gained momentum in the 1990s. Consistent assignment allows the staff member and elder to get to know each other, which in turn builds trust and a feeling of belonging (assuming the match is a good one; if it is not, the elder or their advocate must ask for reassignment). Trust and belonging are top needs identified in Maslow's hierarchy (see chapter 5). The care environment is an elder's home, and he or she is dependent on staff to help meet basic needs. Having rotating staff not only detracts from a sense of home; it is actually detrimental to safety and security, Maslow's most primary need. Gender also must be considered. How comfortable is an older woman with a male caregiver giving her a shower or helping her use the toilet? Some people are indifferent to that; others are not. Finding out whether a facility has consistent assignment, and how often the facility is able to actually implement it, is crucial to establishing the quality of care in that facility.

Staff Financial Compensation

Issues of justice in pay are pertinent in all facilities, no matter their level of care or the population they serve. For instance, staff call off because they are sick, stressed, exhausted, have child care issues, or are facing other family issues that need to be addressed. Because the financial compensation in these facilities is so poor, many staffers juggle two jobs at different facilities. To aggravate matters, they are doing hard physical and psychological work, yet they are the lowest on the totem pole of a strict hierarchy. This also contributes to the "revolving door" problem, i.e., the difficulty of retaining frontline staff. It is increasingly difficult to find people who are willing to work under the conditions offered in most facilities. Status and financial recompense are reserved for the administrator and managing nurses, despite the fact that it is frontline staff who can provide the most pertinent information about a resident. They are rarely consulted because their knowledge is not deemed significant. Frontline workers of today, mostly people of color, are in a similar predicament to nurses and teachers in the years before they unionized.

What is needed is a Dolores Huerta or Cesar Chavez for the caregiving world. It is hard for staff to sustain compassion when little is shown to them. It is a severe indictment of our culture that those who do heart work have the least power and compensation. This perspective is tied to the medical model, which privileges management acumen over social and psychospiritual considerations. Quality-of-life issues for older people are affected by quality-of-life issues for staff. Bill Thomas, one of the most effective change agents in eldercare, confronted these kinds of issues in care environments for years before giving up on facilities. He refers to himself as an "abolitionist" and believes all nursing homes need to be scrapped and a new start made. Needless to say, this has not endeared him to the "industry." Still, Thomas moved the needle in long-term care more than any other individual. It is because of his vision, and that of others who joined him, that federal mandates now include some quality-of-life indicators.

Quality of Life

When ALFs were residences for elders willing and able to use their free time to pursue personal interests, there was little need for more than good basic administration. Currently, most elders enter ALFs with a history of having been socially isolated for some time. Most have at least mild cognitive impairment and have lost the motivation, the self-confidence, and sometimes the ability to get themselves to programs. Unfortunately, ALF regulations have not kept up with these changing demographics. There is no mandate that makes it imperative for staff to assess residents' social interests upon admission and then help them participate in the activities of their choosing. Daily and monthly activity calendars are posted, and whether or not residents engage is left up to them. This is not sufficient. These older adults require reminders, encouragement, and sometimes assistance to participate. This, of course, demands robust, committed, well-trained activity staff, which in turn requires a financial investment from management or ownership.

Thanks to the work of Bill Thomas and the Eden Alternative model he introduced to SNFs (see chapter 9), there are now federal mandates to assess residents when they enter an SNF. There is also required documentation that older people participate in activities of interest. SNF activity staff are responsible for assessing each resident upon admission and coming up with an activity care plan that includes that resident's interests. Staff are also obligated either to ensure that each resident is personally invited to attend activities of choice or to provide stimulating activities in the resident's room. While this does not guarantee good programming or engagement, at least there is an acknowledgment that the resident is impaired and that staff need to remove barriers to participation and offer individual support and encouragement to do so. ALFs would be more lively places if similar state expectations were put into place.

The Medical Model of Care

In all facilities, the primary deterrent to supporting quality of life is an emphasis on efficiency and task completion over psychosocial and spiritual needs. This is particularly acute in CCs and SNFs, where the medical model predominates, but it is also visible in ALFs. Staff have been charged with completing a given task—e.g., getting everyone to the dining room—but Patient A insists on going for a walk. What usually happens is that

Patient A is either ignored or is cajoled or coerced into going to the dining room, because that's the task of the moment, and there is insufficient staff to cater to the needs of the individual. The whole person is not seen, let alone valued. Such a culture of care is directly related to faulty training programs that do not emphasize a person-centered approach. What is taught and what is expected is a skill set tied to proficiency, when what is needed is a "heart set" tied to slow medicine.

Another manifestation of the medical paradigm in SNFs is a paternalistic, patronizing attitude toward residents who are seen as patients. This is somewhat ameliorated in ALFs, where there is less of a focus on medicine. I call this the "Father Knows Best" model of care. It results in staff believing they have the final say over the care of the resident's body. Simply by living in a care environment, residents relinquish the right to make certain decisions about their own care.

Two common examples of problems in this area that can cause a great deal of anguish are walking/falling and eating. Once we reach a certain age, the possibility of falling increases. It is one of the biggest fears about aging because of the repercussions that can ensue. This is especially true in care facilities that have the responsibility of keeping older people safe. Almost everyone knows an older person who fell, broke a hip, had surgery, went through rehab, and never left the nursing home. Everyone dreads this possibility. Facilities take great pains to manage risk by preventing falls. Their added agenda is the fear of being sued for negligence. Thus, they have developed strategies to keep old people safe.

In the so-called "good old days," risk management consisted of staff physically restraining old folks by tying them to their beds or wheelchairs. This ensured they were "safe." Thankfully, regulations ensure this does not occur today; however, facilities have developed other means to achieve the same ends. They use chair or bed alarms to alert staff when a resident tries to get up. Unfortunately, staff become inured to the alarms; and even when they do hear them, by the time they get to the person, that person is already up or down, as the case may be. These alarms add a layer of protection for the facility in terms of liability, but not for the resident. Another strategy is to keep all residents who are at risk of falling in a community room or close to a nursing station where staff can keep an eye on them. When residents attempt to get up, staff admonish or otherwise discourage them. Another method of ensuring compliance is to place impediments in the way so a resident can't get up, such as putting a chairbound resident at a table and locking their wheelchair. The goal of preventing falls significantly limits individual freedom but ensures safety for the facility.

In addition to ambulatory restraints, many facilities use medication as a restraint. This is a very serious and complicated subject that has been thoroughly addressed by Al Power in two successive books. It is now also one of the items state inspectors investigate on their annual assessments. When a resident—usually, though not always, with memory loss—expresses emotion in ways not considered appropriate by facility staff, the go-to intervention is medication to control the person's behavior. It is much easier to give someone a pill than to take the time to explore the source of what might be causing distress. The elimination of risk (preventing the resident from striking another person or staff) and the imperative to maintain a smoothly functioning environment (preventing the resident being disruptive and upsetting others) take precedence.

Of the many problems with this approach, two stand out: the drugs in question are known to have deleterious medical side effects, and they fail to provide any salutary effect. Federal regulations now require facilities to document a decrease in psychotropic drug use among their residents. This is an area where a family member or friend is needed to closely monitor medications when an old person cannot do so on their own. In facilities that have adopted person-centered care, medication is used sparingly. Instead, staff use individualized strategies for resolving residents' behavior problems.

The other problematic issue particular to SNFs (although I have also witnessed this in some ALFs) is feeding people at the end of life. Many times an elder reaches a point where what they consider to be a good quality of life is difficult or impossible to achieve. Often elders like this are not very responsive to their environment and regularly spend the day in a "geri chair" (a large recliner on wheels) or in bed. They are brought to the dining room to be fed, but by this time in their journey, many elders do not want to eat. Perhaps they are choosing abstinence as a path to dying, but persistent staff efforts can override that desire. In addition, toward the end of life many people are at risk of choking, so staff feed them pureed food. This is visually and aesthetically unappetizing, but it is assumed that the old person is too far gone to care or notice. Although there are now molds for kitchens to use that enhance appearance and texture, the extra effort this takes almost guarantees it isn't done.

I once did a sandplay with an elder in an SNF who was in the middle stage of memory loss. She was being strongly encouraged to eat. During her session, she repeatedly mumbled "Take me out of here," and she placed the figure of Pegasus, the mythological winged horse, in a prominent position. This old person obviously knew what she wanted, despite appearances to the contrary. Because we do not give the inner life any kind of credence, especially when a person has memory loss, we don't even see these kinds of appeals. Of course, the possibility of litigation that could result from paying attention and trying to implement an elder's wishes also mitigates against this.

For oldsters who manage to subvert feeding efforts, there are the ubiquitous containers of Ensure (an overly sweet protein drink) that are delivered throughout the day, and the person is encouraged to consume them. What is appropriate in this situation? There are times when food intake is necessary for recovery, and encouragement is appropriate. However, elders at the end of life are not recovering, and overly solicitous efforts to get them to eat are counterproductive. If the resident has not indicated beforehand how they want the end of their life to be managed, then the medical model dictates that they be kept alive for as long as possible, regardless of indications that they do not wish to continue eating or living. For example, an elder might turn his head aside when food is presented, or she may push aside a hand offering food. This action is not deemed meaningful because the medical model of care constrains facilities to operate in terms of black and white. Gray areas open up the possibility of lawsuits and therefore are assiduously avoided.

If you do not want to end up in a state of bare existence at the end of life, it is advisable to ensure that your wishes are known beforehand, while you still have the legal competence to make your wishes known.

Planning Ahead

Prior to admission to a care facility, it is prudent to prepare a document that spells out the elder's personal routines and the kinds of social, cognitive, and spiritual activities they consider meaningful. Such a document is also appropriate to compile for an ALF, especially if the person has memory loss. In SNFs, part of the initial assessment process that staffers are federally mandated to complete now includes preferred times of getting up, eating, going to bed, and bathing, along with activities of interest. Another document is the form called physician orders for life sustaining treatment (POLST), which details some preferential options for medical intervention. If a person is frail and does not have such a form on file with their doctor, a copy can be downloaded from the web (see resource guide in appendix B). The POLST form covers broad categories such as the desire for CPR, a feeding tube, or the use of antibiotics, and therefore does not address the usual day-to-day operations in care environments. Still, it is a worthwhile document to have on file, and most facilities require one.

A movement in end-of-life care that has relevance for the topics of falling and eating is dedicated to empowering patients to make quality-of-life choices when confronted with the possibility of major medical interventions. Surgeon Atul Gawande popularized the movement through his book *Being Mortal.* More recently, physician and researcher Angelo Volandes published a similar book titled *The Conversation.* Both these doctors remind us of the inevitability of death, and both offer compelling arguments for not prolonging life just because it's possible to do so. In words directed to fellow physicians, care workers, and you and me, they advocate a more thoughtful and personal approach to end-of-life care. They focus on encouraging all of us to consider what is important in life and how medical care can support us as human beings who have needs and make choices, rather than being limited to a mere extension of our body's existence. Volandes notes that 98 percent of people want to die in their own homes, while in reality, two-thirds of people sixty-five or older die in a hospital. There is a misalignment between people's desire to die at home and being subjected to unwanted care in medical environments. I highly recommend reading these two books because they are in the forefront of helping our society think about, and reshape, its approach to aging and dying.

The work of Gawande and Volandes can empower the aging person and family members; however, decisions must be made *before* a crisis puts an elder in a facility. Crucial questions to ask have to do with what the old person values. When there is little or no possibility of recovery to the point of X (you fill in the blank with the level of functioning of your choice), ask yourself:

- Do I want someone to keep trying to feed me?

- Do I want Ensure or its equivalent to keep me going?

- If I'm confined to a wheelchair because of potential falling, or only able to walk with staff using a gait belt (a wide belt that is placed around an elder's waist that staff hold onto while walking with the elder), is that acceptable to me?

- Would I rather risk falling and perhaps breaking a leg, arm, hip, or other bone to maintain autonomy?

- Would I be able to adjust to spending all day in a common room (most likely with the TV on) in order to be safe, or would that be anathema to me?

I have witnessed elders in these situations choose to die rather than live under such constraints.

There is a legal document called durable power of attorney (DPOA) that can protect you and help ensure that your wishes are followed. There are two types of DPOA relevant for end-of-life care: one is for health care and the other is for finances. These two separate documents give decision-making power to someone you trust to handle your health and assets if you are no longer able to do so. Some older adults have good relations with their children and feel they can trust their children to follow their wishes, so in that case giving both DPOAs to a child would be natural. Other older people have strained relations with their children, a different value set from their children, or any number of other issues that can result in discord and divisiveness at the end of life. When this is the case, it is best to designate an independent person, such as a fiduciary or lawyer, to retain DPOA for finances at least. Some children have a sense of entitlement, feel they need to take over and be in charge, or are looking for an inheritance. In these situations, giving either DPOA to a child almost always disenfranchises the older person and creates familial discord.

Unless you are certain that your child has your best interests at heart, will follow your directives, and will spend your assets if need be to ensure your well-being *as you see it,* it is best to have your DPOAs with a neutral party. There are many licensed professionals who do this work. If you do not know someone, ask at the local senior center or your county AAA. It is also possible to download these documents from the web and then have them notarized. However, if you can afford to hire an elder-care attorney to help you with this process, I recommend that. There are many intricacies that a blanket document, by its nature, cannot cover.

Consider putting together a binder that includes the documents mentioned; other personal papers; a list of the kinds of care wanted and not wanted; the types of food, music, movies, and books you enjoy; and your achievements and interests that bring you joy. If you were going on a trip, you would plan your itinerary, so why not take a similarly thoughtful approach to your own end-of-life care? Those who are developing the inner life do not find such an endeavor difficult. They have already encountered much in their interior world that is not pleasant, so they can be more sanguine about this exercise. Having worked in aging services for many years, I have witnessed the unnecessary suffering that ensues when these kinds of directives are not in place.

It is very helpful to discuss feelings, thoughts, and desires about care and the end of life with family, the person or people who hold your DPOA, and your primary care physician *while you are still healthy.* Often the person who holds a DPOA needs to step in and advocate for you. This is particularly true if you end up in an SNF, where staff tend to distrust the ability of elders in their care to make appropriate decisions. You could even make a video of yourself talking about the kinds of care you want and don't want. The resource section of this book (appendix B) lists a website (http://caringadvocates.org) put together by physician Stanley Terman that can help guide you through such a process. If you have a video or written document, you should share it with the administrator of your chosen facility *before* moving in. You can also ask the facility administrator to draw up a waiver of liability, which can provide a measure of protection for the facility resulting from any quality-of-life measure you may desire that is contrary to facility policy, such as allowing you to walk even when you are a "fall risk." Facilities may initially balk at these kinds of affidavits, but the more people advocate for them, the more accepted they will become. Talk with a lawyer about how you might make such a document as airtight as possible. Work with advocates for long-term-care reform to have these documents become part of the admission packet.

Advocacy

One indispensable component of making life in any facility livable is having an advocate. Sometimes blatantly and sometimes inadvertently, facility staff ignore what the elder says or wants. Elders with little or no cognitive impairment frequently complain that staff ignore them, talk over their head, or talk to their family members about them as if they were not there. This is not because staff is uncaring; it's because the "Father Knows Best" model of care dominates, and because age bias is alive and well in too many facilities and our culture.

The need for a firm, informed advocate cannot be stressed enough. An advocate can stand up for you when you cannot stand up for yourself. They can insist that things be done in a way that brings meaning to your life, even when that way is contrary to how things are done in the facility. Let's say you like to get up at eight a.m. and read the paper over breakfast, but this interferes with the institutionalized life, where everyone gets up at seven. An advocate can back you up with the powers that be so you can continue to enjoy the routine you find satisfying. This may seem like a small thing, but the reality is that at the end of life, it is the small things that mean the most and that stave off depression. Fortunately, new regulations for SNFs (which are spilling over to CCs) are trying to combat this kind of facility-dictated lifestyle, which is set up for the ease of the facility, not the resident. Although ALFs are inherently less restrictive because they operate on a social model as opposed to a medical one, there too advocates will have plenty of opportunity to stand up for your rights and preferences.

An advocate can also ensure that activity programming is relevant to your needs and interests and that activity staff make an effort to engage you in participating. This is particularly needed in ALFs. For the most part, activity staff are knowledgeable about meeting residents' psychospiritual needs and are amenable to doing what it takes to ensure that these needs are met. This is because they have different training and a mindset geared toward serving the resident. By working with activity staff, an advocate can speak for you when you cannot, and this will go a long way toward enhancing your life.

By now it should be clear to you that care facilities are human institutions. As noted at the beginning of this chapter, they are subject to the same kind of shadow dynamics that pervade the individual psyche. As with so much else in life, institutional living—no matter how much it costs or how fancy the decor—has all the problems associated with managing any large-scale enterprise, such as college dormitories, military operations, and prisons. Problems of inadequate training at all levels, poor financial compensation for the majority of workers, an emphasis on profit over quality of life, fear of litigation, and neglecting the whole person are serious deficiencies in the care of older adults. These will not be corrected overnight. It will take resources, education, and commitment to bring about significant change. We cannot pretend we do not know what needs to be done, and we cannot wait for others to do what it is ours to do. Becoming an informed advocate—raising your voice and your vote now, whenever you have the opportunity—is one of the most effective ways to bring about the change you want. Even though it can feel pointless at times, history shows it is possible to effect change. As we saw in chapter 2, it was the discontent and dissatisfaction of the many that finally pushed Congress to abolish almshouses. The same can happen in our day. To that end, I conclude this chapter with a discussion of what I think is possible if we work together and stay firm.

The Good-Enough Community

Here are some organizational characteristics that, when implemented, create healthy environments for all of us but especially for care facilities. First is that they are nonprofit. Whatever monies are left after expenses go back to the facility in some form: additional staff; staff training; bonus pay; funding for activity equipment; honoraria for musicians, artists, and presenters; special foods or meals; and enhanced environmental features, to name a few options. Second, a livable wage is paid to all, and all are respected for the work they do; that is, the medical hierarchy is eliminated. Third, administrators seek out the voices of residents and line staff and give them preference in decision-making. In other words, administrators serve rather than manage or direct. Fourth, all staff are educated in how to foster community and are actively mentored in implementing what they learn.

With regard to quality of life, facilities need to provide ongoing opportunities for meaningful discussion groups and creativity through writing, art, drama, poetry, clay sculpture, and music. A full-time counselor needs to be on staff to assist both residents and their loved ones with making the kinds of adaptations, changes, and choices that lead to fulfillment at the end of life. So often older people simply need someone to listen, acknowledge, and contextualize their experience. Family members need education in how to identify and work with their feelings while supporting their loved ones. Finally, facilities need to encourage residents to contribute to the life of the community and to give them opportunities to do so. Instead of staff doing everything, staff could support residents in doing more around the facility to better emulate everyday life. It is possible for facilities to become communities that provide settings that are safe yet flexible, autonomous yet congregate, enriching and nourishing body, mind, and spirit. Philosophy of care as it is advertised rather than practiced can be the norm. Quaker-run facilities prove that it is possible to succeed in fostering community.

Given that society is still a long way from providing optimal living situations for old age, entering a facility with eyes open to potential problems is your best protection. Knowledge is power. Knowing what to expect, while initially disheartening, is also empowering. It is also important to remember that life is challenging, and this fact of life continues into old age, when we are often our most vulnerable. Building spiritual muscle ahead of time is no guarantee of ease, but it does enhance our chances of not being completely overpowered by external circumstances.

If we can manage to muster some humor, step back even a small bit from an unpleasant situation, and find compassion for ourselves and others, it can make a tremendous difference. When we no longer have the energy it takes to engage our environment or find meaning in it, then we must rely on trusted others to carry us. This is the meaning of surrender. Life continues until we enter the dying process, and we must continually rise to meet it, mobilizing whatever resources we can.

14

Moving Forward

Our normal waking consciousness, rational consciousness as we call it, is but one special type of consciousness, whilst all about it, parted from it by the filmiest of screens, there lie potential forms of consciousness entirely different.... No account of the universe in its totality can be final which leaves these other forms of consciousness quite disregarded. How to regard them is the question, for they are so discontinuous with ordinary consciousness.

—WILLIAM JAMES, *The Varieties of Religious Experience* (New York: Longmans, Green, and Co., 1902)

Throughout this book I have suggested that there is a deeper perspective we can take as we encounter the many changes that comprise the time of life we call "growing old." This is also true for those caught up in the aging journey through the caregiving experience. A whole new life awaits us when we make the shift from an outer-focused perspective to one focused on the inner world. Aging and caregiving give us the opportunity to experience for ourselves what mystics, philosophers, psychologists, poets, artists, and all those who have stepped off the well-worn path have tried to tell us. There is a whole other world, and it is accessible to us if we look beyond our usual round of preoccupations to the center within. As this chapter's opening quotation tells us, there is normal waking consciousness—egoic consciousness—and there are other forms or levels of consciousness.

When we inform ourselves about end-of-life choices and living arrangements, as discussed in chapters 12 and 13, we are operating on the level of ordinary egoic consciousness. Many of us will never have to face the challenges of facility living, but for those who do, knowing what to expect and planning for it can make the difference between feeling victimized and feeling empowered. Whether you think you will need a facility or are sure you will not, it is healthy to not turn away from the distasteful aspects of presently existing care environments. Imagining oneself in these situations, considering the support you might need, assessing how to obtain this support, and figuring out what you can do to help transform these environments so they reflect the values you want to live by in your later years are all important ego concerns.

However, the process of reflection we undergo to answer ego concerns takes us to the work of self-inquiry. Determining what we need to cultivate in our inner world to turn darkness into light requires shifting to another level or form of consciousness. Jung experienced many forms of consciousness in his life, and he used them as points of exploration. What made him so unusual was his willingness to engage and question whatever arose. This was his gift. It can be ours as well.

The thesis behind this book is that the leisure time that is the hallmark of aging invites us to this deeper level. Liberated from schedules, responsibilities, and outer expectations, we can use our newfound freedom to extricate ourselves from external and internal expectations, explore intuitions and proddings, entertain new ways of being, and take up specialized practices (such as those suggested in chapters 10 and 11) that foster a robust acquaintance with the inner world. This is also true for the caregiver who is overwhelmed with too many responsibilities. Just as the elder must open to previously unexplored territories, the caregiver must do the same but in response to different requirements. How this looks will vary with each person and their philosophical orientation to life.

Our culture envisions aging as a continuation of midlife into old age, and it paints a horrific picture of cognitive loss. The notion that there is something more satisfying than grandchildren, golfing, cruises, and volunteer work is barely recognized. This is not to say there is no place for family, travel, education, volunteering, creativity, or any of the other opportunities afforded by leisure time. Indeed, in order to stay fit emotionally, physically, and mentally, it behooves us to live as fully as we can at any stage of life. These occupations, however, are not sufficient to meet the needs for fullness of life that come to the fore in the second half of life. It's less about what we do than about the way we do it. Jung, more than any other thinker, gives us a way of understanding and talking about positive ways to optimize our time as we age and what some of the internal dynamics we encounter might be. With his incredible erudition in history, philosophy, esoterica, and religion, Jung fashioned a path that he called individuation for the later years. Instead of denying the challenges of aging, he saw them as necessary ingredients to enlarge individual consciousness, and through the individual, the wider world consciousness.

The question is how to make his vision real in our lives. Most of us believe in the notion of development, myself included. However, we often think of development as vertical. We develop in terms of the outer life, by accumulating possessions and titles, and the inner life, by perfecting who we think we are. Development in this sense presupposes certain stages and accomplishments; it is a vertical ascent into greater complexity and differentiation. Our conceptualization of life is that it is lived with forward, upward momentum. This is essentially what we find in Maslow's hierarchy and the Eriksonian model. Maslow's hierarchy identifies the basic needs for well-being. The Eriksons' eight stages lay out the requisite tasks for finding fulfillment in life. As discussed in chapter 3, the first half of life is a heroic journey. The emphasis is on conquering, expanding, and developing. The goal is to build a strong ego, which ideally is connected with the deeper Self. These are all directed upward.

Jung's notion of aging, however, stands in contrast to vertical development. Psychic movement in the last part of life privileges descent over ascent. Hillman called this stage the "involution of aging." This is why in old age we revisit the Eriksonian stages and why Joan Erikson suggested that the ninth stage is a reversal. Maslow's "being" needs are examples of what happens when we get comfortable with the downward movement of psyche: the possibility of transcendence and vitality emerges. Along similar lines, Tornstam's research shows that cosmic, social, and self dimensions naturally manifest in a psychologically mature elder.

From the perspective of living with memory loss, Naomi Feil, Thomas Kitwood, and the person-centered care movement are nudging society to rethink its fear of dementia and to reexamine the outcome of an emphasis on objectivity that reduces the person with cognitive loss to a nonperson. They help us see that for those living with memory loss, the inner life can and does continue, meaning is still available, and when certain prerequisites are met, it is possible for disoriented old people to be at peace. The vision and commitment of these thought leaders awaken us to a more compassionate stance, both to the other and to our own potential.

Descent is not typically valued in our culture, yet to descend is to reclaim one's deeper Self. For this to happen, ego and Self must trade places. Ego dominance yields to an increasing emergence of Self. There are many ways for this to happens. One main way Jung suggested is through a reevaluation of earlier values. In *The Personal and Collective Unconscious*, he puts it this way: "There comes the urgent need to appreciate the value of the opposite of our former ideals, to perceive the error in our former convictions, to recognize the untruth in our former truth and to feel how much antagonism and even hatred lay in what, until now, had passed for love" (Vol. 7, 75).

On the face of it, this is not a very appealing task. It's so much easier to turn away and busy ourselves with everything else. But nature supports this exploration. This is why Hillman says symptoms of the later years are symbols that, if followed, lead us to our depths. To follow such a path is precisely to reorient our values and expectations of life. It is no wonder this is the road less traveled.

We all most likely know old people who refuse to be elders. Unwilling to face the challenges of working with their shadows and re-visioning their values, they attempt to return to a time when life was easier or more satisfying. They may be old, but they refuse to move into the aging process and instead cling to former, outworn modes of thinking, behaving, and feeling. Maybe they deny the aging process entirely, striving to look, act, and dress like an older version of their younger selves; maybe they are angry at the perceived injustices of their life; maybe they chose the route of curmudgeons; maybe they always complain about someone or something; maybe they act like petulant children. In short, they refuse to let aging follow its course. When such patterns become habituated, the person can become possessed by the force of a negative archetype. As Jung noted, in such cases there is a "contraction of forces."

Hopefully, we also know elders who are on their way to an individuated way of life. These are the older adults we naturally gravitate toward. They know who they are, warts and all, yet their focus is on the fruits of life rather than its blemishes. Many are actively engaged at whatever level their ability allows. Some have faith in God; others find answers and sustenance in creative endeavors, however they define that. They are rarely in a bad mood or angry, yet they can be quite fiery and passionate about projects and causes they believe in. They are also able to cry when that is needed. Put simply, they drink deeply from the well of life and know how to balance what comes up from it.

A second way to apply Jung's injunction is to invite reflection, contemplation, and silence into everyday life. As we allow the natural slowing-down process of age to occur, we can find ourselves changed from the inside out as we see previous judgments, self-talk, and orientations more clearly. Habitual responses and reactions can fall away. It is a revolutionary act to open up internal space that allows for reverie. When we attend to some form of daily practice, an essential change takes place at an invisible, unconscious level. We strengthen our access to more positive states and learn to companion ourselves.

A third way to work with the path Jung suggests is to learn to think symbolically when responding to our daily round of activities or caring for a loved one. We're all aware of meaningful coincidences that happen in our lives. Jung called these synchronicities and wrote a book about them. They are seemingly random conjunctions that can delight and puzzle. Synchronicities have been present throughout our lives. It is often only when we slow down, however, that we begin to notice them. They point to a larger field within which we live. Once we look for something, we often see it. Keeping an eye out for meaningful coincidences, images, stories, and encounters in daily life brings joyfulness and meaning.

Symbolic thinking is the primary thought process at work in disorientation. A loved one complains that something is stolen. What is the item? What is its emotional significance to them? Could the missing item be expressing the loss of a former life? A mother who was very beautiful as a young woman accuses her very beautiful daughter of stealing her makeup. Is the mother feeling envious of the daughter and mourning the loss of her own good looks? Another woman has two sons, but in the later stages of memory loss she insists she has two daughters. Did she secretly wish for daughters instead of sons? A man cannot sit still and wanders all over the building. What is he looking for? A woman continually repeats the same stories from her life over and over and over in an effort to accept her current situation. As they interact with the symbolic dimension of life, these elders demonstrate there is more to life than what our ego and cognition determine to be valid.

The archetype of the invalid, proposed by Jungian analyst Adolf Gueggenbuhl-Craig (1923–2008), is a fourth way in which we can recognize our experience. He suggests in *Eros on Crutches* that the older we are, the greater our degree of "invalidism" is. He also notes that most talk about Self in Jungian circles is often focused on the positive: "When we talk about the Self there is much too much said about qualities like roundness, completeness, and wholeness. It is high time that we spoke of the deficiency, the invalidism of the Self.... Man comes to the full realization of himself, of his Self, through his invalidism; completeness is fulfilled through incompleteness" (25).

I would add that this also holds true in society at large if we substitute "ego" for "Self." This is a profound statement for the last part of life, turning our notions and projects of perfection on their heads. It is not an insight any of us rush to embrace. How can it be that imperfection and limitation are part and parcel of psyche's movement toward wholeness? Here we once again come face-to-face with a downward trajectory.

We all look for and desire the positive while doing our best to deny or overlook the imperfect or negative. We want experiences of numinosity. The root of "numinosity," *numen,* comes from Latin and means the presence of a deity or spirit. "Numinosity" is often linked with the word *awesome* when describing mystical experience. Yet the word *awesome* has the same root as *awful,* i.e., *awe-full.* On the one hand, there is awesomeness in the sense of rising above, and on the other, there is awe-full-ness in the sense of "fear and trembling," to borrow the philosopher Kierkegaard's phrase. Aging and caregiving have the capacity to call forth both the dark and the light. Dealing with the personal shadow, revisiting unsettling incidents in one's life, experiencing physical or emotional discomfort, contending with loneliness, coping with a feeling of being overwhelmed, and grappling with existential questions are just a few situations that can take us into the underworld.

How would our lives be different if we gave up the effort to always be independent, appropriate, and in control? Yes, we do need to know that, as in the Greek myth of Persephone, we will return to the world of light; however, the more we struggle against circumstances, the more tightly we are bound to them. Letting go and being with the unwanted seems to be the only way to a broader awareness, empathy, and compassion for ourselves and others. The way in which we think about and live out an understanding of invalidism makes the difference between growing old and growing in wisdom and grace. It is related to the attitude we take to memory loss.

An example of invalidism involves one of the realizations I had while writing this book. For most of my life, I have grappled with my mother's ambition and her indictment of me for not fulfilling what she wanted for herself. As a child, I vacillated between rebellion and acquiescence. In my young adulthood, I worked hard to throw off those maternal imperatives, mostly by trying valiantly to ignore them. As I discovered inner work, I allowed those rejected demands to resurface as I slowly peeled away the onion layers of her expectations and my reactions. Over the years, I have changed significantly; however, some patterns are more intractable than others. One morning in meditation I found myself questioning my authority to write this book. Almost immediately, I heard my mother's voice break the silence with her negative judgments. I started thinking about her and the conditions that formed her into the mother she became. In my mind's eye, she initially appeared large, and then her image shifted; she became small and weak. I was astonished to recognize that after all these years, in the area of my competence I was still the child with this gargantuan mother figure. When the image shifted and she no longer loomed so large, I realized that as a child I had ingested not only her rage at me for disappointing her but also her intense shame based on events in her childhood. All these years I had been carrying both my own and her self-images of weakness, shame, and incompetence.

The writing of this book, which called on my inner authority, summoned the depth of a complex into manifestation. A saying attributed to the Old Testament—"the sins of the father [mother] will be visited on the son [daughter]"—came to me, followed by the Buddha's words to Mara (the equivalent of the devil in Buddhist cosmology)—"I see you, Mara"—just before his enlightenment and throughout his life. I clearly saw in that meditation how I have been living under my mother's authority and unworked psychic life. What she did not resolve in her life was passed on to me. This is how trauma gets passed to the next generation. She did not have the authority to judge me, any more than Mara had the right to question the Buddha's aspiration toward enlightenment. It was a very liberating meditation; however, the shift in perspective is not a once-and-for-all insight. Rather, it's an ongoing process. This is the kind of contemplation that begins to happen in older age, if we are open to the forces of thought and emotion living just below the surface of our life. It takes a long time to free ourselves from habitual beliefs and discover our *daimon*—the talents, abilities, and purpose we each came to this earth to fulfill.

In these kinds of explorations, we unpack experience. As Tornstam's research shows, the psychologically mature elder is no longer driven by ego's habituated patterns, needs for self-aggrandizement, lust for power, or lack thereof. Multiple perspectives are available. The whole is seen along with the parts. The unembellished truths of who we are and who we have been, along with our strengths and our weaknesses, are no longer avoided. As we become less dependent on external validation and authority, we begin to identify what is truly precious for us. Insights come to the open mind and heart, and contentment follows. Often well-being shows up as simple pleasures, such as our garden, family, neighborhood, and small daily events.

I believe similar imperatives are present in the arena of memory loss; however, these manifest and are encountered in very different ways. For those who are disoriented, ego functions are the first to be diminished. One of the most endearing and exasperating things about forgetful elders is that the usual social controls no longer act as gatekeepers. As with young children, unfiltered emotion eclipses more habitual patterns of restraint, creating charged situations for caregivers not accustomed to this level of authenticity. In addition, for some people with forgetfulness, psyche/soul uses this time to rid itself of unwanted and unworked psychological baggage. Both situations can be seen as opportunities rather than dysfunctional brain firings.

"The Guest House" is a poem by Rumi that I have found especially helpful in realigning myself when I am resisting something or caught in some strong emotion:

This being human is a guest house.
Every morning a new arrival.

A joy, a depression, a meanness,
some momentary awareness comes
as an unexpected visitor.

Welcome and entertain them all!
Even if they're a crowd of sorrows,
who violently sweep your house
empty of its furniture.
Still, treat each guest honorably.
He may be clearing you out
for some new delight.

The dark thought, the shame, the malice,
meet them at the door laughing,
and invite them in.

Be grateful for whoever comes,
because each has been sent
as a guide from beyond.

I have returned to this poem so frequently that I now have it memorized. All I have to do is recite the first few lines to experience an attitude adjustment. How we approach an experience makes the difference between being sunk by whatever is happening and seeing a broader landscape beyond the immediate. Frequently, the two happen together, and our experience is both/and. The capacity to welcome whatever comes, trusting that whatever it is can lead to a new delight, is the essence of soul work and elder work.

Physician B. J. Miller offers a stunning example of this work from his life. Following an accident in his midtwenties that left him a triple amputee, he struggled to come to terms with his new life. In a January 2017 article about him in the *New York Times*, Miller is quoted as wondering what would happen if you could "reincorporate your version of reality, of normalcy, to accommodate suffering." As in Rumi's poem, Miller asked himself to entertain a different version of reality. He urged himself to enlarge the way he perceived what had happened to him. In that same article, Miller talks about going a step further by suggesting we can all learn to love not knowing, a very Buddhist perspective. Though Miller's wake-up call happened when he was still a young man, many of us are not pressed into this awareness until our later years. Old age is the time of life when not knowing is a daily companion. The older we are, the more aware we are that death could happen at any time. This awareness can move us to expansion or contraction.

Neuroscience seems to support the expansive dimension. A study of "superagers" at Massachusetts General Hospital showed a similarity in the emotional regions of the brain between young adults and older adults who pushed through the discomfort of exertion, whether the effort was physical or mental. It seems that behaviors and attitudes that ask us to step outside our comfort zones are the very ones that lead to a vigorous interior life. Rumi, Miller, and this research offer us alternate pathways to consider as we look at the vicissitudes of aging and how we can best meet them.

Hillman's notion of an "infolding" psyche evokes the dimension of immanence, while Jung's teleological Self suggests transcendence. Both are needed. The key is a shift in focus from what ego wants to what Self wants. Together these make a whole, contradicting our insistence that only the rational, cognitive domains of experience have legitimacy. Whether we believe in a traditional formulation of God or not, an immutable self or no-self, contextualizing the experience of aging as a journey with a purpose (albeit an unknown one) helps us approach aging more respectfully. We are no longer victims of aging but are empowered to live fully, if differently.

This book has skirted the question of God and self—two of the most profound questions humans have ever asked themselves. It seems the East has focused on self, while the West has chosen to grapple with God. In the end, these two mighty explorations, similar in nature, have the same root. They both go to the very heart of what it is to be human.

This book has attempted to engage this very humanness by encouraging us to reframe aging and cognitive loss in a broader, deeper context. Buddhist tradition has a wonderful metaphor I have found very useful in this regard. Indra's net is a poetic image of a vast web with a jewel at each point of connection. It stretches in all directions, each jewel reflecting all the other jewels in an endlessly exquisite vision of holographic interconnectedness. We are each a facet of that web, and each of us affects those around us, radiating out to larger and larger communities. By considering the various perspectives discussed in this book, you have the opportunity to consciously choose what you radiate out to others. No matter what your external conditions are, when you bring presence, care, and a deep understanding to yourself, you can foster love over fear and healing over sickness and darkness.

In conclusion, I offer my own definition of self, which is linked to the image of Indra's net and which I have painstakingly birthed during my life's journey. Jung's archetypal Self is Indra's net. It has been called many names, including God, throughout history. At the core of every human being there exists a reflection of Self, a sparkling jewel. Because it resides within, it is personal; but because a similar jewel also resides in everyone (and everything), it is also transpersonal, meaning it transcends the personal. Self pushes us toward wholeness, no matter our circumstances. As we approach our death, this movement becomes more urgent and relevant. It is our choice whether to heed the call. Those who turn inward have a quality of greater light, and society calls them wise. For some, Self has been occluded due to trauma in childhood or later. In these cases, Self has gone underground, and the person may only be aware of its absence in feelings of depression or disconnection. At times like these, another person, such as a therapist, friend, caregiver, or confidant, is needed to hold the one who is lost in an "I-Thou" relationship until the lost one can claim her inner wholeness, as Miller did. To find Self is to truly live before one dies.

I leave you with a remark Jung made in his early eighties, recorded in *Memories, Dreams, Reflections:* "The meaning of my existence is that life has addressed a question to me. Or, conversely, I myself am a question which is addressed to the world, and I must communicate my answer, for otherwise I am dependent upon the world's answer" (358).

Appendix A:
Ritual Collage

BY DORENE MAHONEY, MA

The wordless occurrences which are called forth [from the uncon-scious] … demand to be individually shaped in and by each man's life and work. They are images sprung from the life, the joys and sorrows, of our ancestors; and to life they seek to return, not in experience only, but in deed. Because of their opposition to the conscious mind they cannot be translated straight into our world; hence a way must be found that can mediate between conscious and unconscious reality.

—C. G. JUNG, *Two Essays on Analytical Psychol-ogy,* translated by R. F. C. Hull, 2nd ed.; vol. 8 of *The Collected Works of C. G. Jung,* edited by Herbert Read, Michael Fordham, Gerhard Adler, and William McGuire (Princeton, NJ: Princeton University Press, 1972)

C. G. Jung coined *active imagination* as a broad term for any number of individual practices one might use to tap into nonrational and uncon-scious material and to access the liminal space between conscious and unconscious reality. Guided meditation is one method of active imagi-nation. It helps the practitioner quiet the mind and access a deeper level of awareness. Like meditation, creating a collage can take one to a place outside of our logical thinking.

As a nonrational medium, collage is also effective at expressing feelings that one may be aware of but that are difficult to articulate.

Collage may also help one make sense of unconscious material that intrudes upon daily life. For example, when one is unable to understand their feelings, or when feelings are beyond one's capacity for words, a simple collage is very effective at revealing those feelings. By casting those feelings into images and then expressing them onto paper—i.e., in getting them outside of oneself—the feelings are transformed in some important way.

To create a ritual collage you will need the following:

- magazines, scissors, and glue sticks

- genuine curiosity and openness to the process—it is *not* art; it's process

- expectation that something potent will emerge, without attachment to what that might be

A finished collage is rich with symbolism and tells a vivid story of something that wants to be born into consciousness at this time.

Creating a Ritual Collage

Notice how your body feels. Wherever you feel tension in your body, release it. Follow your breath in and out, relaxing a little more with each exhale.

Choose a magazine and turn the pages. When you encounter images that evoke a response in your body—that *draw* or *repel* you—use the scissors to cut them out. When you finish with a magazine, take another.

Work silently, as if the activity were sacred, but with no agenda other than to create a collage from the pictures you cut.

When you feel a sense of impatience, boredom, or completion, leave the magazines and select a backing.

Trim the images in a way that feels right to you.

Move the images around on the backing until you feel satisfied with the arrangement. Then glue them down.

Engaging with Your Collage

Once you've finished your collage, put it in a place where you will see it often. Each day, spend a few minutes looking at your collage and journaling about it. Notice its tone, color scheme, shapes, image themes, and any possible messages or interpretations captured in it.

What feelings are evoked in you when you gaze upon the collage? What insights do you notice? What connections become evident?

Does your collage exhibit synchronicities between your feelings and other arenas of your life?

What might your collage be saying about you today and in the future?

Do you recall dreams that might mirror the messages in your collage?

Does the meaning or tone of your collage transform over time? What wants to emerge—to be born—from your unconscious at this time?

Guided Visualization

Settle yourself comfortably. Take a few deep breaths in through the mouth and out from the belly. Pay attention as the breath moves through your body.

When you feel settled, bring a current challenge or an uncomfortable mood to mind—a depression, anxiety, conflict, pain, or the like.

Let it float into your awareness and watch what is going on inside you as you turn your attention to it. Pay attention to what is happening in your body; notice where the feeling/thought is located in the body. Does it have weight? Color? Sound? Texture? Temperature? Stay with watching.

Here are some questions to consider that can help you maintain a focus on your chosen challenge or mood:

- Do you feel the urge to resist it? Do you feel yourself pushing the challenge or mood away?

- Do you find yourself feeling distracted? Muddled? Foggy? Hungry?

- Notice any voices or images that accompany the mood. What advice are the voices giving? What tone are the voices using? Whose voices are they?

- Is this a familiar mood? Can you recall when you first started to be aware of it? What was happening in your life at the time? What did you do when you first noticed it?

- How have you been with this mood over your life so far? What have you discovered about yourself because of it?

Other questions may flow from these. When you come out of your meditation or reverie, jot down what you learned. See if the challenge/ mood shifted in any way, and if so, how. See if you have a slightly different relationship to it now than you did before.

Appendix B: Resource Guide

Books on Aging
(not included in the annotated bibliography)

Atwell, Robert. *Soul Unfinished: Finding Happiness, Taking Risks and Trusting God as We Grow Older.*

Baker, Beth. *Old Age in a New Age.*

Baldwin, Christina. *Life's Companion: Journal Writing as a Spiritual Quest.*

Birren, James, and Donna Deutchman. *Guiding Autobiography Groups with Older Adults.*

Campbell, Joseph. *The Hero's Journey.*

Chittister, Joan. *The Gift of Years.*

Freedman, Marc. *Encore: Finding Work That Matters in the Second Half of Life.*

Gendlin, Eugene. *Focusing.*

Goff, David "Lucky," and Alexandra Hart. *The Age of Actualization.*

Grosskopf, Barry. *Healing the Generations: How Understanding Your Family Legacy Can Transform Your Life.*

Hanson, Rick. *Hardwiring Happiness.*

Kübler-Ross, Elisabeth. *On Death and Dying.*

Lane, Beldon. *The Solace of Fierce Landscapes.*

Lindley, Daniel. *On Life's Journey: Always Becoming.*

Lustbader, Wendy. *Life Gets Better.*

———. *What's Worth Knowing.*

Maslow, Abraham. *The Farther Reaches of Human Nature.*

Moon, Susan. *This Is Getting Old.*

Moore, Thomas. *Ageless Soul: The Lifelong Journey toward Meaning and Joy.*

Palmer, Parker. *On the Brink of Everything: Grace, Gravity, and Getting Old.*

Salzberg, Sharon. *A Heart as Wide as the World.*

Sawin, Leslie, Lionel Corbett, and Michael Carbine, editors. *Jung and Aging: Possibilities and Potentials for the Second Half of Life.*

Shabahangi, Nadar, and Bogna Szymkiewicz. *Deeper into the Soul.*

Siegel, Daniel. *The Mindful Brain.*

Simons, Philip. *Learning to Fall: The Blessings of an Imperfect Life.*

Solie, David. *How to Say It to Seniors.*

Stewart, Susan Avery. *Winter's Graces: The Surprising Gifts of Later Life.*

Thomas, Bill. *In the Arms of Elders.*

———. *Second Wind: Navigating the Passage to a Slower, Deeper, and More Connected Life.*

———. *Tribes of Eden.*

Volandes, Angelo. *The Conversation.*

Wiman, Christian. *My Bright Abyss: Meditation of a Modern Believer.*

Books on Memory Loss
(not included in the annotated bibliography)

Angelica, Jade. *Where Two Worlds Touch.*

Bresnahan, Rita. *Walking Each Other Home: Moments of Grace and Possibility in the Midst of Alzheimer's.*

Bryden, Christine. *Dancing with Dementia.*

Hoblitzelle, Olivia Ames. *Ten Thousand Joys and Ten Thousand Sorrows: A Couple's Journey through Alzheimer's.*

Kitwood, Thomas. *Dementia Reconsidered: The Person Comes First.*

Parker, Charlotte, and Virginia Parker. *Return to Joy: A Family's Initiation into the Mysteries of Dementia.*

Sawatsky, Jarem. *Dancing with Elephants.*

Snyder, Lisa. *Living Your Best with Early-Stage Alzheimer's.*

Taylor, Richard. *Alzheimer's from the Inside Out.*

Voris, Ed, Nadar Shabahangi, and Patrick Fox. *Conversations with Ed: Waiting for Forgetfulness: Why Are We So Afraid of Alzheimer's Disease?*

Poets Whose Work Often Focuses on the Inner Life

- Raymond Carver

- Leonard Cohen

- John Fox—www.poeticmedicine.org/about-john-fox%2C-cpt.html

- Hafiz

- Tony Hoagland—www.poetryfoundation.org/poets/tony-hoagland

- Alison Luterman—www.alisonluterman.net

- Clare Morris

- Mark Nepo—http://marknepo.com

- John O'Donohue—www.johnodonohue.com

- Rumi

- Naomi Shihab Nye—www.poetryfoundation.org/poets/naomi -shihab-nye

- David Whyte—www.davidwhyte.com

Websites on Aging

- Advance directive for basic activities of daily living—www.hsag .com/contentassets/df8e53c36037416abcb7a1e667b1f79b/c2 _iatb-dementia-care-llc--my-way-an-advanced-directive_508.pdf

- Aging Life Care Association (similar to Eldercare Locator, below)—www.aginglifecare.org

- California Advocates for Nursing Home Reform (also includes assisted living facilities)—www.canhr.org

- California Registry—www.calregistry.com
- Compassion and Choices—https://compassionandchoices.org
- Daughterhood Circles (an online resource center that connects you with local groups and information when you are providing care for an older adult)—www.daughterhood.org/circles-2
- Eldercare Locator (helps identify services for elders across the country)—https://eldercare.acl.gov
- National Association of Area Agencies on Aging—www.n4a.org
- National Placement and Referral Alliance (helps identify facilities across the country)—https://npralliance.org
- National POLST (physician orders for life-sustaining treatment) Paradigm—http://polst.org
- *On Old Age I: A Conversation with Joan Erikson at 90* (film of interview with Joan Erikson)—www.davidsonfilms.com/products/on-old-age-i-a-conversation-with-joan-erikson-at-90
- Pioneer Network—www.pioneernetwork.net
- Soul 2 Soul (memory loss blog by Odile Lavault)—https://soul2soul-seniors.com
- Stanley Terman (living wills and care planning for the future)—http://caringadvocates.org
- Story Corps (website that records stories of older adults)—https://storycorps.org
- Bill Thomas:
    - https://drbillthomas.org
    - https://changingaging.org
    - https://myminka.com
- Village to Village Network—www.vtvnetwork.org
- Well Connected (previously called Senior Center without Walls; brings senior center activities into the home by telephone)—http://covia.org/services/well-connected

- "What Is Person-Centered Care and Why Is It Important?"—http://healthinnovationnetwork.com/system/ckeditor_assets/attachments/41/what_is_person-centred_care_and_why_is_it_important.pdf

Websites on Meditation and Spiritual Practices

- Center for Action and Contemplation (Richard Rohr's website)—https://cac.org
- ContemplAgeing (Jane Thibault's blog; you can find her article "Aging as a Natural Monastery" on this site)—www.contemplageing.com/jane-thibault
- Contemplative Outreach (Christian Centering Prayer)—www.centeringprayer.com
- "The Dream Work Toolkit" (Jeremy Taylor's webpage on working with dreams)—www.jeremytaylor.com/dream_work/dream_work_toolkit/index.html
- "8 Steps to Practice a Chakra Meditation"—http://aboutmeditation.com/chakra-meditation
- "5 Steps of Feeding Your Demons" (meditation developed by Tsultrim Allione)—http://taramandala.org/about-kapala-training/the-process
- Guided Mindfulness Meditation Practices with Jon Kabat-Zinn—www.mindfulnesscds.com
- How to Practice *Lectio Divina*—www.beliefnet.com/faiths/catholic/2000/08/how-to-practice-lectio-divina.aspx
- Ignatian Spirituality—www.ignatianspirituality.com/ignatian-prayer/the-spiritual-exercises
- Insight Meditation Society—www.dharma.org
- International Focusing Institute (focusing meditation developed by Eugene Gendlin)—www.focusing.org
- "Jungian Active Imagination & Hypnagogia"—www.bodysoulandspirit.net/hypnagogia/what/define.shtml

- "On the Meaning of: OM MANI PADME HUM," by the Dalai Lama—www.sacred-texts.com/bud/tib/omph.htm
- Orthodox Christian Prayer of the Heart—www.prayerofheart.com
- "Overcoming Spiritual Darkness: The Practice of *Japa*"—https://yogainternational.com/article/view/overcoming-spiritual-darkness-the-practice-of-japa
- Palouse Mindfulness (free mindfulness-based stress reduction course)—https://palousemindfulness.com
- "Praying with Icons"—www.ssje.org/2013/02/26/praying-with-icons-br-james-koester
- Progoff Intensive Journal Program for Self-Development—http://intensivejournal.org/index.php
- Recollective Awareness Meditation—http://recollectiveawareness.org
- "The Science behind Guided Imagery"—www.huffpost.com/entry/guided-imagery-cancer-patients_b_1026296
- Sharon Salzberg's website—www.sharonsalzberg.com/meditations
- Spirit Rock Meditation Center—www.spiritrock.org
- Transcendental Meditation—www.tm.org
- "Visualization Techniques to Affirm Your Desired Outcomes: A Step-by-Step Guide"—www.jackcanfield.com/blog/visualize-and-affirm-your-desired-outcomes-a-step-by-step-guide
- "What Exactly Is Vipassana Meditation?"—https://tricycle.org/magazine/vipassana-meditation
- Zenlightentment (basics of Zen Buddhism)—www.zenlightenment.net
- *Zikr* (meditation from the Islamic tradition)—www.zikr.co.uk

ANNOTATED SELECTED BIBLIOGRAPHY

Applewhite, Ashton. *This Chair Rocks: A Manifesto Against Ageism.* New York: Celadon Books, 2019.

This book seeks to awaken the reader to personal and societal bias against growing old and looks at some of the challenges older people face from a realistic and positive perspective.

Baines, Barry K. *Ethical Wills.* Boston: Da Capo Lifelong Books, 2006.

Dr. Baines explains his approach and reasoning behind writing ethical wills, and he gives readers a how-to guide. The workbook that accompanies this book, titled *The Ethical Will Writing Guide Workbook,* is an excellent resource for groups.

Chinen, Allan. *In the Ever After: Fairy Tales for the Second Half of Life.* Asheville, NC: Chiron Publications, 2002.

A compilation of fairy tales from around the world that reflects the challenges and opportunities of aging. After each tale, the author adds interpretive comments from a psychological and spiritual perspective to lead to further reflection.

Cohen, Gene D. *The Creative Age.* New York: William Morrow, 2000.

Focuses on the creative power generated by age and experience, using quotes and citations from many older artists, scientists, philosophers, and the like. This work shows the reader how to tap their inner source to enrich and transform their later years.

————. *The Mature Mind: The Positive Power of the Aging Brain.* New York: Basic Books, 2006.

A redefinition of the "golden years" that moves from an emphasis on loss to a positive perspective. The book draws on scientific research and interviews with older adults to illustrate how the mind continues to grow and flourish into old age.

Cole, Thomas. *Journey of Life: A Cultural History of Aging in America.* Cambridge, UK: Cambridge University Press, 1992.

This book is both a cultural history of aging and a contribution to the public dialogue about the meaning and significance of later life. It traces images of the life course and shows how our culture is beginning to recover the spiritual dimensions of later life and to envision new opportunities for growth.

Dass, Ram. *Still Here.* New York: Riverhead Books, 2000.

Written by the spiritual guru for the boomer generation after he suffered a major stroke that resulted in paralysis and aphasia. This book is filled with personal stories and observations about today's culture and most importantly about how the author was able to use the experience of a stroke to deepen his spiritual awareness and understanding. As this book was going to press in late 2019, Ram Dass died at the age of eighty-eight.

Erikson, Erik, and Joan Erikson. *The Life Cycle Completed: Extended Version.* New York: W. W. Norton & Company, 1998.

Reviews the Eriksons' original eight stages of life from the vantage point of being ninety years old, and adds a ninth stage that covers old-old age.

Feil, Naomi. *The Validation Breakthrough.* Towson, MD: Health Professions Press, 2012.

This book outlines the theory of validation therapy as developed by Feil. It goes into depth describing the various stages of disorientation and is full of examples of how to communicate lovingly and effectively with those who are struggling with memory loss. Feil is a retired MSW-prepared social worker.

Gawande, Atul. *Being Mortal.* New York: Metropolitan Books, 2014.

Using research and personal experience as a physician, Gawande talks frankly about the interventions of modern medicine and how they do not always enhance quality of life in older age or cancer treatment.

Guggenbuhl-Craig, Adolf. *The Old Fool and the Corruption of Myth.* Translated by Dorothea Wilson. Thompson, CT: Spring Publications, 1998.

This book by a Jungian analyst takes a hard look at the realities of aging, acknowledges the cultural pressure to want all elders to be wise, and offers an alternative, balanced perspective.

Hillman, James. *The Force of Character and the Lasting Life.* New York: Random House, 1999.

For Hillman, a Jungian analyst, the final years have a very important purpose: the fulfillment and confirmation of one's character. In this book he explains how one's true nature emerges as we become older. In areas of life ranging from "Waking at Night" (chapter 5) to "Heart Failure" (chapter 13), Hillman connects the seemingly mundane or hopeless with a deeper truth seeking emergence.

———. *The Soul's Code.* New York: Penguin Random House, 2017.

This book introduces Hillman's "acorn theory," the idea that we all have a calling that is our fate. How we address our particular circumstances or fail to do so determines our character. In old age, our fate stands out because we now have time to reflect on the twists and turns of our life and to claim that life.

Hollis, James. *Creating a Life: Finding Your Individual Path.* Toronto, ON: Inner City Books, 2001.

———. *On This Journey We Call Our Life: Living the Questions.* Toronto, ON: Inner City Books, 2003.

———. *Swamplands of the Soul: New Life in Dismal Places.* Toronto, ON: Inner City Books, 1996.

Hollis is a Jungian analyst who was originally a professor of literature. All of his books focus on issues in the second half of life from a depth psychology perspective, and they all are easily accessible to the average reader.

Jung, C. G. *Memories, Dreams, Reflections.* Edited by Aniela Jaffe. Translated by Richard and Clara Winston. New York: Vintage Books, 1961.

One of the most readable of Jung's works, he wrote it when he was in his early eighties. After he died his secretary, Aniela Jaffe, edited it. It is an excellent introduction to his life as seen through his eyes, and it touches on all the major features of his thought as they play out in the course of his life.

―――. "The Stages of Life." In *Structure & Dynamics of the Psyche,* translated by R. F. C. Hull, 387–403. 2nd ed. Vol. 8 of *The Collected Works of C. G. Jung,* edited by Herbert Read, Michael Fordham, Gerhard Adler, and William McGuire. Princeton, NJ: Princeton University Press, 1969.

Another very accessible work of Jung's that focuses on the development of consciousness and the role of problems in that development. This is an excellent introduction to how Jung conceptualizes the path of individuation.

Leder, Drew. *Spiritual Passages.* New York: Tarcher, 1997.

A wonderful book that is both a workbook and a reader. The author presents the various challenges of aging and addresses them from the perspectives of the world's spiritual traditions. Each chapter has meditations and exercises to help readers integrate the material.

Linn, Matthew, Sheila Fabricant, and Dennis Linn. *Healing the Eight Stages of Life.* Mahwah, NJ: Paulist Press, 1988.

Using Erik Erikson's developmental model of the eight stages of life, the authors offer a way to heal wounds and move toward integration in older age through prayer, memory, life, and attention. Two of the authors are Jesuits, and the third has a master's of divinity.

Luke, Helen. *Old Age: Journey into Simplicity.* Sandpoint, ID: Morning Light Press, 1988.

Five essays reflecting on old age, written by a noted Jungian analyst while in her old age. Using Homer, Dante, Shakespeare, and T. S. Eliot, the author fleshes out the challenges and life-giving responses required for continued growth as we age.

Lustbader, Wendy. *Counting on Kindness.* New York: Free Press, 1993.

A sensitive book that explores dependency from the perspective of the person receiving care as well as the person giving care. The book opens a window on the interior world of dependency and shows how to regain a sense of power and purpose. Lustbader is a retired MSW-prepared social worker.

Moody, Harry. *The Five Stages of the Soul.* New York: Penguin Random House, 1998.

Although applicable to any time of life, this book is especially relevant to older age, when we acknowledge that the major task of the second half of life is spiritual development. The author combines psychology, religion, myth, and literature to name and elaborate on the stages and to show, through the example of many people, the nature of the spiritual journey. Moody practices Sufism, the mystical branch of Islam.

Nouwen, Henri, and Walter Gaffney. *Aging: The Fulfillment of Life.* New York: Image Books, 1976.

An inspirational book for those who are elderly and caregivers. This is the type of book to read in short paragraphs and savor in quiet reflection. Scenes of people and nature are interspersed throughout to add to the book's contemplative nature. Nouwen was a Catholic priest.

Pipher, Mary. *Another Country.* New York: Riverhead Books, 1999.

This is a book for everyone seeking to glimpse the reality of the landscape of age. It is a field guide to another country, a place most of us will one day visit and where we will be affected by the changes, challenges, joys, and sadnesses of growing older. The book is based on interviews with families and older people and is recounted through the eyes of the author, a therapist.

———. *Women Rowing North.* London: Bloomsbury Publishing, 2019.

This is Pipher's most recent book, about women in their seventies and older.

Power, Allen. *Dementia beyond Disease.* Towson, MD: Health Professions Press, 2016.

This is Dr. Power's second book. His first is *Dementia Beyond Drugs.* In both books he advocates for a better quality of care for elders living with memory loss. His books are full of examples of how care that is thoughtful and respectful lightens the experience of disorientation for elders and their caregivers.

Richmond, Lewis. *Aging as a Spiritual Practice.* Farmington Hills, MI: Thorndike Press, 2016.

Richmond is a Buddhist priest and meditation teacher in the Zen tradition. Working from within that tradition, he offers an understanding of how to work with the various mind states that arise as we age. Each chapter ends with a contemplative reflection to ground the material.

Rohr, Richard. *Falling Upwards: A Spirituality for the Two Halves of Life.* San Francisco: Jossey-Bass, 2011.

A thorough exploration of the tasks of the first and second halves of life. Rohr is a Franciscan priest who has studied Jung and Eastern meditative traditions. Although the book is written using Christian imagery, there is much to recommend it to non-Christians.

Sarton, May. *Encore: A Journal of the Eightieth Year.* New York: W. W. Norton & Company, 1995.

Personal reflections on being eigthy from an American poet, author, and memorist.

Schacter-Shalomi, Rabbi Zalman. *From Age-ing to Sage-ing.* New York: Grand Central Publishing, 2014.

Written from the author's personal experience and based on research in consciousness studies, life extension, human potential, transpersonal psychology, and spiritual traditions, this seminal work seeks nothing less than to transform the older adult into an elder or wisdom keeper for the culture. Through theory, story, and concrete exercises, this book leads the reader on a journey from age-ing to sage-ing.

Scott-Maxwell, Florida. *The Measure of My Days*. New York: Penguin Books, 1979.

Written in the style of a notebook, this book reflects on the victories and defeats of aging. The author, a playwright and Jungian analyst, was in her mideighties when she wrote these reflections.

Shalit, Erel. *The Cycle of Life*. Sheridan, WY: Fisher King Press, 2011.

This book uses the metaphor of a journey through life to help readers find meaning in their lives. He starts with childhood and moves to adolescence, youth, later adulthood, and old age. His book is rich in imagery from Greek myth and Jungian thought. Shalit was an Israeli Jungian analyst.

Sherman, Edmund. *Contemplative Aging: A Way of Being in Later Life*. New York: Gordian Knot, 2010.

A retired professor of social welfare, Sherman wrote this book for those who want to experience a more aware way of being in later life. The book covers philosophical, psychological, and spiritual writers as well as research in the field of aging.

Thibault, Jane Marie. *A Deepening Love Affair: The Gift of God in Later Life*. Nashville: Upper Room Books, 1998.

The author writes, "I have written this book for the mature adult who is spiritually discontented. The state of being spiritually discontented is an extremely significant state of being. It can lead either to a radical deepening of faith or to a virtual abandonment of living faith. The difficulty is that the answer lies within." Written from a Christian perspective.

Thibault, Jane Marie, and Richard R. Morgan. *Pilgrimage into The Last Third of Life: 7 Gateways to Spiritual Growth*. Nashville, Upper Room Books, 2012.

This work is Jane's latest contribution to an appreciation of the spiritual possibilities in late life. It is written with a retired minister who is living with his wife in assisted living. Each chapter is brief with salient reflection questions at the end that go to the heart of the joys and challenges of living into old age. It is a wonderful book for discussion groups, particularly in facilities.

Thomas, William H. *What Are Old People For?* St. Louis: Vanderwyk & Burnham, 2004.

Written by the leader of the Eden Alternative—an alive, humane, and compassionate approach to eldercare in nursing homes—this book looks at the prejudices of modern society against the elderly and explores the value and meaning of old people to our culture.

Tornstam, Lars. *Gerotranscendence.* New York: Springer Publishing Co., 2005.

Describes his theory of potential in late life based on longitudinal research with Swedish elders over many years. It is meant to influence the conversation about aging by providing information about developmental changes that show increased life satisfaction as we age. Tornstam's thought is influenced by Jung and Erikson.

INDEX

ACKNOWLEDGMENTS

There is a saying that it takes a village to raise a child. I say it takes a village of devoted friends and colleagues to write a book. Without the love and support I received from so many friends, this book would never have seen the light of day. Every time I pick up a book, I go first to the table of contents and then to the acknowledgments. Who are the people who helped birth this book? It is always a cadre of people who have blessed the author's life, and seeing who those people are always gives me a flavor of what the book will be like.

First and foremost among this book's village is Janet Keyes. When I first announced my desire to write this book, Janet immediately volunteered to be my reader and editor. For untold hours the two of us met and went over each chapter line by line. Her love, perspicacity, and steady inquiry turned my sometimes inarticulate leanings and academic language into a readable work.

Janet Hewins diligently read through each chapter and offered her firsthand experience of aging. Her tweaking enlarged the range of the discussion. Much gratitude is also due to my elder friends Martha Coleman, Dolores McGill, Father Jim Sloan, Joy Bishop, and Ingrid Borland for their unflagging encouragement of my work and their willingness to share their experiences.

Specific thanks go to numerous friends who strengthened individual chapters based on their professional or personal experience: Maureen Kelly, for her expertise in aging-related matters and her willingness to venture into the unknown territory of Jung, which forced me to make concepts accessible; Odiel Lavault, for her skill in validation therapy and memory care and for her exactness with words; Marita Grudzen, for pointing out the desirableness of encouraging others to translate this book into the lived experience of elders with diverse cultural and ethnic experiences; Judy Sarno, Emily Kunsler, and Dorene Mahoney for helping to make my writing clearer; and Lea Tenneriello, for offering suggestions from her experience living in a facility.

Thanks to mentor and friend Clare Morris for the use of her poetry, and to John Fox and Coleman Barks for the generous and gracious use of their poetry; to Marianne Morgan of the C. G. Jung Institute in San Francisco, who ensured that my Jung quotations have accurate references; to Marianne York, photographer extraordinaire and fellow traveler from whom all good comes; and to Maria Chaia for helping me explore my soul these many years.

My deepest thanks to my editor, Shayna Keyles. I used to wonder what editors actually did before my experience with Shayna. Now I know. They winnow the chaff from the wheat. I can truly say this book did not come together until I worked with Shayna's edits. She forced me to dig down to the bottom of my soul and bring out its treasure.

Recognition is also due to Zoe Francesca, who introduced my work to her colleague Susan Bumps at North Atlantic Books, thus initiating the publishing process and saving me countless fruitless hours of hunting for publishers.

Finally, my lifelong gratitude goes to Maureen Wesolowski, who has afforded me a beautiful living space at a ridiculously low cost. Without her generosity, I would not have had the resources required to attempt such an endeavor.

Most of all I want to thank all those named and unnamed for believing in me and this effort when I lost the thread and succumbed to my Achilles' heel.

This work rides on the back of many thinkers. It is a synthesis of their thought with experiences from my life, hopefully presented in a format that makes their work easily accessible. I have done my best to credit ideas and explain what I think an author is saying. I apologize in advance for any errors or misunderstandings that my work may generate, and I deeply thank all those who have, knowingly and unknowingly, contributed to my growth and this work.

ABOUT THE AUTHOR

SANDI PETERS has a master's degree in psychology and has been working in the field of gerontology since 1986. Her area of specialty is life span development and the possibilities for renewal in older age. As a student of C. G. Jung, she has particular interest in the role of symbolic expression in older age, especially for those with memory loss. Sandi is an avid swimmer (especially in open water), teaches swimming to adults, and is a longtime meditator and seeker. She lives in Berkeley, California, and can be reached at sandi4eldercare@gmail.com.

About North Atlantic Books

North Atlantic Books (NAB) is an independent, nonprofit publisher committed to a bold exploration of the relationships between mind, body, spirit, and nature. Founded in 1974, NAB aims to nurture a holistic view of the arts, sciences, humanities, and healing. To make a donation or to learn more about our books, authors, events, and newsletter, please visit www.northatlanticbooks.com.

North Atlantic Books is the publishing arm of the Society for the Study of Native Arts and Sciences, a 501(c)(3) nonprofit educational organization that promotes cross-cultural perspectives linking scientific, social, and artistic fields. To learn how you can support us, please visit our website.